Trends in Functional Programming

Trends in Functional Programming

Volume 9

Edited by

Peter Achten, Pieter Koopman, & Marco T. Morazán

intellect Bristol, UK / Chicago, USA

First published in the UK in 2009 by
Intellect Books, The Mill, Parnall Road, Fishponds, Bristol, BS16 3JG, UK

First published in the USA in 2009 by
Intellect Books, The University of Chicago Press, 1427 E. 60th Street, Chicago,
IL 60637, USA

A catalogue record for this book is available from the British Library.

Cover Design: Holly Rose

ISBN 978-1-84150-277-9

Printed and bound by Gutenberg Press, Malta.

Contents

Preface   **v**

1   Prediction of Linear Memory Usage for First-Order Functional Programs   **1**
Brian Campbell   **Best student paper**

2   Dependent Types for Distributed Arrays   **17**
Wouter Swierstra, Thorsten Altenkirch   **Best student paper**

3   Size Analysis of Algebraic Data Types   **33**
Alejandro Tamalet, Olha Shkaravska, Marko van Eekelen

4   Confluence for Non-Full Functional Dependencies   **49**
Tom Schrijvers, Martin Sulzmann

5   A Leaner Specification for GADTs   **65**
Arie Middelkoop, Atze Dijkstra, S. Doaitse Swierstra

6   One Vote for Type Families in Haskell!   **81**
Louis-Julien Guillemette, Stefan Monnier

7   Optimization of Dynamic, Hybrid Signal Function Networks   **97**
Neil Sculthorpe, Henrik Nilsson

8   Short Cut Fusion for Effects   **113**
Neil Ghani, Patricia Johann

9   Towards a Verified STM   **129**
Liyang HU, Graham Hutton

10 Complexity Certification of C++ Template Metaprogramming   **145**
Emanuele Covino, Giovanni Pani

11 Lightweight Invariants with Full Dependent Types   **161**
Edwin Brady, Christoph Herrmann, Kevin Hammond

Preface

This is Volume 9 in the *Trends in Functional Programming* (TFP) series and contains the peer-reviewed papers of TFP 2008: the Ninth Symposium on Trends in Functional Programming. TFP 2008 was co-located with the Sixth International Summer School on Advanced Functional Programming (AFP 2008). Both events were hosted in the venue Center Parcs 'Het Heijderbos', a holiday resort in the woodlands near Nijmegen, The Netherlands.

The TFP international symposia are dedicated to promoting new research directions in the field of functional programming and to investigating the relationship between functional programming and other branches of Computer Science. TFP strives to be a venue where novel and upcoming research is presented in a friendly and lively setting. The symposia use a post-symposium review process model. This year work was accepted for presentation at the symposium based either on an extended abstract or on a full article. The submissions were scanned by the programme committee to ensure they were within the scope of the symposium and contained enough novel material for an interesting oral presentation. TFP 2008 received 33 submissions of which 29 were accepted for presentation. After the symposium, authors were invited to submit full articles, which take into account the feedback received before and during the symposium, to the formal review process. The revised articles were refereed using international academic standards by the programme committee. The programme committee received 23 revised papers of which eleven were accepted for publication in this volume.

The roots of TFP lie in Scotland, with the Glasgow Functional Programming Workshop series that ran from 1988 to 1998. It was renamed as the Scottish Functional Programming Workshop in 1999, and was renamed once more as Symposium on Trends in Functional Programming in 2003 in Edinburgh. Subsequent meetings took place in Munich, Germany (2004), Tallinn, Estonia (2005), Nottingham, England (2006), and New York City, USA (2007).

TFP pays special attention to Ph.D. students, acknowledging that they play a key role in developing new trends. Authors of submissions describing work done mostly by students can request additional feedback from the programme committee before the formal review process. Upon such a request, a submission receives special attention by a selected programme committee member to provide early feedback on the paper. In addition to providing extra feedback to student submissions, TFP also offers a best student paper award. The recipient of the award is selected by the programme committee. To be eligible for the award, the work described in an article must have been done mostly by students and the paper itself must have been written mostly by students. This year the programme committee decided to honour two excellent student articles:

- *Prediction of Linear Memory Usage for First-Order Functional Programs* by Brian Campbell, and

- *Dependent Types for Distributed Arrays* by Wouter Swierstra and Thorsten Altenkirch.

These best student articles are the first two chapters of this volume. The remainder of this volume is organized along the research themes: *types* (Chapters 3–6), *reactive systems* (Chapter 7), *program transformation* (Chapters 8–9), and *reasoning* (Chapters 10–11).

TFP 2008 was attended by 50 academic researchers, students, and industry professionals. About a third of the audience also participated in AFP 2008. In order to stimulate friendship and collaboration between participants, TFP 2008 followed the TFP tradition of having a social event which included a guided tour in the city center of Nijmegen, the oldest city of the Netherlands, a visit to a beer brewery, and the symposium dinner which took place on a restaurant boat at the Waal riverside in Nijmegen. To further stimulate interactions between participants, there were 20-minute coffee breaks between every two talks. Finally, TFP 2008 had two invited talks. We were honored to have Prof. Henk Barendregt from the Radboud University Nijmegen speak about *'Simple, Recursive, and Intersection Types'* and to have Gert Veldhuizen van Zanten from Getronics PinkRoccade speak about *'Functional Programming and Business Applications'*.

ACKNOWLEDGEMENTS

We thank all the speakers and all the authors for contributing and participating in TFP 2008. We thank the members of the programme committee and the sub-reviewers for their hard work which was invaluable in the development of this volume. A heart-felt thank you goes to Simone Meeuwsen for her great help in organizing both AFP and TFP. Ever since 1999, the TFP proceedings have been published by Intellect. We acknowledge their help and support in publishing this series and this volume. We gratefully acknowledge the generous support of Getronics Pink Roccade, The Nederlandse Organisatie voor Wetenschappelijk Onderzoek (NWO), and the Netherlands Defence Academy. Finally, we thank the TFP steering committee for their support in making TFP 2008 a success.

Peter Achten and **Pieter Koopman**
programme committee Chairs and Editors
Marco T. Morazán
Symposium Chair and Editor

Nijmegen, December 2008

TFP 2008 ORGANIZATION

Symposium Chair:	Marco T. Morazán	Seton Hall University
Programme Chair:	Peter Achten	Radboud University Nijmegen
	Pieter Koopman	Radboud University Nijmegen
Treasurer:	Greg Michaelson	Heriot-Watt University
Local Arrangements:	Simone Meeuwsen	Radboud University Nijmegen

TFP 2008 PROGRAMME COMMITTEE

Peter Achten (co-Chair)	Radboud University Nijmegen
Andrew Butterfield	Trinity College
Manuel Chakravarty	University of New South Wales
John Clements	California Poly State University
Matthias Felleisen	Northeastern University
Jurriaan Hage	Utrecht University
Michael Hanus	Christian-Albrechts Universität zu Kiel
Ralf Hinze	University of Oxford
Graham Hutton	University of Nottingham
Johan Jeuring	Utrecht University
Pieter Koopman (co-Chair)	Radboud University Nijmegen
Shriram Krishnamurthi	Brown University
Hans-Wolfgang Loidl	Ludwig-Maximilians Universität München
Rita Loogen	Philipps-Universität Marburg
Greg Michaelson	Heriot-Watt University
Marco T. Morazán (Symposium Chair)	Seton Hall University
Sven-Bodo Scholz	University of Hertfordshire
Ulrik Schultz	University of Southern Denmark
Clara Segura	Universidad Complutense de Madrid
Olin Shivers	Northeastern University
Phil Trinder	Heriot-Watt University
Varmo Vene	University of Tartu
Viktória Zsók	Eötvös Loránd University

ADDITIONAL REVIEWERS

Andreas Abel	Jevgeni Kabanov	Henrik Nilsson
Jost Berthold	Tamás Kozsik	Ricardo Peña
Greg Cooper	Sean Leather	Zoltán Porkoláb
Xiao Yan Deng	José Pedro Magalhães	Alexey Rodriguez
Péter Diviánszky	Manuel Montenegro	Attila Ulbert
Marko van Eekelen	Dominic Mulligan	Vesal Vojdani
Lu Fan	Härmel Nestra	Abyd Al Zain

Chapter 1

Prediction of Linear Memory Usage for First-Order Functional Programs

Brian Campbell[1]
Category: Research Paper
Best Student Paper

Abstract: Hofmann and Jost have presented a type inference system for a pure first-order functional language which uses linear programming to give linear upper bounds on heap memory usage with respect to the input size. We present an extended analysis which infers bounds for heap and stack space requirements, and which uses more expressive post-evaluation bounds to model a common pattern of stack space use.

1.1   INTRODUCTION

Knowing strict upper bounds on the memory usage of a program can guarantee that it will operate without exhausting the available resources. This is particularly important in highly constrained environments, such as smart cards, especially where failures are difficult or expensive to recover from. Hofmann and Jost have presented a type-based approach [6] which can automatically infer such upper bounds for the heap memory usage of a wide range of programs where that usage is linear in the size of the input.

However, their analysis does not include stack memory, so some forms of excessive memory consumption may go unnoticed. In this paper we extend their system to infer linear bounds on the stack, heap or total memory used by pro-

---

[1]Laboratory for Foundations of Computer Science, University of Edinburgh, `Brian.Campbell@ed.ac.uk`. This work was partially supported by the MRG project (IST-2001-33149) and the ReQueST project (EPSRC EP/C537068/1).

1

$$P := \text{let } B \mid \text{let } B \; P \qquad B := D \mid D \text{ and } B \qquad D := f(x_1, \ldots, x_p) = e_f$$

$$e := * \mid \text{true} \mid \text{false} \mid x \mid f(x_1, \ldots, x_p) \mid \text{let } x = e_1 \text{ in } e_2 \mid \text{if } x \text{ then } e_t \text{ else } e_f$$

$$\mid (x_1, x_2) \mid \text{match } x \text{ with } (x_1, x_2) \to e$$

$$\mid \text{inl}(x) \mid \text{inr}(x) \mid \text{match } x \text{ with inl}(x_l) \to e_l \mid \text{inr}(x_r) \to e_r$$

$$\mid \text{nil} \mid \text{cons}(x_h, x_t) \mid \text{match } x \text{ with nil} \to e_n \mid \text{cons}(x_h, x_t) \to e_c$$

$$\mid \text{match}' \; x \text{ with nil} \to e_n \mid \text{cons}(x_h, x_t) \to e_c$$

FIGURE 1.1. Syntax

grams, and incorporate tail call optimization in a flexible manner. Of particular interest is the temporary nature of stack memory usage, which would cause difficulties with a straightforward adaption of the heap analysis. We have overcome this by allowing more precise estimates of free memory *after* an expression has been executed by relating it to both the size of the result *and* the size of variables in the context. This requires some care when part of the result appears in the context. The result is an analysis that copes with many common cases of these stack requirements, while maintaining a reasonable complexity and a single analysis for heap and stack requirements.

Finally, we show the soundness of the new analysis with respect to the operational semantics of the language.

1.2 THE LANGUAGE

The language is a simple first-order call-by-value functional programming language. For consistency, it is the one considered by Hofmann and Jost. The syntax for programs is given in Figure 1.1, where f is a function name, $*$ is the value of unit type, x and x_i are variable names and the e_i are subexpressions. Programs, P, take the form of a number of function definitions, D, arranged in mutually recursive groups, B.

Note the use of variables rather than subexpressions in many places; this corresponds to requiring that the program is in a 'let-normal' form, similar to A-normal form [5], to make the evaluation order explicit and allow the typing rules to be simpler. However, partial compilation of programs of interest is required to put them into that form before we can obtain bounds. Indeed, Jost's implementation of the heap space inference uses an intermediate language produced from a high–level language as part of the Mobile Resource Guarantees project [10].

To reason about heap space we require some mechanism to limit the lifetime of heap allocated data, so we mark places in the code where deallocation could safely occur. In this language only list elements are heap allocated and we distinguish between (potentially) destructive match expressions and benign, 'read-only', match' ones. There is more than one possible implementation of heap management using these marks, but we do not need to pick one. The only subtlety is that it must prevent memory fragmentation from inflating memory usage. See Hofmann and Jost's paper [6] for more discussion on this point.

We presume the existence of some external analysis which ensures that match is used safely so that no data is deallocated while live references to it exist, a property called *benign sharing*. Aspinall and Hofmann's usage aspects [1] or Konečný's DEEL typing [11] are suitable systems. They also provide a conservative estimate of the set of variables that do not overlap on the heap with the result of a given expression in the program. We will make use of this separation property in Section 1.4.

The types are $T := 1 \mid \text{bool} \mid T \otimes T \mid T + T \mid \mathsf{L}(T)$ for unit, boolean, pairs, sums and lists, respectively. The analysis will annotate the types to indicate resource requirements. The language can be extended with richer first-order types such as integers and arbitrary algebraic datatypes without affecting the results. Function signatures are of the form $T_1, \ldots, T_p \to T$.

A simple example of a program in this language is a function to negate a list of booleans:

```
let notlist(l) =
  match' l with nil -> nil | cons(h,t) ->
    let hh = if h then false else true in
    let tt = notlist t in
      cons(hh,tt)
```

The function uses `match'` so that the argument, `l`, is left intact. As a result, the function needs extra heap memory equal to the space occupied by the argument. Using the destructive match instead would allow it to run without requiring extra heap space, but that would only be suitable if the input list is never used again. Regardless of the variant used, the function requires stack space proportional to the length of the argument.

1.2.1 Operational Semantics

Values v in the operational semantics consist of unit, booleans, pairs, variants ($\text{inl}(v)$ and $\text{inr}(v)$ for value v) and heap locations $l \in \text{loc}$ for lists. An environment S maps variables to values, and a store σ maps locations to (value, location) pairs for each list element. A special location null is presumed which can represent nil. The operational semantics is given in Figures 1.2 and 1.3, with judgements of the form

$$m, S, \sigma \vdash^{f,t} e \rightsquigarrow v, \sigma', m'$$

meaning that with m units of free memory, the environment S and the store σ, the expression e (from function f, in tail position if t is true) can be evaluated to value v, with the new store σ' and m' units of free memory. The evaluation of a whole program is realized by the evaluation of a chosen 'initial' function $f(x_1, \ldots, x_p)$ on some arguments $v_1, \ldots, v_p$,

$$m, [x_1 \mapsto v_1, \ldots, x_p \mapsto v_p], \sigma \vdash^{\text{initial,false}} e_f \rightsquigarrow v, \sigma', m',$$

where e_f is the body of f.

The operational semantics uses two auxiliary functions to define the memory requirements. The first, $\text{size}(v)$, gives the amount of heap memory required to store a value v. In the present setting only list elements are heap allocated, so v is always the pair of a list element's contents and the location of the next element. Secondly, $\text{stack}(f,g,t)$ gives the size of the stack frame required to call function f from g, in tail position iff t is true. (We assume a fixed frame size for the evaluation of each function, although the system could be adapted to change the frame size when evaluating expressions involving binding.)

Definitions of these functions depend on the concrete implementation, and precise values could be obtained from the compiler. In the examples here we will take the simpler approach of assigning uniform sizes–essentially counting the number of objects or stack frames rather than their exact sizes. Heap space can be considered alone by fixing $\text{stack}(f,g,t)$ to be zero everywhere, and stack space by fixing $\text{size}(v)$ to be zero.

Some common choices for $\text{stack}(f,g,t)$ are to assign every function f a single frame size, $\text{frame}(f)$, and set $\text{stack}(f,g,t) = \text{frame}(f)$ for all g,t to model a compiler with no tail call optimization. Alternatively, we could use

$$\text{stack}(f,g,t) = \left\{ \begin{array}{ll} \text{frame}(f) & \text{if } t = \text{false} \\ \text{frame}(f) - \text{frame}(g) & \text{otherwise} \end{array} \right.$$

for general tail call optimization (where the stack may shrink as well as grow).

Thus tail-calls are modelled by a combination of the tail position flags and the stack function. Thanks to the use of let-normal form, only the E-LET rule and E-FUN rule have premises with different flags to their conclusion because only the E-LET rule can introduce a subexpression that is not in tail position.

We will also require an unmetered form of the operational semantics, where the resource amounts are dropped from all of the rules. Judgements then take the form $S, \sigma \vdash e \leadsto v, \sigma'$.

We also need to formalize the guarantees that we expect a benign sharing analysis to give. For E-MATCHCONS the 'dead' location should not be accessible from the 'live' variables that the subexpression may use,

$$l \notin \mathscr{R}(\sigma, S[h \mapsto v_h][t \mapsto v_t] \upharpoonright \text{FV}(e_2)),$$

and for E-LET the parts of the heap needed for e_2 should not be altered by match expressions in e_1,

$$\sigma \upharpoonright \mathscr{R}(\sigma, S \upharpoonright \text{FV}(e_2)) = \sigma_0 \upharpoonright \mathscr{R}(\sigma, S \upharpoonright \text{FV}(e_2)),$$

where $\mathscr{R}(\sigma, S)$ is the set of locations in σ reachable from S.

The separation property can also be formalized. For any expression e in the program, the benign sharing analysis should provide a set of variables $V_e \subseteq \text{FV}(e)$ that do not overlap with the result of e. More precisely, given an evaluation $S, \sigma \vdash e \leadsto v, \sigma'$ in the program we have $\mathscr{R}(\sigma, S \upharpoonright V_e) \cap \mathscr{R}(\sigma', v) = \emptyset$. These properties may be derived from (for example) the correctness theorem of [11].

$$\frac{}{m,S,\sigma \vdash^{g,t} * \rightsquigarrow *,\sigma,m} \text{(E-UNIT)} \qquad \frac{c \in \{\text{true},\text{false}\}}{m,S,\sigma \vdash^{g,t} c \rightsquigarrow c,\sigma,m} \text{(E-BOOL)}$$

$$\frac{}{m,S,\sigma \vdash^{g,t} x \rightsquigarrow S(x),\sigma,m} \text{(E-VAR)}$$

$$\frac{S(x_1)=v_1 \ \dots \ S(x_p)=v_p \qquad m,[y_1 \mapsto v_1,\dots,y_p \mapsto v_p],\sigma \vdash^{f,\text{true}} e_f \rightsquigarrow v,\sigma',m'}{\text{the } y_i \text{ are the symbolic arguments in the definition of } f}$$
$$\frac{}{m+\text{stack}(f,g,t),S,\sigma \vdash^{g,t} f(x_1,\dots,x_p) \rightsquigarrow v,\sigma',m'+\text{stack}(f,g,t)} \text{(E-FUN)}$$

$$\frac{m,S,\sigma \vdash^{g,\text{false}} e_1 \rightsquigarrow v_0,\sigma_0,m_0 \qquad m_0,S[x \mapsto v_0],\sigma_0 \vdash^{g,t} e_2 \rightsquigarrow v,\sigma',m'}{m,S,\sigma \vdash^{g,t} \text{let } x=e_1 \text{ in } e_2 \rightsquigarrow v,\sigma',m'} \text{(E-LET)}$$

$$\frac{S(x)=\text{true} \qquad m,S,\sigma \vdash^{g,t} e_t \rightsquigarrow v,\sigma',m'}{m,S,\sigma \vdash^{g,t} \text{if } x \text{ then } e_t \text{ else } e_f \rightsquigarrow v,\sigma',m'} \text{(E-IFTRUE)}$$

$$\frac{S(x)=\text{false} \qquad m,S,\sigma \vdash^{g,t} e_f \rightsquigarrow v,\sigma',m'}{m,S,\sigma \vdash^{g,t} \text{if } x \text{ then } e_t \text{ else } e_f \rightsquigarrow v,\sigma',m'} \text{(E-IFFALSE)}$$

$$\frac{v=(S(x_1),S(x_2))}{m,S,\sigma \vdash^{g,t} (x_1,x_2) \rightsquigarrow v,\sigma,m} \text{(E-PAIR)}$$

$$\frac{S(x)=(v_1,v_2) \qquad m,S[x_1 \mapsto v_1][x_2 \mapsto v_2],\sigma \vdash^{g,t} e \rightsquigarrow v,\sigma',m'}{m,S,\sigma \vdash^{g,t} \text{match } x \text{ with } (x_1,x_2) \rightarrow e \rightsquigarrow v,\sigma',m'} \text{(E-PAIRELIM)}$$

$$\frac{S(x)=v}{m,S,\sigma \vdash^{g,t} \text{inl}(x) \rightsquigarrow \text{inl}(v),\sigma,m} \qquad \frac{S(x)=v}{m,S,\sigma \vdash^{g,t} \text{inr}(x) \rightsquigarrow \text{inr}(v),\sigma,m}$$
$$\text{(E-INL)} \qquad\qquad\qquad\qquad \text{(E-INR)}$$

FIGURE 1.2.   Operational semantics

1.3   OVERVIEW

We now present an overview of the Hofmann-Jost heap space analysis and our extensions to bound the stack space requirements.

The Hofmann-Jost system assigns hypothetical amounts of free memory to data structures in proportion to their sizes. Conditions are imposed on the assignments so that the total amount at any point in an evaluation would be sufficient for all allocations and assignments of these amounts to newly constructed data. In particular, the amount assigned to the initial arguments will be an upper bound of the total heap memory requirements of the entire program.

This is an amortized analysis, using the *physicist's view* of amortization described by Tarjan [12]. Following Tarjan, we call these hypothetical amounts of free memory *potential*. The Hofmann-Jost analysis assigns potential to data structures using type annotations, and side conditions on the typing rules ensure that the assignments are sufficient for all allocations.

The Hofmann-Jost system annotates typings and function signatures with non–

$$\frac{S(x) = \mathsf{inl}(v_0) \qquad m, S[x_l \mapsto v_0], \sigma \vdash^{g,t} e_l \rightsquigarrow v, \sigma', m'}{m, S, \sigma \vdash^{g,t} \mathsf{match}\ x\ \mathsf{with}\ \mathsf{inl}(x_l) \rightarrow e_l \mid \mathsf{inr}(x_r) \rightarrow e_r \rightsquigarrow v, \sigma', m'} \quad \text{(E-MatchInl)}$$

$$\frac{S(x) = \mathsf{inr}(v_0) \qquad m, S[x_r \mapsto v_0], \sigma \vdash^{g,t} e_r \rightsquigarrow v, \sigma', m'}{m, S, \sigma \vdash^{g,t} \mathsf{match}\ x\ \mathsf{with}\ \mathsf{inl}(x_l) \rightarrow e_l \mid \mathsf{inr}(x_r) \rightarrow e_r \rightsquigarrow v, \sigma', m'} \quad \text{(E-MatchInr)}$$

$$\frac{}{m, S, \sigma \vdash \mathsf{nil} \rightsquigarrow \mathsf{null}, \sigma, m} \quad \text{(E-Nil)}$$

$$\frac{v = (S(h), S(t)) \qquad l \notin \mathrm{dom}(\sigma)}{m + \mathrm{size}(v), S, \sigma \vdash^{g,t} \mathsf{cons}(h, t) \rightsquigarrow l, \sigma[l \mapsto v], m} \quad \text{(E-Cons)}$$

$$\frac{S(x) = \mathsf{null} \qquad m, S, \sigma \vdash^{g,t} e_1 \rightsquigarrow v, \sigma', m'}{m, S, \sigma \vdash^{g,t} \mathsf{match}\ x\ \mathsf{with}\ \mathsf{nil} \rightarrow e_1 \mid \mathsf{cons}(h, t) \rightarrow e_2 \rightsquigarrow v, \sigma', m'} \quad \text{(E-MatchNil)}$$

$$\frac{\begin{array}{c} S(x) = l \qquad \sigma(l) = (v_h, v_t) \\ m + \mathrm{size}((v_h, v_t)), S[h \mapsto v_h][t \mapsto v_t], \sigma \backslash l \vdash^{g,t} e_2 \rightsquigarrow v, \sigma', m' \end{array}}{m, S, \sigma \vdash^{g,t} \mathsf{match}\ x\ \mathsf{with}\ \mathsf{nil} \rightarrow e_1 \mid \mathsf{cons}(h, t) \rightarrow e_2 \rightsquigarrow v, \sigma', m'}$$
$$\text{(E-MatchCons)}$$

$$\frac{S(x) = \mathsf{null} \qquad m, S, \sigma \vdash^{g,t} e_1 \rightsquigarrow v, \sigma', m'}{m, S, \sigma \vdash^{g,t} \mathsf{match}'\ x\ \mathsf{with}\ \mathsf{nil} \rightarrow e_1 \mid \mathsf{cons}(h, t) \rightarrow e_2 \rightsquigarrow v, \sigma', m'} \quad \text{(E-Match'Nil)}$$

$$\frac{\begin{array}{c} S(x) = l \qquad \sigma(l) = (v_h, v_t) \\ m, S[h \mapsto v_h][t \mapsto v_t], \sigma \vdash^{g,t} e_2 \rightsquigarrow v, \sigma', m' \end{array}}{m, S, \sigma \vdash^{g,t} \mathsf{match}'\ x\ \mathsf{with}\ \mathsf{nil} \rightarrow e_1 \mid \mathsf{cons}(h, t) \rightarrow e_2 \rightsquigarrow v, \sigma', m'}$$
$$\text{(E-Match'Cons)}$$

FIGURE 1.3.   Operational semantics continued

negative rational values[2] in two places. First, we add 'before' and 'after' amounts to typing judgements and function signatures to represent constant amounts of potential. The constraints on these will mirror the operational semantics, requiring the 'before' annotation at an allocation to be at least as large as the amount to be allocated, and the 'after' annotation to be correspondingly lower. Similarly, a relative increase in the annotations is permitted when typing a deallocation.

Second, we place annotations on list types to denote 'per-element' amounts of potential. So a list x of type $\mathsf{L}(T, k)$ represents a free memory requirement of $k \times |x|$ units, and at a $\mathsf{cons}(h, x)$ expression we require that the 'after' annotation must be k *extra* units lower to compensate for the longer list. Then wherever an element is taken from a list with that type using match, the constraints in the typing allow k more units in the constant memory annotation. More intuitively, the cons reserves k units of free memory per element, and the match releases it again for use.

In this way we can represent affine memory requirements. For example, the

---

[2]Fractional annotations can arise naturally in this system. For example, if we require a cell for every second element of a boolean list l, then l will have the type $\mathsf{L}(\mathsf{bool}, \frac{1}{2})$.

`notlist` function might be given the function signature

$$\mathtt{notlist} : \mathsf{L}(\mathsf{bool}, 3), 0 \to \mathsf{L}(\mathsf{bool}, 2), 0,$$

which says that if it is invoked with a boolean list x and $3 \times |x| + 0$ cells of memory are free, then all of the allocations in the function will succeed, and some boolean list y will be returned along with $2 \times |y| + 0$ free cells for later use. Note that this typing is not unique; we consider other values for the annotations below.

Allocating a constant length list can transform a 'constant' amount of potential into a 'per-element' one. For example, in

$$\cdot, 9 \vdash \mathsf{cons}(\mathsf{false}, \mathsf{cons}(\mathsf{false}, \mathsf{cons}(\mathsf{false}, \mathsf{nil}))) : \mathsf{L}(\mathsf{bool}, 2), 0$$

with the empty context $\cdot$ and 9 units of potential, we consume 3 cells for allocations, then the remaining $6 = 3 \times 2$ units satisfy the 'per-element' annotation of the list, 2.

To infer these annotations the typing rules give linear constraints that their values must satisfy. We can use standard linear programming techniques to solve these constraints to find a minimal set of satisfying annotations.

The straightforward part of adapting the Hofmann-Jost analysis to include stack space in the bounds is to adjust the constraints to require extra potential at each function call for the stack space required. To model tail call optimization we reproduce the tail position information from the operational semantics in the typing rules. Note that it would be sound to use a more conservative $\mathrm{stack}(f, g, t)$ function in the type system than a particular implementation requires. This allows the analysis to provide coarser upper bounds which covers multiple implementations of the language.

However, the temporary nature of stack memory usage is not handled well by the straightforward adaptions above. A simple example involves the non-tail-recursive list length function,

```
let length(l) = match' l with nil -> 0
               | cons(h,t) -> let n = length(t) in 1+n
```

where one stack frame per element (i.e. $|l|$ frames) is required. This stack memory is free again after the function returns, but only a constant amount of potential can be assigned to the result because there is no annotation on the result's type that is capable of representing $|l|$ frames. Hence, should we attempt to use the function twice on the same argument,

```
let twicelength(l) =
  let n1 = length(l) in let n2 = length(l) in n1+n2
```

then the analysis sums the requirements of the two `length l` calls. So the best stack memory bound on `twicelength` is twice the actual usage. While this example is contrived, reuse of variables (and the corresponding requirement for stack space) occurs frequently, such as when consulting a lookup table repeatedly.

For a more subtle example consider the function

```
let andlists(l1, l2) =
  match' l1 with nil -> nil | cons(h1,t1) ->
  match' l2 with nil -> nil | cons(h2,t2) ->
    let h = if h1 then h2 else false in
    let t = andlists(t1, t2) in cons(h,t)
```

which computes the pairwise boolean 'and' of two lists. The size of either list would be an appropriate upper bound on the stack space required, because the actual amount used is the size of the shorter list. A straightforward adaption of Hofmann-Jost as outlined above can infer this without difficulty. (In these examples we estimate only the stack memory because the problem affects stack space analysis more acutely, so let size $\equiv 0$ and stack$(f,g,t) = 1$ for all f,g,t.)

Now consider using andlists twice, with the same first argument:

```
let andlists2(l1, l2, l3) =
  let r1 = andlists(l1, l2) in
  let r2 = andlists(l1, l3) in (r1, r2)
```

The actual stack bound is $\min\{|\text{l1}|, \max\{|\text{l2}|, |\text{l3}|\}\} + 1$ frames. We do not handle maxima in our analysis (this is considerably more involved, and the topic of future work), but we would still expect to be able to infer a bound of $|\text{l1}| + 1$ frames. However, a straightforward adaption would again simply sum the requirements because the post-evaluation potential for the first call can only be expressed in terms of the result, r1. Ideally, we ought to be able to reuse the potential initially assigned to l1 at the second function call.

We achieve this reuse by adding a second 'give-back' annotation to list types which indicates an amount to be passed to the 'normal' annotation of a future use of the variable. The above functions will then have types whose constraints allow the following solutions:

$$\text{length}: \mathsf{L}(T, 1 \rightsquigarrow 1), 0 \rightarrow \mathsf{int}, 0$$
$$\text{twicelength}: \mathsf{L}(T, 1 \rightsquigarrow 1), 1 \rightarrow \mathsf{int}, 1$$
$$\text{andlists}: \mathsf{L}(\mathsf{bool}, 1 \rightsquigarrow 1), \mathsf{L}(\mathsf{bool}, 0 \rightsquigarrow 0), 0 \rightarrow \mathsf{L}(\mathsf{bool}, 0 \rightsquigarrow 0), 0$$
$$\text{andlists2}: \mathsf{L}(\mathsf{bool}, 1 \rightsquigarrow 1), \mathsf{L}(\mathsf{bool}, 0 \rightsquigarrow 0), \mathsf{L}(\mathsf{bool}, 0 \rightsquigarrow 0), 1$$
$$\rightarrow \mathsf{L}(\mathsf{bool}, 0 \rightsquigarrow 0) \otimes \mathsf{L}(\mathsf{bool}, 0 \rightsquigarrow 0), 1$$

These signatures mean that if any of these functions is given a list l as the first argument, then $1 \times |l|$ stack frames are sufficient for evaluation, and that those $1 \times |l|$ stack frames will be free afterwards.[3] As the free memory afterwards is expressed as an annotation on l, its reuse will be taken into account when typing a subsequent occurrence of l.

To use these extra annotations, we provide an alternative to the Hofmann-Jost rule for contraction which takes advantage of the 'give-back' annotation. We choose to adapt the LET rule to ensure that the uses of the variables involved (Δ)

---

[3]Plus one more for twicelength and andlists2, due to the extra function call.

occur sequentially. We also change the rules for match so that their constraints not only 'release' the potential for each list element, but also 'reserve' the give-back potential.

1.4 THE TYPE SYSTEM

To formalize the system, we need a precise notion of the meaning of the annotations. The annotated types are

$$T_a := 1 \mid \text{bool} \mid T_a \otimes T_a \mid (T_a, k_l) + (T_a, k_r) \mid \mathsf{L}(T_a, k \rightsquigarrow k'),$$

where k_l, k_r, k and k' are constraint variables. Sum types are also annotated to reflect different resource requirements depending upon the choice made, but are not assigned a give-back annotation because the separation condition we use to ensure soundness requires the values involved to be heap allocated. To link the annotations to amounts of memory, we define a function which sums the annotations over every reachable value, and extend it to environments:

$$\Upsilon : \text{heap} \times \text{val} \times T_a \to \mathbb{Q}^+,$$
$$\Upsilon(\sigma, *, 1) = \Upsilon(\sigma, c, \text{bool}) = \Upsilon(\sigma, \text{null}, \mathsf{L}(T, k \rightsquigarrow k')) = 0,$$
$$\Upsilon(\sigma, (v_1, v_2), T_1 \otimes T_2) = \Upsilon(\sigma, v_1, T_1) + \Upsilon(\sigma, v_2, T_2),$$
$$\Upsilon(\sigma, \text{inl}(v), (T_l, k_l) + (T_r, k_r)) = k_l + \Upsilon(\sigma, v, T_l),$$
$$\Upsilon(\sigma, \text{inr}(v), (T_l, k_l) + (T_r, k_r)) = k_r + \Upsilon(\sigma, v, T_r),$$
$$\Upsilon(\sigma, l, \mathsf{L}(T, k \rightsquigarrow k')) = \Upsilon(\sigma, \sigma(l), T \otimes \mathsf{L}(T, k \rightsquigarrow k')) + k,$$
$$\Upsilon(\sigma, S, \Gamma) = \sum_{x \in \text{dom}(\Gamma)} \Upsilon(\sigma, S(x), \Gamma(x)).$$

For example, if x is a list of booleans, then $\Upsilon(\sigma, S(x), \mathsf{L}(\text{bool}, k \rightsquigarrow k'))$ is k times the length of x. Similarly, we define a counterpart to measure the potential for the give-back annotations:

$$\Upsilon' : \text{heap} \times \text{val} \times T_a \times \text{loc} \to \mathbb{Q}^+$$
$$\Upsilon'(\sigma, *, 1, l) = \Upsilon'(\sigma, c, \text{bool}, l) = \Upsilon'(\sigma, \text{null}, \mathsf{L}(T, k \rightsquigarrow k'), l) = 0$$
$$\Upsilon'(\sigma, (v_1, v_2), T_1 \otimes T_2, l) = \Upsilon'(\sigma, v_1, T_1, l) + \Upsilon'(\sigma, v_2, T_2, l)$$
$$\Upsilon'(\sigma, \text{inl}(v), (T_l, k_l) + (T_r, k_r), l) = \Upsilon'(\sigma, v, T_l, l)$$
$$\Upsilon'(\sigma, \text{inr}(v), (T_l, k_l) + (T_r, k_r), l) = \Upsilon'(\sigma, v, T_r, l)$$
$$\Upsilon'(\sigma, l', \mathsf{L}(T, k \rightsquigarrow k'), l) = \Upsilon'(\sigma, \sigma(l'), T \otimes \mathsf{L}(T, k \rightsquigarrow k'), l) + \begin{cases} k' & \text{if } l' = l \\ 0 & \text{otherwise} \end{cases}$$

The amount is measured *per heap location l* so that we can use the heap separation condition in the LET case of the proof.

Throughout, we adopt the convention that for any type $\mathsf{L}(T, k \rightsquigarrow k')$ we add the constraint $k \geq k'$ to prevent unused variables in the context receiving unbounded give-back annotations. This reduces the amount of clutter in the type system.

$$\frac{}{\Gamma, n \vdash_{\Sigma}^{g,t} * : 1, n' \mid \{n \geq n'\}} \text{ (UNIT)} \qquad \frac{c \in \{\mathsf{true},\mathsf{false}\}}{\Gamma, n \vdash_{\Sigma}^{g,t} c : \mathsf{bool}, n' \mid \{n \geq n'\}} \text{ (BOOL)}$$

$$\frac{x \in \mathrm{dom}(\Gamma)}{\Gamma, n \vdash_{\Sigma}^{g,t} x : \Gamma(x), n' \mid \{n \geq n'\}} \text{ (VAR)}$$

$$\frac{\begin{array}{c} \Sigma(f) = (T_1, \ldots, T_p, k \to T, k') \\ \Phi = \{n \geq k + \mathsf{stack}(f, g, t), n - k + k' \geq n'\} \end{array}}{\Gamma, x_1 : T_1, \ldots, x_p : T_p, n \vdash_{\Sigma}^{g,t} f(x_1, \ldots, x_p) : T, n' \mid \Phi} \text{ (FUN)}$$

$$\frac{\begin{array}{c} \Gamma_1, \Delta_1, n \vdash_{\Sigma}^{g,\mathsf{false}} e_1 : T_0, n_0 \mid \Phi_1 \qquad \Gamma_2, \Delta_2, x : T_0, n_0 \vdash_{\Sigma}^{g,t} e_2 : T, n' \mid \Phi_2 \\ \Delta = \Delta_1 \succ \Delta_2 \mid \Phi_3 \qquad \text{Values for } \Delta \text{ are separate from the result of } e_1 \end{array}}{\Gamma_1, \Gamma_2, \Delta, n \vdash_{\Sigma}^{g,t} \mathsf{let}\ x = e_1\ \mathsf{in}\ e_2 : T, n' \mid \Phi_1 \cup \Phi_2 \cup \Phi_3} \text{ (LET)}$$

$$\frac{\Gamma, n \vdash_{\Sigma}^{g,t} e_t : T, n' \mid \Phi_1 \qquad \Gamma, n \vdash_{\Sigma}^{g,t} e_f : T, n' \mid \Phi_2}{\Gamma, x : \mathsf{bool}, n \vdash_{\Sigma}^{g,t} \mathsf{if}\ x\ \mathsf{then}\ e_t\ \mathsf{else}\ e_f : T, n' \mid \Phi_1 \cup \Phi_2} \text{ (IF)}$$

$$\frac{}{\Gamma, x_1 : T_1, x_2 : T_2, n \vdash_{\Sigma}^{g,t} (x_1, x_2) : T_1 \otimes T_2, n' \mid \{n \geq n'\}} \text{ (PAIR)}$$

$$\frac{\Gamma, x_1 : T_1, x_2 : T_2, n \vdash_{\Sigma}^{g,t} e : T, n' \mid \Phi}{\Gamma, x : T_1 \otimes T_2, n \vdash_{\Sigma}^{g,t} \mathsf{match}\ x\ \mathsf{with}\ (x_1, x_2) \to e : T, n' \mid \Phi} \text{ (PAIRELIM)}$$

FIGURE 1.4. Typing rules for expressions

The typing rules for expressions in the basic system are given in Figures 1.4 and 1.5, and use the size and stack functions from the operational semantics, except that size now operates on types rather than values. This assumes that all values of the same type require the same storage. As before, heap or stack space can be considered on its own by setting one of the functions to zero everywhere.

Typing judgements for expressions take the form

$$\Gamma, n \vdash_{\Sigma}^{g,t} e : T, n' \mid \Phi$$

where Γ is the typing context, n is an amount of potential before evaluation (in addition to that from the type annotations), n' is the corresponding amount after evaluation, T is the annotated type of e, Σ contains the function signatures, g is the function in which the expression appears, t is the tail position flag and Φ is the set of constraints on annotations that must hold for a valid typing.

The function signatures now take the form $T_1, \ldots, T_p, k \to T, k'$ where T_i and T are the annotated types for the arguments and the result and k and k' are extra amounts of potential required and released (analogous to n and n' above).

The typing rules for function definitions are given in Figure 1.6. They check that mutually recursive blocks of functions and entire programs are well–typed, with functions conforming to their function signatures in Σ. A program P is well-typed if we can derive $\vdash_{\Sigma} P \Rightarrow \Phi$ for some Φ.

There are two rules for contraction. The SHARE rule is equivalent to its coun-

$$\frac{}{\Gamma, x : T_l, n \vdash_{\Sigma}^{g,t} \mathsf{inl}(x) : (T_l, k_l) + (T_r, k_r), n' \mid \{n \geq k_l + n'\}} \quad \text{(INL)}$$

$$\frac{}{\Gamma, x : T_r, n \vdash_{\Sigma}^{g,t} \mathsf{inr}(x) : (T_l, k_l) + (T_r, k_r), n' \mid \{n \geq k_r + n'\}} \quad \text{(INR)}$$

$$\frac{\Gamma, x_l : T_l, n_l \vdash_{\Sigma}^{g,t} e_l : T, n' \mid \Phi_l \qquad \Gamma, x_r : T_r, n_r \vdash_{\Sigma}^{g,t} e_r : T, n' \mid \Phi_r}{\Gamma, x : (T_l, k_l) + (T_r, k_r), n \vdash_{\Sigma}^{g,t} \mathsf{match}\ x\ \mathsf{with}\ \mathsf{inl}(x_l) \rightarrow e_l \mid \mathsf{inr}(x_r) \rightarrow e_r : T, n' \mid \Phi}$$
$$\Phi = \Phi_l \cup \Phi_r \cup \{n_l = n + k_l, n_r = n + k_r\}$$
$$\text{(SUMELIM)}$$

$$\frac{}{\Gamma, n \vdash_{\Sigma}^{g,t} \mathsf{nil} : \mathsf{L}(T, k \rightsquigarrow k'), n' \mid \{n \geq n'\}} \quad \text{(NIL)}$$

$$\frac{\Phi = \{n \geq k + n' + \mathsf{size}(T \otimes \mathsf{L}(T,k))\}}{\Gamma, h : T, t : \mathsf{L}(T, k \rightsquigarrow k'), n \vdash_{\Sigma}^{g,t} \mathsf{cons}(h,t) : \mathsf{L}(T, k \rightsquigarrow k'), n' \mid \Phi} \quad \text{(CONS)}$$

$$\frac{\Gamma, n \vdash_{\Sigma}^{g,t} e_n : T', n' \mid \Phi_n \qquad \Gamma, h : T, t : \mathsf{L}(T, k \rightsquigarrow k'), n_c \vdash_{\Sigma}^{g,t} e_c : T', n'_c \mid \Phi_c}{\Gamma, x : \mathsf{L}(T, k \rightsquigarrow k'), n \vdash_{\Sigma}^{g,t} \mathsf{match}\ x\ \mathsf{with}\ \mathsf{nil} \rightarrow e_n \mid \mathsf{cons}(h,t) \rightarrow e_c : T', n' \mid \Phi}$$
$$\Phi = \Phi_n \cup \Phi_c \cup \{n_c = n + k + \mathsf{size}(T \otimes \mathsf{L}(T,k)), n'_c = n' + k'\}$$
$$\text{(LISTELIM)}$$

$$\frac{\Gamma, n \vdash_{\Sigma}^{g,t} e_n : T', n' \mid \Phi_n \qquad \Gamma, h : T, t : \mathsf{L}(T, k \rightsquigarrow k'), n_c \vdash_{\Sigma}^{g,t} e_c : T', n'_c \mid \Phi_c}{\Gamma, x : \mathsf{L}(T, k \rightsquigarrow k'), n \vdash_{\Sigma}^{g,t} \mathsf{match'}\ x\ \mathsf{with}\ \mathsf{nil} \rightarrow e_n \mid \mathsf{cons}(h,t) \rightarrow e_c : T', n' \mid \Phi}$$
$$\Phi = \Phi_n \cup \Phi_c \cup \{n_c = n + k, n'_c = n' + k'\}$$
$$\text{(LISTELIM')}$$

$$\frac{\Gamma, a : T_1, b : T_2, n \vdash_{\Sigma}^{g,t} e : T', n' \mid \Phi \qquad T = T_1 \oplus T_2 \mid \Phi'}{\Gamma, x : T, n \vdash_{\Sigma}^{g,t} e[x/a, x/b] : T', n' \mid \Phi \cup \Phi'} \quad \text{(SHARE)}$$

FIGURE 1.5. **Typing rules for expressions (continued)**

terpart in Hofmann-Jost. It splits the potential between two uses of the variable. Informally, we require this splitting because the total bound on the free memory required with respect to some variable x is the sum of the bounds with respect to each individual use of x. The auxiliary rules in Figure 1.7 formalize this splitting, which ensures that the types' annotations sum pairwise to the combined type. For example, the judgement

$$\mathsf{L}(\mathsf{bool}, k \rightsquigarrow k') = \mathsf{L}(\mathsf{bool}, k_1 \rightsquigarrow k'_1) \oplus \mathsf{L}(\mathsf{bool}, k_2 \rightsquigarrow k'_2) \mid \{k = k_1 + k_2, k' = k'_1 + k'_2\}$$

allows $\mathsf{L}(\mathsf{bool}, 3 \rightsquigarrow 3) = \mathsf{L}(\mathsf{bool}, 2 \rightsquigarrow 2) \oplus \mathsf{L}(\mathsf{bool}, 1 \rightsquigarrow 1)$, splitting three units per element between two uses of the list. The rule can also be used to reduce an annotation so that two types match.

The second (new) form of contraction is part of the LET rule. This allows the potential given-back in e_1 to be used in e_2. The 4-place relation $\cdot = \cdot \succ \cdot \mid \cdot$ given in Figure 1.8 formalizes the use of the give-back annotations. For example, the

$$\frac{\Sigma(f) = (T_1, \ldots, T_p, k \to T, k') \qquad x_1 : T_1, \ldots, x_p : T_p, k \vdash_{\Sigma}^{f,\text{true}} e_f : T, k' \mid \Phi}{\vdash_{\Sigma} f(x_1, \ldots, x_p) = e_f \Rightarrow \Phi}$$

$$\frac{\vdash_{\Sigma} D \Rightarrow \Phi \qquad \vdash_{\Sigma} B \Rightarrow \Phi'}{\vdash_{\Sigma} D \text{ and } B \Rightarrow \Phi \cup \Phi'} \qquad \frac{\vdash_{\Sigma} B \Rightarrow \Phi}{\vdash_{\Sigma} \text{let } B \Rightarrow \Phi} \qquad \frac{\vdash_{\Sigma} B \Rightarrow \Phi \qquad \vdash_{\Sigma} P \Rightarrow \Phi'}{\vdash_{\Sigma} \text{let } B \, P \Rightarrow \Phi \cup \Phi'}$$

FIGURE 1.6.   **Typing rules for function definitions**

$$\overline{1 = 1 \oplus 1 \mid \emptyset} \qquad\qquad \overline{\text{bool} = \text{bool} \oplus \text{bool} \mid \emptyset}$$

$$\frac{T = T_1 \oplus T_2 \mid \Phi \qquad T' = T_1' \oplus T_2' \mid \Phi'}{T \otimes T' = (T_1 \otimes T_1') \oplus (T_2 \otimes T_2') \mid \Phi \cup \Phi'}$$

$$\frac{T = T_1 \oplus T_2 \mid \Phi \qquad T' = T_1' \oplus T_2' \mid \Phi'}{\Phi_0 = \Phi \cup \Phi' \cup \{k = k_1 + k_2, k' = k_1' + k_2'\}}{(T, k) + (T', k') = (T_1, k_1) + (T_1', k_1') \oplus (T_2, k_2) + (T_2', k_2') \mid \Phi_0}$$

$$\frac{T = T_1 \oplus T_2 \mid \Phi}{\mathsf{L}(T, k \rightsquigarrow k') = \mathsf{L}(T_1, k_1 \rightsquigarrow k_1') \oplus \mathsf{L}(T_2, k_2 \rightsquigarrow k_2') \mid \Phi \cup \{k = k_1 + k_2, k' = k_1' + k_2'\}}$$

FIGURE 1.7.   **Rules for splitting annotations**

judgement

$$x : \mathsf{L}(\text{bool}, k \rightsquigarrow k') = x : \mathsf{L}(\text{bool}, k_1 \rightsquigarrow k_1') \succ x : \mathsf{L}(\text{bool}, k_2 \rightsquigarrow k_2')$$
$$\mid \{k \geq k_1, k - k_1 + k_1' \geq k_2, k_2' \geq k'\}$$

means that at the first use of x, k_1' out of the k_1 annotation is only needed temporarily, so it can be reused at the second occurrence of x (as part of k_2).

The separation condition for Δ and the result of e_1 in LET is required to ensure that no give-back potential is assigned to both e_1's result and Δ_1. For example, the identity function `let identity l = l` can be given the function signature

$$\text{identity} : \mathsf{L}(\text{bool}, 1 \rightsquigarrow 1), 0 \to \mathsf{L}(\text{bool}, 1 \rightsquigarrow 1), 0.$$

If we did not require separation we could use the potential assigned to `l` twice in an expression `let x = identity l in ... x ... l ...`, once for x and once for l (via the 'give-back' annotation), and the space bound would be too low.

We presumed in Section 1.2 the availability of 'benign sharing' analyses that can give a conservative estimate of the set of variables satisfying the separation condition. For instance, Konečný's DEEL typing [11] can be used. Thus we can use this set during type inference to decide which variables from the context to put into Δ. Then we construct Δ_1 and Δ_2 from Δ using fresh constraint variables and derive the set of constraints Φ_3 from the rules for $\succ$.

$$\overline{1 = 1 \succ 1 \mid \emptyset} \qquad\qquad \overline{\mathsf{bool} = \mathsf{bool} \succ \mathsf{bool} \mid \emptyset}$$

$$\frac{T = T_1 \succ T_2 \mid \Phi \qquad T' = T_1' \succ T_2' \mid \Phi'}{T \otimes T' = (T_1 \otimes T_1') \succ (T_2 \otimes T_2') \mid \Phi \cup \Phi'}$$

$$\frac{T = T_1 \succ T_2 \mid \Phi \qquad T' = T_1' \succ T_2' \mid \Phi' \qquad \Phi'' = \{k = k_1 + k_2, k' = k_1' + k_2'\}}{(T,k) + (T',k') = (T_1,k_1) + (T_1',k_1') \succ (T_2,k_2) + (T_2',k_2') \mid \Phi \cup \Phi' \cup \Phi''}$$

$$\frac{T = T_1 \succ T_2 \mid \Phi \qquad \Phi' = \{k \geq k_1, k - k_1 + k_1' \geq k_2, k_2' \geq k'\}}{\mathsf{L}(T,k \rightsquigarrow k') = \mathsf{L}(T_1,k \rightsquigarrow k_1') \succ \mathsf{L}(T_2,k_2 \rightsquigarrow k') \mid \Phi \cup \Phi'}$$

$$\frac{\forall x \in \mathrm{dom}(\Delta).\; \Delta(x) = \Delta_1(x) \succ \Delta_2(x) \mid \Phi_x}{\Delta = \Delta_1 \succ \Delta_2 \mid \cup_{x \in \mathrm{dom}(\Delta)} \Phi_x}$$

FIGURE 1.8.   Rules for contraction in let expressions

We also need to adapt other rules so that the give-back annotations reflect free memory at runtime which is not accounted for by other annotations. The LISTELIM$'$ rule adds the 'normal' list annotation to the constant annotation when typing the **cons** subexpression because we are extracting an element from x. Our replacement rule also requires the amount for the 'give-back' annotation to be returned afterwards for a later use of x: We also adapt LISTELIM in the same way.

1.4.1   Soundness

The soundness of this analysis with respect to the operational semantics can now be given. The intuition is that any well–typed expression can be executed with the amount of free memory predicted by the annotations $(n + \Upsilon(\sigma, S, \Gamma))$, and the annotations also conservatively predict the free memory afterwards. Moreover, execution will not consume any extra free memory (q) that may be available.

Note that $\Upsilon(\sigma, S, \Gamma)$ is defined when the variables in Γ have corresponding values in S and σ that are of the correct type. The $\max\{0, \ldots\}$ is present in the 'after' bound to prevent newly allocated data structures interfering with the potential calculation.

Theorem 1.1. *If an expression e in a well-typed program has a typing*

$$\Gamma, n \vdash_{\Sigma}^{g,t} e : T, n' \mid \Phi$$

with an assignment of non–negative rationals to constraint variables which satisfies the constraints generated for the whole program, and an evaluation

$$S, \sigma \vdash e \rightsquigarrow v, \sigma',$$

which satisfies the benign sharing conditions, and $\Upsilon(\sigma, S, \Gamma)$ is defined, then for any $q \in \mathbb{Q}^+$ and $m \in \mathbb{N}$ such that $m \geq n + \Upsilon(\sigma, S, \Gamma) + q$ we have

$$m, S, \sigma \vdash^{g,t} e \rightsquigarrow v, \sigma', m'$$

where $m' \geq n' + \sum_{l \in \text{loc}} \max\{0, \Upsilon'(\sigma, S, \Gamma, l) - \Upsilon'(\sigma', v, T, l)\} + \Upsilon(\sigma', v, T) + q$.

Proof. (Sketch.) We proceed by simultaneous induction on the evaluation and typing derivations. The evaluation terminates, so the derivation of the evaluation must be finite. The SHARE rule is the only one which has no counterpart in the operational semantics, so we consider it separately.

SHARE. We have $\Gamma = \Gamma_0, x : T$ and $S = S_0[x \mapsto v_x]$ for some Γ_0 and S_0 where $v_x = S(x)$, so

$$m \geq n + \Upsilon(\sigma, S, \Gamma) + q = n + \Upsilon(\sigma, S_0[a \mapsto v_x, b \mapsto v_x], (\Gamma_0, a : T_1, b : T_2)) + q$$

by the linearity of Υ with respect to $\oplus$. Thus by substitution of a and b for x in the appropriate parts of the execution derivation, we can apply the induction hypothesis and obtain the result by the linearity of Υ'.

LET. Using the definition of Υ, Υ' and $\succ$ it can be shown that $\Upsilon(\sigma, S, \Delta) \geq \Upsilon(\sigma, S, \Delta_1)$,

$$\Upsilon(\sigma, S, \Delta) - \Upsilon(\sigma, S, \Delta_1) + \sum_{l \in \text{loc}} \Upsilon'(\sigma, S, \Delta_1, l) \geq \Upsilon(\sigma, S, \Delta_2)$$

and $\Upsilon'(\sigma, S, \Delta_2, l) \geq \Upsilon'(\sigma, S, \Delta, l)$. The first is used to apply the induction hypothesis to e_1. The remainder $\Upsilon(\sigma, S, \Delta) - \Upsilon(\sigma, S, \Delta_1)$ is kept aside for e_2 by incorporating it into the constant q.

To form the precondition for applying the induction hypothesis to e_2 we note that $\Upsilon'(\sigma_0, v_0, T_0, l) = 0$ for all $l \in \mathcal{R}(\sigma, S \upharpoonright \text{dom}(\Delta_1))$ can be deduced from the separation condition $\mathcal{R}(\sigma, S \upharpoonright \text{dom}(\Delta)) \cap \mathcal{R}(\sigma_0, v_0) = \emptyset$. So

$$\sum_{l \in \text{loc}} \max\{0, \Upsilon'(\sigma, S, \Delta_1, l) - \Upsilon'(\sigma_0, v_0, T_0, l)\} = \sum_{l \in \text{loc}} \Upsilon'(\sigma, S, \Delta_1, l),$$

after which the second property using the amount left aside is sufficient. Then using the third property the result of the induction hypothesis for e_2 can be transformed to show the result for the let.

The other cases take two forms. Those with a subexpression (IF, PAIRELIM, SUMELIM, LISTELIM, LISTELIM$'$) adjust the context as necessary, extracting part of the amount from an annotation if matching something, then invoke the induction hypothesis. The others (UNIT, BOOL, VAR, PAIR, INL, INR, NIL, CONS) use $\Upsilon(\sigma, v, A) \geq \sum_{l \in \text{loc}} \Upsilon'(\sigma, v, T, l)$ to deal with unused parts of the context and then follow from simple arithmetic manipulations. Function application (FUN) mixes the two forms. $\square$

We can extend the result to the whole program:

Corollary 1.2. *Suppose a well–typed program has an initial function f, and arguments for f are given as values $v_1, \ldots, v_p$ with an initial store σ. If*

$$\Sigma(f) = T_1, \ldots, T_p, k \to T', k'$$

then any execution of $f(v_1, \ldots, v_p)$ will require at most

$$\Upsilon(\sigma, [x_1 \mapsto v_1, \ldots, x_p \mapsto v_p], (x_1 : T_1, \ldots, x_p : T_p)) + \mathrm{stack}(f) + k$$

units of memory, for any assignment of non–negative rationals to constraint variables which satisfies the generated constraints.

The soundness result can be extended to non-terminating programs, by adjusting the operational semantics to allow the execution to be terminated at any point. The proof then shows that any such partial execution also respects the inferred memory bound, although not necessarily the bound on m'. Moreover, if the tail call optimization extension is not used, then obtaining a stack space bound also gives us a bound on the call depth, guaranteeing termination. The 'resource polymorphism' extension suggested by Hofmann and Jost which allows functions to have different signatures at different points in the program can also be applied. A full proof of the soundness theorem for the analysis with these extensions and a slightly larger language can be found in [2].

An implementation of the give-back system with tail-recursion analysis has been produced,[4] based upon Jost's `lfd_infer` [10]. This system has only a small linear increase in the number of constraints and variables in the linear programs used, and so should enjoy efficiency similar to Jost's system.

1.5 RELATED AND FURTHER WORK

There are other examples of the use of type systems to provide guarantees on memory usage. Pareto and Hughes [8] gave a system based on *sized-types* which can be used to check heap and stack memory bounds expressed in Presburger arithmetic, using explicit regions to handle deallocation. Crary and Weirich [4] present a flexible type system to certify execution time. Both of these systems check bounds, but do not infer them, although Chin and Khoo's work has used transitive closure and widening operations to infer sizes in the form of Presburger formulae on the input's size [3].

Jost has extended the basic analysis in [6] to include higher-order functions along with some other improvements [9], and one potential avenue of further work is to merge that with the enhancements presented in this paper. Hofmann and Jost have also presented a type system (without inference) for checking resource bounds of object-oriented programs [7].

Another area of interest is to introduce annotations which give resource bounds in terms of the *depth* of data structures, rather than their total size. Ongoing work in this area [2, Chapters 6 and 7] involves representing several alternate annotations in contexts, for example, one for each branch of a tree. This should be especially useful for inferring stack bounds of programs using tree–structured data. It may also express bounds that are the maximum of two other bounds, which would be useful for examples like `andlists2` in Section 1.3.

---

[4]Available from `http://homepages.inf.ed.ac.uk/bcampbe2/tfp08/`.

1.6 CONCLUSION

We have shown how to add stack bounds to Hofmann and Jost's analysis, and a mechanism for obtaining better overall bounds by using more expressive post-evaluation calculation of potential. This is particularly important for obtaining good stack space bounds because of its temporary nature.

REFERENCES

[1] D. Aspinall, M. Hofmann, and M. Konečný. A type system with usage aspects. *Journal of Functional Programming*, 18(2):141–178, 2008.

[2] B. Campbell. *Type-based amortized stack memory prediction*. PhD thesis, University of Edinburgh, 2008.

[3] W.-N. Chin and S.-C. Khoo. Calculating sized types. *Higher Order and Symbolic Computation*, 14(2-3):261–300, 2001.

[4] K. Crary and S. Weirich. Resource bound certification. In *Proceedings of the 27th ACM SIGPLAN-SIGACT symposium on Principles of Programming Languages (POPL)*, pages 184–198, New York, NY, USA, 2000. ACM Press.

[5] C. Flanagan, A. Sabry, B. F. Duba, and M. Felleisen. The essence of compiling with continuations. In *Proceedings of the ACM SIGPLAN 1993 Conference on Programming Language Design and Implementation (PLDI)*, pages 237–247. ACM Press, 1993.

[6] M. Hofmann and S. Jost. Static prediction of heap space usage for first-order functional programs. In *Proceedings of the 30th ACM Symposium on Principles of Programming Languages (POPL)*, New Orleans, 2003. ACM Press.

[7] M. Hofmann and S. Jost. Type-based amortised heap-space analysis (for an object-oriented language). In P. Sestoft, editor, *Proceedings of the 15th European Symposium on Programming (ESOP), Programming Languages and Systems*, volume 3924 of *LNCS*, pages 22–37. Springer-Verlag, 2006.

[8] J. Hughes and L. Pareto. Recursion and dynamic data-structures in bounded space: towards embedded ML programming. In *Proceedings of the 4th ACM SIGPLAN International Conference on Functional Programming (ICFP)*, pages 70–81. ACM Press, 1999.

[9] S. Jost. ARTHUR: A resource-aware typesystem for heap-space usage reasoning. http://www.tcs.informatik.uni-muenchen.de/~jost/publication.html, 2004.

[10] S. Jost. lfd_infer: an implementation of a static inference on heap space usage. In *Proceedings of Second Workshop on Semantics, Program Analysis and Computing Environments for Memory Management (SPACE)*, 2004.

[11] M. Konečný. Functional in-place update with layered datatype sharing. In *Typed Lambda Calculi and Applications (TLCA): 6th International Conference*, volume 2701 of *Lecture Notes in Computer Science*, pages 195–210. Springer-Verlag, 2003.

[12] R. E. Tarjan. Amortized computational complexity. *SIAM Journal on Algebraic and Discrete Methods*, 6(2):306–318, 1985.

Chapter 2

Dependent Types for Distributed Arrays

Wouter Swierstra[1] and Thorsten Altenkirch[1]
Category: Research Paper
Best Student Paper

Abstract: Locality–aware algorithms over distributed arrays can be very difficult to write. Yet such algorithms are becoming more and more important as desk-
top machines boast more and more processors. We show how a dependently-typed
programming language can help develop such algorithms by hosting a domain–
specific embedded language that ensures every well–typed program will only ever
access local data. Such static guarantees can help catch programming errors early
on in the development cycle and maximize the potential speedup that multicore
machines offer. At the same time, the functional specification of effects we provide facilitates the testing of and reasoning about algorithms that manipulate distributed arrays.

2.1 INTRODUCTION

Computer processors are not becoming significantly faster. To satisfy the demand
for more and more computational power, manufacturers are now assembling computers with multiple microprocessors. It is hard to exaggerate the impact this will
have on software development: tomorrow's programming languages must em-
brace parallel programming on multicore machines.

Researchers have proposed several new languages to maximize the potential
speedup that multicore processors offer [2, 6, 7, 8, 12, 18]. Although all these
languages are different, they share the central notion of a *distributed array*, where
the elements of an array may be distributed over separate processors or even over
separate machines. To write efficient code, programmers must ensure that processors only access *local* parts of a distributed array—it is much faster to access data

---

[1]University of Nottingham, {wss,txa}@cs.nott.ac.uk.

stored locally than remote data on another core.

When writing such locality-aware algorithms it is all too easy to make subtle mistakes. Programming languages such as X10 require all arrays operations to be local [8]. Any attempt to access non-local data results in an exception. To preclude such errors, Grothoff et al. have designed a type system, based on a dependently–typed lambda calculus, for a small core language resembling X10 that is specifically designed to guarantee that programs only access local parts of a distributed array [9]. Their proposed system is rather intricate and consists of a substantial number of complicated type rules that keep track of locality information.

In this paper, we explore an alternative avenue of research. Designing and implementing a type system from scratch is a lot of work. New type systems typically require extensive proofs of various meta-theoretical results. Instead, we show how to tailor a powerful type system to enforce certain properties resulting in a *domain-specific embedded type system*. We immediately inherit all the desirable properties of our dependently–typed host type system, such as subject reduction, decidable type checking, and principle typing. Functional programmers have studied domain-specific embedded languages for years [11]; the time is ripe to take these ideas one step further.

In previous work [20], we described a pure specification of several parts of the IO monad, the interface between pure functional languages such as Haskell [16] and the 'real world.' By providing functional, executable specifications we can test, debug, and reason about impure programs as if they were pure. When we release the final version of our code, we can replace our pure specifications with their impure, more efficient, counterparts. In the presence of dependent types, we will show how our specifications can provide even stronger static guarantees about our programs. To this end, we make several novel contributions:

- We begin by giving a pure specification of arrays (Section 2.3). Due to our rich type system, the specification is *total*: there is no way to access unallocated memory; there are no 'array index out of bounds' exceptions. As a result, these specifications can not only be used to *program* with, but also facilitate *formal proofs* about array algorithms.

- Distributed arrays pose more of a challenge (Section 2.4). Not only do we attend to locality constraints, but we must also accommodate place-shifting operators. The pure specification we present is, once again, executable and total: it can be interpreted both as a domain-specific embedded language for writing algorithms on distributed arrays and as an executable denotational model for specifying and proving properties of such algorithms.

- Finally, we demonstrate how programmers may write their own locality-aware control structures. We implement a simple distributed algorithm using these control structures, and conclude by discussing the limitations of our approach and directions for further research (Section 2.5).

Throughout this paper, we will use the dependently–typed programming language Agda [1, 15] as a vehicle of explanation. In fact using lhs2TeX [13], the sources of this paper generate an Agda program that can be compiled and executed.[1] We will briefly introduce the syntax by means of several examples, as it may be unfamiliar to many readers.

2.2 AN OVERVIEW OF AGDA

Data types in Agda can be defined using a similar syntax to that for Generalized Algebraic Data Types, or GADTs, in Haskell [17]. For example, consider the following definition of the natural numbers.

> **data** *Nat* : $\star$ **where**
> *Zero* : *Nat*
> *Succ* : *Nat* $\to$ *Nat*

There is one important difference with Haskell. We must explicitly state the *kind* of the data type that we are introducing; in particular, the declaration *Nat* : $\star$ states that *Nat* is a base type.

We can define functions by pattern matching and recursion, just as in any other functional language. To define addition of natural numbers, for instance, we could write:

> $\_ + \_ :$ *Nat* $\to$ *Nat* $\to$ *Nat*
> *Zero* $+ m = m$
> *Succ n* $+ m = $ *Succ* $(n + m)$

Note that Agda uses underscores to denote the positions of arguments when defining new operators.

Polymorphic lists are slightly more interesting than natural numbers:

> **data** *List* $(a : \star) : \star$ **where**
> *Nil* : *List a*
> *Cons* : $a \to$ *List a* $\to$ *List a*

To uniformly parameterize a data type, we can write additional arguments to the left of the copula. In this case, we add $(a : \star)$ to our data type declaration to state that lists are type *constructors*, parameterized over a type variable *a* of kind $\star$.

Just as we defined addition for natural numbers, we can define an operator that appends one list to another:

> *append* : $(a : \star) \to$ *List a* $\to$ *List a* $\to$ *List a*
> *append a Nil* $ys = ys$
> *append a* (*Cons x xs*) $ys = $ *Cons x* (*append a xs ys*)

The *append* function is polymorphic. In Agda, such polymorphism can be introduced via the *dependent function space*, written $(x : a) \to y$, where the variable *x* may occur in the type *y*. This particular example of the dependent function space is not terribly interesting: it corresponds to parametric polymorphism. Later we

---

[1]The resulting code is available from the first author's website.

will encounter more interesting examples, where *types* depend on *values*.

One drawback of using the dependent function space for such parametric polymorphism, is that we must explicitly instantiate polymorphic functions. For example, the recursive call to *append* in the *Cons* case takes a type as its first argument. Fortunately, Agda allows us to mark certain arguments as *implicit*. Using implicit arguments, we could also define *append* as in any other functional language:

$$append : \{a : \star\} \rightarrow List\ a \rightarrow List\ a \rightarrow List\ a$$
$$append\ Nil \qquad\quad ys = ys$$
$$append\ (Cons\ x\ xs)\ ys = Cons\ x\ (append\ xs\ ys)$$

Arguments enclosed in curly brackets, such as $\{a : \star\}$, are implicit: we do not write a to the left of the equals sign and do not pass a type argument when we make a recursive call. The Agda type checker will automatically instantiate this function whenever we call it, much in the same way as type variables are automatically instantiated in Haskell.

Besides polymorphic data types, Agda also supports *indexed families*. Like Haskell's GADTs, indexed families allow a data type's constructors to have different codomains. Indexed families, however, are more general as they also capture data types that are indexed by *values* instead of types. For example, we can define the family of finite types:

$$\textbf{data}\ Fin : Nat \rightarrow \star\ \textbf{where}$$
$$Fz : \{n : Nat\} \rightarrow Fin\ (Succ\ n)$$
$$Fs : \{n : Nat\} \rightarrow Fin\ n \rightarrow Fin\ (Succ\ n)$$

The type *Fin n* corresponds to a finite type with n distinct values. For example, *Fin* 1 is isomorphic to the unit type; *Fin* 2 is isomorphic to *Bool*. Note that the argument n is left implicit in both the constructors of *Fin*. From the types of these constructors, it is easy to see that *Fin* 0 is uninhabited. For every n, the *Fs* constructor embeds *Fin n* into *Fin* (*Succ n*); the *Fz* constructor, on the other hand, adds a single new element to *Fin* (*Succ n*) that was not in *Fin n*. By induction it is easy to see that *Fin n* does indeed have n elements.

Agda has many other features, such as records and a module system, that we will hardly use in this paper. Although there are a few more concepts we will need, we will discuss them as they pop up in later sections.

2.3 MUTABLE ARRAYS

With this brief Agda tutorial under our belt, we can start our specification of mutable arrays. We will specify three different operations on arrays: the creation of new arrays; reading from an array; and updating a value stored in an array. Before we can define the behaviour of these operations, however, we need to introduce several data types to describe the layout and contents of memory. Using these data types, we can proceed by defining an *IO* type that captures the syntax of array operations. Finally, we will define a *run* function that describes how the array operations affect the heap, assigning semantics to our syntax. This semantics can be used to simulate and reason about computations on mutable arrays in a pure functional language. When compiled, however, these operations should be replaced by their more efficient, low-level counterparts.

To keep things simple, we will only work with flat arrays storing natural numbers. This is, of course, a drastic oversimplification. The techniques we present here, however, can be adapted to cover multidimensional arrays that may store different types of data (Section 2.5).

To avoid confusion between numbers denoting the size of an array and the data stored in an array, we introduce the *Data* type synonym. Throughout the rest of this paper, we will use *Data* to refer to the data stored in arrays; the *Nat* type will always refer to the size of an array.

$Data : \star$
$Data = Nat$

Using the *Fin* type, we can give a functional specification of arrays of a fixed size by mapping every index to the corresponding value.

$Array : Nat \rightarrow \star$
$Array\ n = Fin\ n \rightarrow Data$

How should we represent the heap? We need to be a bit careful—as the heap will store arrays of different sizes, its type should explicitly state how many arrays it stores and how large each array is. To accomplish this, we begin by introducing a data type representing the *shape* of the heap:

$Shape : \star$
$Shape = List\ Nat$

The *Shape* of the heap is simply a list of natural numbers, representing the size of the arrays stored in memory.

We can now define a *Heap* data type that is indexed by a *Shape*. The *Empty* constructor corresponds to an empty heap; the *Alloc* constructor adds an array of size n to any heap of shape ns to build a larger heap with the layout *Cons n ns*.

data *Heap* : *Shape* $\rightarrow \star$ **where**
  Empty : *Heap Nil*
  Alloc : $\{n : Nat\} \rightarrow \{ns : Shape\} \rightarrow$
    Array n $\rightarrow$ *Heap ns* $\rightarrow$ *Heap* (*Cons n ns*)

Finally, we will want to model references, denoting locations in the heap. A value of type *Loc n ns* corresponds to a reference to an array of size n in a heap with shape ns. The *Loc* data type shares a great deal of structure with the *Fin* type. Every non-empty heap has a *Top* reference; we can weaken any existing reference to denote the same location in a larger heap using the *Pop* constructor.

data *Loc* : *Nat* $\rightarrow$ *Shape* $\rightarrow \star$ **where**
  Top : $\{n : Nat\} \rightarrow \{ns : Shape\} \rightarrow Loc\ n$ (*Cons n ns*)
  Pop : **forall** $\{n\ k\ ns\} \rightarrow Loc\ n\ ns \rightarrow Loc\ n$ (*Cons k ns*)

Note that in the type signature of the *Pop* constructor, we omit the types of three implicit arguments and quantify over them using the **forall** keyword. When we use the **forall**-notation, the types of *n*, *k*, and *ns* are inferred from the rest of the signature by the Agda type checker. Alternatively, we could also have written the more verbose:

$$Pop : \{n : Nat\} \rightarrow \{k : Nat\} \rightarrow \{ns : Shape\} \rightarrow$$
$$Loc\ n\ ns \rightarrow Loc\ n\ (Cons\ k\ ns)$$

We will occasionally use the **forall**-notation to make large type signatures somewhat more legible.

With these data types in place, we can define a data type capturing the syntax of the permissible operations on arrays. Crucially, the *IO* type is indexed by *two* shapes: a value of type *IO a ns ms* denotes a computation that takes a heap of shape *ns* to a heap of shape *ms* and returns a result of type *a*. This pattern of indexing operations by an initial and final 'state' is a common pattern in dependently–typed programming [14].

> **data** *IO* (*a* : ⋆) : *Shape* → *Shape* → ⋆ **where**
>   *Return* : {*ns* : *Shape*} → *a* → *IO a ns ns*
>   *Write* : **forall** {*n ns ms*} →
>   *Loc n ns* → *Fin n* → *Data* → *IO a ns ms* → *IO a ns ms*
>   *Read* : **forall** {*n ns ms*} →
>   *Loc n ns* → *Fin n* → (*Data* → *IO a ns ms*) → *IO a ns ms*
>   *New* : **forall** {*ns ms*} →
>   (*n* : *Nat*) → (*Loc n* (*Cons n ns*) → *IO a* (*Cons n ns*) *ms*) →
>   *IO a ns ms*

The *IO* type has four constructors. The *Return* constructor returns a pure value of type *a* without modifying the heap. The *Write* constructor takes four arguments: the location of an array of size *n*; an index in that array; the value to write at that index; and the rest of the computation. Similarly, reading from an array requires a reference to an array and an index. Instead of requiring the data to be written, however, the last argument of the *Read* constructor may refer to data that has been read. Finally, the *New* constructor actually changes the size of the heap. Given a number *n*, it allocates an array of size *n* on the heap; the second argument of *New* may then use this fresh reference to continue the computation in a larger heap.

The *IO* data type is a *parameterized monad* [3]—that is, a monad with *return* and bind operators that satisfy certain coherence conditions with respect to the *Shape* indices.

> *return* : {*a* : ⋆} → {*ns* : *Shape*} → *a* → *IO a ns ns*
> *return x* = *Return x*
>
> _⋙_ : **forall** {*a b ns ms ks*} →
>   *IO a ns ms* → (*a* → *IO b ms ks*) → *IO b ns ks*
> *Return x* ⋙ *f*   = *f x*
> *Write a i x wr* ⋙ *f* = *Write a i x* (*wr* ⋙ *f*)
> *Read a i rd* ⋙ *f* = *Read a i* (λ*x* → *rd x* ⋙ *f*)
> *New n io* ⋙ *f*   = *New n* (λ*a* → *io a* ⋙ *f*)

The return of the *IO* data type lifts a pure value into a computation that can run on a heap of any size. Furthermore, *return* does not modify the shape of the heap. The bind operator, $\gg=$, can be used to compose monadic computations. To sequence two computations, the heap resulting from the first computation must be a suitable starting point for the second computation. This condition is enforced by the type of the bind operator:

To actually program using these array operations, we need to introduce smart constructors. For example, we could define the *readArray* function as follows:

> *readArray*: **forall** $\{n\,ns\} \rightarrow Loc\,n\,ns \rightarrow Fin\,n \rightarrow IO\,Data\,ns\,ns$
> *readArray a i = Read a i Return*

There is a slight problem with this definition. As we allocate new memory, the size of the heap changes; correspondingly, we must explicitly modify any existing pointers to denote locations in a larger heap. We can achieve this by revising the above definition slightly, applying the *inj* function to weaken references:

> *inj*: **forall** $\{ms\,ns\,n\} \rightarrow Loc\,n\,ns \rightarrow Loc\,n\,(append\,ms\,ns)$
> *inj* $\{Nil\}$ $i = i$
> *inj* $\{Cons\,k\,ks\}\,i = Pop\,(inj\,i)$

For the purpose of this paper, however, we will ignore this technicality. The first definition will suffice for the examples we cover. For a more comprehensive discussion, we refer to the first author's forthcoming thesis [19].

Denotational model   We have described the syntax of array computations using the *IO* data type, but we have not specified how these computations *behave*. Recall that we can model arrays as functions from indices to natural numbers:

> *Array*: $Nat \rightarrow \star$
> *Array n = Fin n \rightarrow Data*

Before specifying the behaviour of *IO* computations, we define several auxiliary functions to update an array and lookup a value stored in an array.

> *lookup*: **forall** $\{n\,ns\} \rightarrow Loc\,n\,ns \rightarrow Fin\,n \rightarrow Heap\,ns \rightarrow Data$
> *lookup Top* $i\,(Alloc\,a\,\_) = a\,i$
> *lookup* $(Pop\,k)\,i\,(Alloc\,\_\,h) = lookup\,k\,i\,h$

The *lookup* function takes a reference to an array *l*, an index *i* in the array at location *l*, and a heap, and returns the value stored in the array at index *i*. It dereferences *l*, resulting in a function of type $Fin\,n \rightarrow Data$; the value stored at index *i* is the result of applying this function to *i*.

Next, we define a pair of functions to update the contents of an array.

> *updateArray*: $\{n : Nat\} \rightarrow Fin\,n \rightarrow Data \rightarrow Array\,n \rightarrow Array\,n$
> *updateArray i d a* = $\lambda j \rightarrow$ **if** $i \equiv j$ **then** *d* **else** *a j*

> *updateHeap*: **forall** $\{n\,ns\} \rightarrow$
> $Loc\,n\,ns \rightarrow Fin\,n \rightarrow Data \rightarrow Heap\,ns \rightarrow Heap\,ns$
> *updateHeap Top* $i\,x\,(Alloc\,a\,h) = Alloc\,(updateArray\,i\,x\,a)\,h$
> *updateHeap* $(Pop\,k)\,i\,x\,(Alloc\,a\,h) = Alloc\,a\,(updateHeap\,k\,i\,x\,h)$

The *updateArray* function overwrites the data stored at a single index. The function *updateHeap* updates a single index of an array stored in the heap. It proceeds by dereferencing the location on the heap where the desired array is stored and updates it accordingly, leaving the rest of the heap unchanged.

We now have all the pieces in place to assign semantics to *IO* computations. The *run* function below takes a computation of type *IO a ns ms* and an initial heap of shape *ns* as arguments, and returns a pair consisting of the result of the computation and the final heap of shape *ms*.

data *Pair* $(a:\star)$ $(b:\star):\star$ **where**
    pair : $a \to b \to Pair\ a\ b$

run : **forall** $\{a\ ns\ ms\} \to IO\ a\ ns\ ms \to Heap\ ns \to Pair\ a\ (Heap\ ms)$
run (*Return x*) *h*   = *pair x h*
run (*Read a i rd*) *h*   = *run* (*rd* (*lookup a i h*)) *h*
run (*Write a i x wr*) *h* = *run wr* (*updateHeap a i x h*)
run (*New n io*) *h*   = *run* (*io Top*) (*Alloc* ($\lambda i \to Zero$) *h*)

The *Return* constructor simply pairs the result and heap; in the *Read* case, we lookup the data from the heap and recurse with the same heap; for the *Write* constructor, we recurse with an appropriately modified heap; finally, when a new array is created, we extend the heap with a new array that stores *Zero* at every index, and continue recursively. Note that, by convention, the *Top* constructor always refers to the most recently created reference. Our smart constructors will add additional *Pop* constructors when new memory is allocated.

We refer to this specification as a denotational model. As Agda is a programming language based on type theory, we may also view it as a constructive set theory. In that sense, the *run* function constitutes a denotational semantics of mutable arrays. By implementing these semantics in Agda, we build an executable denotational model in Agda's underlying type theory.

Example Using our smart constructors and the monad operators, we can now define functions that manipulate arrays. For example, the swap function exchanges the value stored at two indices:

swap : **forall** $\{n\ ns\} \to Loc\ n\ ns \to Fin\ n \to Fin\ n \to IO\ ()\ ns\ ns$
swap a i j = *readArray a i* $\gg\!\!=\lambda vali \to$
        readArray a j $\gg\!\!=\lambda valj \to$
        writeArray a i valj $\gg$
        writeArray a j vali

In a dependently–typed programming language such as Agda, we can prove properties of our code. For example, we may want to show that swapping the contents of any two array indices twice, leaves the heap intact :

swapProp : **forall** $\{n\ ns\} \to$
    $(l:Loc\ n\ ns) \to (i:Fin\ n) \to (j:Fin\ n) \to (h:Heap\ ns) \to$
    $(h \equiv snd\ (run\ (swap\ l\ i\ j \gg swap\ l\ i\ j)\ h))$

The proof requires a lemma about how *updateHeap* and *lookupHeap* interact and is not terribly interesting in itself. The fact that we can formalize such properties and have our proof verified by a computer is much more exciting.

2.4 DISTRIBUTED ARRAYS

Arrays are usually represented by a continuous block of memory. *Distributed arrays*, however, can be distributed over different *places*—where every place may correspond to a different core on a multiprocessor machine, a different machine on the same network, or any other configuration of interconnected computers.

We begin by determining the type of places where data is stored and code is executed. Obviously, we do not want to fix the type of all possible places prematurely: you may want to execute the same program in different environments. Yet regardless of the exact number of places, there are certain operations you will always want to perform, such as iterating over all places, or checking when two places are equal.

We therefore choose to abstract over the *number* of places in the module we will define in the coming section. Agda allows modules to be paramaterised:

module *DistrArray* (*placeCount* : *Nat*) **where**

When we import the *DistrArray* module, we are obliged to choose the number of places. Typically, there will be one place for every available processor. From this number, we can define a data type corresponding to the available places:

Place : $\star$
Place = *Fin placeCount*

The key idea underlying our model of locality-aware algorithms is to index computations by the place where they are executed. The new type declaration for the *IO* monad corresponding to operations on *distributed* arrays will become:

data *DIO* (*a* : $\star$) : *Shape* → *Place* → *Shape* → $\star$ **where**

You may want to think of a value of type *DIO a ns p ms* as a computation that can be executed at place *p* and will take a heap of shape *ns* to a heap of shape *ms*, yielding a final value of type *a*.

We strive to ensure that any well-typed program written in the *DIO* monad will never access data that is not local. The specification of distributed arrays now poses a twofold problem: we want to ensure that the array manipulations from the previous section are 'locality-aware', that is, we must somehow restrict the array indices that can be accessed from a certain place; furthermore, X10 facilitates several *place-shifting* operations that change the place where certain chunks of code are executed. As we shall see in the rest of this section, both these issues can be resolved quite naturally.

Regions, Points, and Distributed Arrays

Before we define the *DIO* monad, we need to introduce several new concepts. In what follows, we will try to stick closely to X10's terminology for distributed arrays. Every array is said to have a *region* associated with it. A region is a set of valid index points. A *distribution* specifies a place for every index point in a region.

Once again, we will only treat flat arrays storing natural numbers and defer any discussion about how to deal with more complicated data structures for the moment. In this simple case, a region merely determines the size of the array.

> *Region* : $\star$
> *Region* = *Nat*

As we have seen in the previous section, we can model array indices using the *Fin* data type:

> *Point* : *Region* $\rightarrow$ $\star$
> *Point n* = *Fin n*

To model distributed arrays, we now need to consider the distribution that specifies *where* this data is stored. In line with existing work [9], we assume the existence of a fixed distribution. Agda's **postulate** expression allows us to assume the existence of a distribution, without providing its definition.

> **postulate**
>> *distr* : **forall** $\{n\ ns\} \rightarrow Loc\ n\ ns \rightarrow Point\ n \rightarrow Place$

Although we have implemented several of X10's combinators for defining distributions, we do not have the space to cover them here.

Now that we have all the required auxiliary data types, we proceed by defining the *DIO* monad. As it is a bit more complex than the data types we have seen so far, we will discuss every constructor individually.

The *Return* constructor is analogous to one we have seen previously for the *IO* monad: it lifts any pure value into the *DIO* monad.

> *Return* : $\{p : Place\} \rightarrow \{ns : Shape\} \rightarrow a \rightarrow DIO\ a\ ns\ p\ ns$

The *Read* and *Write* operations are more interesting. Although they correspond closely to the operations we have seen in the previous section, their type now keeps track of the place where they are executed. Any read or write operation to point *pt* of an array *l* can *only* be executed at the place specified by the distribution. This invariant is enforced by the types of our constructors:

> *Read* : **forall** $\{n\ ns\ ms\} \rightarrow$
>> $(l : Loc\ n\ ns) \rightarrow (pt : Point\ n) \rightarrow$
>> $(Data \rightarrow DIO\ a\ ns\ (distr\ l\ pt)\ ms) \rightarrow$
>> $DIO\ a\ ns\ (distr\ l\ pt)\ ms$
>
> *Write* : **forall** $\{n\ ns\ ms\} \rightarrow$
>> $(l : Loc\ n\ ns) \rightarrow (pt : Point\ n) \rightarrow Data \rightarrow$
>> $DIO\ a\ ns\ (distr\ l\ pt)\ ms \rightarrow$
>> $DIO\ a\ ns\ (distr\ l\ pt)\ ms$

In contrast to *Read* and *Write*, new arrays can be allocated at any place.

> *New* : **forall** $\{p\ ns\ ms\} \rightarrow$
>> $(n : Nat) \rightarrow$
>> $(Loc\ n\ (Cons\ n\ ns) \rightarrow DIO\ a\ (Cons\ n\ ns)\ p\ ms) \rightarrow$

DIO a ns p ms

Finally, we add a constructor for a place-shifting operator. Using this *At* operator lets us execute a computation at another place.

At : **forall** $\{p\ ns\ ms\ ps\} \rightarrow$
$\quad (q : Place) \rightarrow DIO\ ()\ ns\ q\ ms \rightarrow DIO\ a\ ms\ p\ ps \rightarrow DIO\ a\ ns\ p\ ps$

Note that we will discard the result of the computation that is executed at another place. We therefore require this computation to return an element of the unit type.

We can add our smart constructors for each of these operations, as we have done in the previous section. We can also show that *DIO* is indeed a parameterized monad. We have omitted the definitions of the *return* and bind operators for the sake of brevity:

return : **forall** $\{ns\ a\ p\} \rightarrow a \rightarrow DIO\ a\ ns\ p\ ns$

$\_ \ggg \_$: **forall** $\{ns\ ms\ ks\ a\ b\ p\} \rightarrow$
$\quad DIO\ A\ ns\ p\ ms \rightarrow (A \rightarrow DIO\ B\ ms\ p\ ks) \rightarrow DIO\ B\ ns\ p\ ks$

It is worth noting that the bind operator $\ggg$ can only be used to sequence operations at the same place.

Denotational model

To run a computation in the *DIO* monad, we follow the *run* function defined in the previous section closely. Our new *run* function, however, must be locality-aware. Therefore, we parameterize the *run* function explicitly by the place where the computation is executed.

run : **forall** $\{a\ ns\ ms\} \rightarrow$
$\quad (p : Place) \rightarrow DIO\ a\ ns\ p\ ms \rightarrow Heap\ ns \rightarrow Pair\ a\ (Heap\ ms)$
run p (*Return x*) *h* $\qquad = pair\ x\ h$
run .(*distr l i*) (*Read l i rd*) *h* $\quad = run\ (distr\ l\ i)\ (rd\ (lookup\ l\ i\ h))\ h$
run .(*distr l i*) (*Write l i x wr*) *h* = **let** $h' = updateHeap\ l\ i\ x\ h$
$\qquad\qquad\qquad\qquad\qquad\qquad$ **in** *run* (*distr l i*) *wr h'*
run p (*New n io*) *h* $\qquad\qquad = run\ p\ (io\ Top)\ (Alloc\ (\lambda i \rightarrow Zero)\ h)$
run p (*At q io1 io2*) *h* $\qquad\quad = run\ p\ io2\ (snd\ (run\ q\ io1\ h))$

Now we can see that the *Read* and *Write* operations may not be executed at *any* place. Recall that the *Read* and *Write* constructors both return computations at the place *distr l i*. When we pattern match on a *Read* or *Write*, we know exactly what the place argument of the *run* function must be. Correspondingly, we do not pattern match on the place argument—we know that the place can only be *distr l i*. Agda's syntax allows us to prefix expressions by a single period, provided we know that there is only one possible value an argument may take. This may be unfamiliar to many functional programmers who are used to thinking of patterns being built-up from variables and constructors: *distr l i* is an expression, not a pattern! The situation is somewhat similar to pattern matching on GADTs in Haskell, which introduces equalities between *types*. The *DIO* monad, however, is indexed by values. As a result, pattern matching in the presence of dependent types may introduce equalities between *values*.

The other difference with respect to the previous *run* function, is the new case for the *At* constructor. In that case, we sequence the two computations *io1* and *io2*. To do so, we first execute the *io1* at *q*, but discard its result; we continue executing the second computation *io2* with the heap resulting from the execution of *io1* at the location *p*. Conforming to previous proposals [10], we have assumed that *io1* and *io2* are performed synchronously—executing *io1* before continuing with the rest of the computation. Using techniques to model concurrency that we have presented previously [20], we believe we could give a more refined treatment of the X10's *globally asynchronous/locally synchronous* semantics and provide specifications for X10's clocks, *finish*, and *force* constructs.

Locality-aware combinators

Using the place-shifting operator *at*, we can define several locality-aware control structures. With our first-class distribution and definition of *Place*, we believe there is no need to define more primitive operations.

The distributed map, for example, applies a function to all the elements of a distributed array at the place where they are stored. We define it in terms of an auxiliary function, *for*, that iterates over all the indices of an array:

$$for: \textbf{forall } \{n\ ns\ p\} \rightarrow (Point\ n \rightarrow DIO\ ()\ ns\ p\ ns) \rightarrow DIO\ ()\ ns\ p\ ns$$
$$for\ \{Succ\ k\}\ dio = dio\ Fz \gg (for\ \{k\}\ (dio\ .\ Fs))$$
$$for\ \{Zero\} \quad dio = return\ ()$$

$$dmap: \textbf{forall } \{n\ ns\ p\} \rightarrow (Data \rightarrow Data) \rightarrow Loc\ n\ ns \rightarrow DIO\ ()\ ns\ p\ ns$$
$$dmap\ f\ l = for\ (\lambda i \rightarrow at\ (distr\ l\ i)\ (readArray\ l\ i \ggeq \lambda x \rightarrow$$
$$writeArray\ l\ i\ (f\ x)))$$

Besides *dmap*, we implement two other combinators: *forallplaces* and *ateach*. The *forallplaces* operation executes its argument computation at all available places. We define it using the *for* function to iterate over all places. The *ateach* function, on the other hand, is a generalization of the distributed map operation. It iterates over an array, executing its argument operation once for every index of the array, at the place where that index is stored.

$$forallplaces: \textbf{forall } \{p\ ns\} \rightarrow$$
$$((q\!:\!Place) \rightarrow DIO\ ()\ ns\ q\ ns) \rightarrow DIO\ ()\ ns\ p\ ns$$
$$forallplaces\ io = for\ (\lambda i \rightarrow at\ i\ (io\ i))$$

$$ateach: \textbf{forall } \{n\ ns\ p\} \rightarrow$$
$$(l\!:\!Loc\ n\ ns) \rightarrow ((pt\!:\!Point\ n) \rightarrow DIO\ ()\ ns\ (distr\ l\ pt)\ ns) \rightarrow$$
$$DIO\ ()\ ns\ p\ ns$$
$$ateach\ l\ io = for\ (\lambda i \rightarrow at\ (distr\ l\ i)\ (io\ i))$$

Example   We will now show how to write a simple algorithm that sums all the elements of a distributed array. To do so efficiently, we first locally sum all the values at every place. To compute the total sum of all the elements of the array, we add together all these local sums. In what follows, we will need the following auxiliary function, *increment*:

$$increment : \textbf{forall} \; \{n \; ns \; p\} \rightarrow$$
$$(l : Loc \; n \; ns) \rightarrow (i : Fin \; n) \rightarrow Nat \rightarrow (distr \; l \; i \equiv p) \rightarrow DIO \; () \; ns \; p \; ns$$
$$increment \; l \; i \; x \; Refl = readArray \; l \; i \ggg \lambda y \rightarrow writeArray \; l \; i \; (x + y)$$

Note that *increment* is a bit more general than strictly necessary. We could return a computation at *distr l i*, but instead we choose to be a little more general: *increment* can be executed at any place, as long as we have a proof that this place is equal to *distr l i*. The $\equiv$-type is inhabited by single constructor *Refl*.

We can use the *increment* function to define a simple sequential *sum* function:

$$sum : \textbf{forall} \; \{n \; ns \; p\} \rightarrow Loc \; n \; ns \rightarrow Loc \; 1 \; ns \rightarrow DIO \; () \; ns \; p \; ns$$
$$sum \; l \; out = ateach \; l \; (\lambda i \rightarrow readArray \; l \; i \ggg \lambda n \rightarrow$$
$$at \; (distr \; out \; Fz) \; (increment \; out \; Fz \; n \; Refl))$$

The *sum* function takes an array as its argument, together with a reference to a single-celled array, *out*. It reads every element of the array, and increments *out* accordingly.

Finally, we can use both these functions to define a parallel sum:

$$psum : \textbf{forall} \; \{n \; ns\} \rightarrow$$
$$(l : Loc \; n \; ns) \rightarrow (localSums : Loc \; placeCount \; ns) \rightarrow$$
$$((i : Place) \rightarrow distr \; localSums \; i \equiv i) \rightarrow$$
$$(out : Loc \; 1 \; ns) \rightarrow DIO \; Nat \; ns \; (distr \; out \; Fz) \; ns$$
$$psum \; l \; localSums \; locDistr \; out =$$
$$ateach \; l \; (\lambda i \rightarrow (readArray \; l \; i \ggg \lambda n \rightarrow$$
$$increment \; localSums \; (distr \; l \; i) \; n \; (locDistr \; (distr \; l \; i))))$$
$$\ggg sum \; localSums \; out$$
$$\ggg readArray \; out \; Fz$$

The *psum* function takes four arguments: the array *l* whose elements you would like to sum; an array *localSums* that will store the intermediate sums; an assumption regarding the distribution of this array; and finally, the single-celled array to which we write the result. For every index *i* of the array *l*, we read the value stored at index *i*, and increment the corresponding local sum. We then add together the local sums using our previous sequential *sum* function, and return the final result. We use our assumption about the distribution of the *localSums* array when calling the increment function. Without this assumption, we would have to use the place-shifting operation *at* to update a (potentially) non-local array index.

There are several interesting issues that these examples highlight. First of all, as our *at* function only works on computations returning a unit type, the results of intermediate computations must be collected in intermediate arrays.

More importantly, however, whenever we want to rely on properties of the global distribution, we need to make explicit assumptions in the form of proof arguments. This is rather unfortunate: it would be interesting to research how a specific distribution can be associated with an array when it is created. This would hopefully allow for a more fine-grained treatment of distributions and eliminate the need for explicit proof arguments.

2.5 DISCUSSION

Using a dependently–typed host language, we have shown how to implement a domain-specific library for distributed arrays, together with an embedded type system that guarantees all array access operations are both safe and local. In contrast to existing work [10], we have not designed a specific set of type rules; instead, we have shown how equivalent properties can be enforced by a general-purpose language with dependent types. We have provided semantics for our library in the form of a total, functional specification. Although our semantics may not take the form of deduction rules, they are no less precise or concise. Besides these functional specifications are both executable and amenable to computer-aided formal verification. More generally, we hope that this approach can be extended to other domains: a dependently–typed language accommodates domain specific libraries with their own embedded type systems.

Having said this, there are clearly several serious limitations of this work as it stands. We have had to make several simplifying assumptions. First and foremost, we have assumed that every array only stores natural numbers, disallowing more complex structures such as multidimensional arrays. This can be easily fixed by defining a more elaborate *Shape* data type. In its most general form, we could choose our *Shape* data type as a list of types; a heap then corresponds to a list of values of the right type.[2] We decided to restrict ourself to this more simple case for the purpose of presentation. We believe that there is no fundamental obstacle preventing us from incorporating the rich region calculus offered by X10 in the same fashion.

Furthermore, our pure model is rather naive. It would be interesting to explore a more refined model, where every place maintains its own heap. As our example in the previous section illustrated, assuming the presence of a global distribution does not scale well. Decorating every array with a distribution upon its creation should help provide locality-information when it is needed.

We have not discussed how code in the *IO* or *DIO* monad is actually compiled. At the moment, Agda can only be compiled to Haskell. Agda does provide several pragmas to customize how Agda functions are translated to their Haskell counterparts. The ongoing effort to support data parallelism in Haskell [4, 5] may therefore provide us with a most welcome foothold.

There are many features of X10 that we have not discussed here at all. Most notably, we have refrained from modelling many of X10's constructs that enable asynchronous communication between locations, even though we would like to do so in the future.

Finally, we should emphasize that we need to explore larger examples to ac-

---

[2]There are some technical details involving 'size problems' that are beyond the scope of this paper. The standard technique of introducing a universe, closed under natural numbers and arrays, should resolve these issues.

quire a better understanding of how this approach scales. At the moment, we cannot predict how efficient the resulting code will be; we do not know how difficult it will be to reason about large, realistic distributed algorithms. Unfortunately, we do not have the space to explore such examples further in this paper. Despite these many limitations, however, we believe this paper provides an important first stepping-stone for such further work.

Acknowledgements We wish to express our gratitude to Jens Palsberg for our interesting discussions; to Ulf Norell for his fantastic new incarnation of Agda; and to Mauro Jaskelioff, Nicolas Oury, Liyang HU, and the anonymous reviewers for their helpful comments on a draft version of this paper.

REFERENCES

[1] T. Agda Team. Agda. `http://www.cs.chalmers.se/~ulfn/Agda`.

[2] E. Allen, D. Chase, V. Luchangco, J.-W. Maessen, S. Ryu, G. L. S. Jr., and S. Tobin-Hochstadt. The Fortress language specification. Technical report, Sun Microsystems, Inc., 2005.

[3] R. Atkey. Parameterised notions of computation. In *Proceedings of the Workshop on Mathematically Structured Functional Programming*. British Computer Society, 2006.

[4] M. M. Chakravarty, G. Keller, R. Lechtchinsky, and W. Pfannenstiel. Nepal – Nested Data-Parallelism in Haskell. In *Euro-Par 2001: Parallel Processing, 7th International Euro-Par Conference*, volume LNCS 2150, 2001.

[5] M. M. Chakravarty, R. Leshchinskiy, S. Peyton Jones, G. Keller, and S. Marlow. Data Parallel Haskell: A status report. *Proceedings of the 2007 Workshop on Declarative Aspects of Multicore Programming*, 2007.

[6] B. Chamberlain, S. Deitz, M. B. Hribar, and W. Wong. Chapel. Technical report, Cray Inc., 2005.

[7] B. L. Chamberlain, S.-E. Choi, E. C. Lewis, C. Lin, L. Snyder, and D. Weathersby. ZPL: A machine independent programming language for parallel computers. *Software Engineering*, 26(3), 2000.

[8] P. Charles, C. Grothoff, V. Saraswat, C. Donawa, A. Kielstra, K. Ebcioglu, C. von Praun, and V. Sarkar. X10: an object-oriented approach to non-uniform cluster computing. In *OOPSLA '05*, 2005.

[9] C. Grothoff, J. Palsberg, and V. Saraswat. Safe arrays via regions and dependent types. Submitted for publication.

[10] C. Grothoff, J. Palsberg, and V. Saraswat. A type system for distributed arrays. Unpublished draft.

[11] P. Hudak. Building domain-specific embedded languages. *ACM Computing Surveys*, 28, 1996.

[12] B. Liblit and A. Aiken. Type systems for distributed data structures. In *POPL '00: Proceedings of the 27th ACM SIGPLAN-SIGACT Symposium on Principles of Programming Languages*, pages 199–213, 2000.

[13] A. Löh. lhs2tex. `http://people.cs.uu.nl/andres/lhs2tex/`.

[14] J. McKinna and J. Wright. A type-correct, stack-safe, provably correct, expression compiler in Epigram. To appear in the *Journal of Functional Programming*.

[15] U. Norell. *Towards a Practical Programming Language Based on Dependent Type Theory*. PhD thesis, Chalmers University of Technology, 2007.

[16] S. Peyton Jones, editor. *Haskell 98 Language and Libraries – The Revised Report*. Cambridge University Press, 2003.

[17] S. Peyton Jones, D. Vytiniotis, S. Weirich, and G. Washburn. Simple unification-based type inference for GADTs. In *ICFP '06: Proceedings of the Eleventh ACM SIGPLAN International Conference on Functional Programming*, 2006.

[18] S.-B. Scholz. Single Assignment C — efficient support for high-level array operations in a functional setting. *Journal of Functional Programming*, 13(6):1005–1059, 2003.

[19] W. Swierstra. *A Functional Specification of Effects*. PhD thesis, University of Nottingham, 2008.

[20] W. Swierstra and T. Altenkirch. Beauty in the beast: a functional semantics of the awkward squad. In *Proceedings of the ACM SIGPLAN Haskell Workshop*, 2007.

Chapter 3

Size Analysis of Algebraic Data Types

Alejandro Tamalet, Olha Shkaravska, Marko van Eekelen[1]
Category: Research

Abstract: We present a size-aware type system for a first-order functional language with algebraic data types, where types are annotated with polynomials over size variables. We define how to generate typing rules for each data type, provided its user–defined size function meets certain requirements. As an example, a program for balancing binary trees is type checked. The type system is shown to be sound with respect to the operational semantics in the class of shapely functions. Type checking is shown to be undecidable, however, decidability for a large subset of programs is guaranteed.

3.1 INTRODUCTION

Embedded systems or server applications often have limited resources available. Therefore, it can be important to know in advance how much time or memory a computation is going to take, for instance, to determine how much memory should at least be put in a system to enable all desired operations. This helps to prevent abrupt termination on small devices like mobile phones and Java cards as well as on powerful computers running memory exhaustive computations like GRID applications and model generation. Analyzing resource usage is also interesting for optimizations in compilers, in particular optimizations of memory allocation and garbage collection techniques. An accurate estimation of heap usage enables preallocation of larger chunks of memory instead of allocating memory cells separately when needed, leading to a better cache performance. Size verification can

---

[1] All authors are members of the Digital Security Section, Institute for Computing and Information Sciences, Radboud University, Nijmegen, The Netherlands; {`A.Tamalet,` `O.Shkaravska, M.vanEekelen`}`@cs.ru.nl`. This work is sponsored by the Netherlands Organization for Scientific Research (NWO) under grant nr. 612.063.511.

be used to avoid memory exhaustion which helps to prevent attacks that exploit it, like some 'Denial of Service' attacks. Size-aware type systems can also be used to prove termination of finite computations or progression of infinite ones (see the related work section).

Decisions regarding these (and related) problems should be based on formally verified upper bounds of resource consumption. A detailed analysis of these bounds requires knowledge of the sizes of the data structures used throughout the program (see [11]).

As part of the AHA project, we study in this paper a *type-and-effect system* for a strict first-order functional language with algebraic data types, where types are annotated with size information. We focus on *shapely* function definitions in this language, where shapely means that the size of their output is polynomial with respect to the sizes of its arguments. Formally, if $size_{\tau_i} : \tau_i \to \mathcal{N}$ are the size functions of the types τ_i for $i = 1..k+1$, a function $f : \tau_1 \times \ldots \times \tau_k \to \tau_{k+1}$ is shapely if there exists a polynomial p on k variables such that

$$\forall x_1 : \tau_1, \ldots, x_k : \tau_k \, . \, size_{\tau_{k+1}}(f(x_1, \ldots, x_k)) = p(size_{\tau_1}(x_1), \ldots, size_{\tau_k}(x_k))$$

For instance, if we take for lists their length to be their size, then appending two lists is shapely because the size of the output is the sum of the sizes of the inputs. However, a function that conditionally deletes an element from a list is not shapely because the size of the output can be the same as the size of the input or one less, which can not be expressed with a unique polynomial. The definition can be easily extended to size functions that return tuples of natural numbers.

We have previously shown for a basic language (whose only types are integers and lists) and a simplified size-aware type system, that type checking is undecidable in general, but decidable under a syntactical restriction [9]. Type inference through a combination of dynamic testing and type checking was developed in [12]. A demonstrator for type checking and type inference is available at www.aha.cs.ru.nl.

In this paper we extend this analysis to algebraic data types. We show a procedure to generate size-aware typing rules for an algebraic data type, provided its size function has a given form. Furthermore, for any data type we define a *canonical size function* which is used in case no size function is defined by the user. We prove soundness of the type system with respect to its operational semantics, which allows sharing. In the presence of sharing, the size annotations can be interpreted as an upper bound on the amount of memory used to allocate the result. Type checking is shown to be undecidable, however, the syntactic restriction introduced in [9] can be used to guarantee decidability. We also give an example that shows that the type system is incomplete.

This paper is organized as follows. In Section 3.2 we define the language and the type system, and we give generic typing rules for user–defined size functions. In Section 3.3 we deal with soundness, decidability and completeness issues. Section 3.4 discusses a possible extension to the language and future work. Section 3.5 comments on related work and Section 3.6 draws conclusions.

3.2 SIZE-AWARE TYPE SYSTEM WITH ALGEBRAIC DATA TYPES

We start this section by introducing the working language and types with size annotations followed by an example with binary trees in 3.2.2. Subsection 3.2.3 shows how to obtain typing rules from a size function that meets the requirements stated in 3.2.1.

3.2.1 Language and Types

We define a type and effect system in which types are annotated with polynomial size expressions:

$$p ::= c \mid n \mid p+p \mid p-p \mid p*p$$

where c is a rational number and n denotes a size variable that ranges over natural numbers. A zero-order type can be one of the primitive data types (boolean and integers), a type variable or size annotated algebraic data type:

$$\tau ::= \texttt{Bool} \mid \texttt{Int} \mid \alpha \mid T^{p_1,\dots,p_n}(\tau_1,\dots,\tau_m)$$

An algebraic data type is annotated with a tuple of polynomials. This allows one to measure different aspects of an element of that type, for instance, the number of times each constructor is used. To simplify the presentation we will usually write just $T^{\mathrm{p}}(\overline{\tau})$.

The sets $FV(\tau)$ and $FSV(\tau)$ of the free type and free size variables of τ, are defined inductively in the obvious way. Let τ° denote a zero-order type whose size annotation contains just constants or size variables. First-order types are assigned to shapely functions over values of τ°-types.

$$\begin{aligned} \tau^f ::= \quad & \tau_1^\circ \times \dots \times \tau_k^\circ \to \tau_{k+1} \\ & \text{such that } FSV(\tau_{k+1}) \subseteq FSV(\tau_1^\circ) \cup \dots \cup FSV(\tau_k^\circ) \end{aligned}$$

We work with a fairly simple first-order language over these types. The following grammar defines the syntax of the language, where b ranges over booleans and ι over integers, x denotes a program variable of a zero-order type, C stands for a constructor name and f for a function name.

$$\begin{aligned} d \quad &::= \texttt{data } T(\overline{\alpha}) = C_1(\overline{\tau}_1(\overline{\alpha})) \mid \dots \mid C_r(\overline{\tau}_r(\overline{\alpha})) \\ a \quad &::= b \mid \iota \mid f(\overline{x}) \mid C(\overline{x}) \\ e \quad &::= a \mid \texttt{letfun } f(\overline{x}) = e_1 \texttt{ in } e_2 \\ & \quad\mid \texttt{let } x = a \texttt{ in } e \mid \texttt{if } x \texttt{ then } e_1 \texttt{ else } e_2 \\ & \quad\mid \texttt{match } x \texttt{ with } \mid C_1(\overline{x}_1) \Rightarrow e_{C_1} \mid \dots \mid C_r(\overline{x}_r) \Rightarrow e_{C_r} \\ pr \quad &::= d^* \, e \end{aligned}$$

On the data type definition we have abused of the notation: only type constructors may have type variables as parameters. Types appearing on the right-hand side of the definition of a data type must not have free size variables. We prohibit head-nested let-expressions and restrict subexpressions in function calls to variables to make type checking straightforward. Program expressions of a general form can be equivalently transformed into expressions of this form. It is useful to think of this as an intermediate language. We also assume that the language has the typical basic operations on integers and booleans, but their study is omitted since they do not involve size annotations.

In order to add size annotations to an algebraic data type, it must be decided what to measure. Because of polymorphism, one can measure only the outer structure, e.g., since the size of $\mathsf{List}(\alpha)$ must be defined for any α, the size of a $\mathsf{List}(\mathsf{Tree}(\mathsf{Int}))$ will be just the length of the list. But, because the size is part of the type, all the elements of the list must have the same size, which allows the user to compute the total size once the sizes of the trees are known. Another consequence of polymorphism is that one usually needs to count the number of times each constructor is used to build an element. A size function for

$$\mathsf{data\ TreeAB}(\alpha, \beta) = \mathsf{Empty} \mid \mathsf{Leaf}(\alpha) \mid \mathsf{Node}(\beta, \mathsf{TreeAB}(\alpha, \beta), \mathsf{TreeAB}(\alpha, \beta))$$

should return the number of empties, leaves and nodes. Any size function for these trees that returns a single natural number is losing information and the user will not be able to calculate the total size once α and β are known. One may not want to count the number of times some constructor is used because it can be deduced from the others or it is constant, e.g., any finite list has always one nil constructor cell. Ignoring some constructors can also make a function definition shapely as in the case of a function that can return trees of type TreeAB with different number of empties and leaves, but always the same number of nodes. If all the constructors cells are counted, such a function is not shapely, however, if only nodes are counted, it is shapely.

We require a size function for $T(\overline{\alpha})$ to be total and have the form

$$size_T(C_i(x_{i1}, \ldots, x_{ik_i})) = \mathsf{c}_i + \sum_{j=1}^{k_i} \gamma(x_{ij})$$

where $x_{ij} : T_{ij}$, c_i is a non-negative integer or a tuple of non-negative integers and

$$\gamma(x_{ij}) = \begin{cases} size_T(x_{ij}) & \text{if } T_{ij}(\overline{\alpha}) = T(\overline{\alpha}) \\ 0 & \text{otherwise} \end{cases}$$

Henceforth, we will assume that every size function satisfies these requirements. The motivation for this is twofold. On one hand linearity is needed for decidability (see 3.3.2) and on the other hand, requiring the recursive calls of the size function to be applied to (some of) the arguments of the constructors, allows us to relate their sizes with the annotations of the respective types in the context (see 3.2.3).

A *canonical size function* for $T(\overline{\alpha})$ is a size function where each c_i is 1_i^r, the tuple of arity r (the number of constructors of T) with all zeros except for a 1 on the i-th position. It is always possible to obtain a canonical size function for a given algebraic data type, and there is only one way to construct it, thus it is unique for that type. When no size function for a type is provided by the user, its canonical size function is used. We write s_T for the canonical size function of $T(\overline{\alpha})$. For instance, s_{List} is a function that takes a polymorphic list l and returns $(1, length(l))$, since it is defined as:

$$s_{\text{List}}(\text{Nil}) = (1, 0)$$
$$s_{\text{List}}(\text{Cons}(hd, tl)) = (0, 1) + s_{\text{List}}(tl)$$

We say that a size function for T is *sensible* if it returns the exact amount of occurrences of each constructor of T in its argument. Recall that an inductive type is an initial algebra of the endofunctor corresponding to its constructors. Because we do not allow free size variables in the definitions of data types, we can always 'flatten' any algebraic data type of our language, and obtain an isomorphic *polynomial inductive type*. It is not difficult to prove [10] that the canonical size function of an polynomial inductive type is sensible.

A context Γ is a finite mapping from zero-order variables to zero-order types. A signature Σ is a finite function from function names to first-order types. A typing judgement is a relation of the form $D; \Gamma \vdash_\Sigma e \colon \tau$, where D is a set of *Diophantine* equations (i.e., with integer solutions) that constrains the possible values of the size variables, and Σ contains a type assumption for the function that is going to be type checked along with the signatures of the functions used in its definition. The entailment $D \vdash \mathsf{p} = \mathsf{p}'$ means that $\mathsf{p} = \mathsf{p}'$ is derivable from the equations in D, while $D \vdash \tau = \tau'$ means that τ and τ' have the same underlying type and equality of their size annotations is derivable.

The typing rules for the language, excluding the ones for data types, are shown in Figure 3.1. In the FUNAPP rule, C is used to deal with functions where the input size variables are repeated, as in the type of matrix multiplication: $\text{List}^n(\text{List}^k(\texttt{Int})) \times \text{List}^k(\text{List}^m(\texttt{Int})) \to \text{List}^n(\text{List}^m(\texttt{Int}))$. If such a function is instantiated with lists of type $\text{List}^{p_1}(\text{List}^{p_2}(\texttt{Int}))$ and $\text{List}^{q_1}(\text{List}^{q_2}(\texttt{Int}))$, we add the condition $p_2 = q_1$ to C. For more details on the use of this rule see [10].

3.2.2 Example: Binary Trees

Consider the following definition of binary trees:

$$\texttt{data Tree}(\alpha) = \text{Empty} \mid \text{Node}(\alpha, \text{Tree}(\alpha), \text{Tree}(\alpha))$$

The canonical size function for Tree is:

$$s_{\text{Tree}}(\text{Empty}) = (1, 0)$$
$$s_{\text{Tree}}(\text{Node}(v, l, r)) = (0, 1) + s_{\text{Tree}}(l) + s_{\text{Tree}}(r)$$

Conforming to s_{Tree}, an annotated binary tree has the form $\text{Tree}^{e,n}(\alpha)$, where e is the number of Empty constructors (the leaves of the tree) and n is the number of nodes. We want to obtain typing rules for binary trees that will enable us to statically check the values of e and n when the binary tree is the result of a shapely function. We need one rule per constructor and one rule for pattern matching a binary tree. An empty tree has one leaf and no node, thus:

$$\frac{}{D;\Gamma \vdash_\Sigma b\colon \texttt{Bool}} \; \text{BCONST} \qquad \frac{}{D;\Gamma \vdash_\Sigma \iota\colon \texttt{Int}} \; \text{ICONST}$$

$$\frac{D \vdash \tau = \tau'}{D;\Gamma, x\colon \tau \vdash_\Sigma x\colon \tau'} \; \text{VAR}$$

$$\frac{\Gamma(x) = \texttt{Bool} \qquad D;\Gamma \vdash_\Sigma e_t\colon \tau \qquad D;\Gamma \vdash_\Sigma e_f\colon \tau}{D;\Gamma \vdash_\Sigma \texttt{if } x \texttt{ then } e_t \texttt{ else } e_f\colon \tau} \; \text{IF}$$

$$\frac{x \notin dom(\Gamma) \qquad D;\Gamma \vdash_\Sigma e_1\colon \tau_x \qquad D;\Gamma, x\colon \tau_x \vdash_\Sigma e_2\colon \tau}{D;\Gamma \vdash_\Sigma \texttt{let } x = e_1 \texttt{ in } e_2\colon \tau} \; \text{LET}$$

$$\frac{\begin{array}{c} \Sigma(f) = \tau_1^\circ \times \cdots \times \tau_k^\circ \to \tau_{k+1} \\ x_1\colon \tau_1^\circ, \ldots, x_k\colon \tau_k^\circ \vdash_\Sigma e_1\colon \tau_{k+1} \qquad D;\Gamma \vdash_\Sigma e_2\colon \tau' \end{array}}{D;\Gamma \vdash_\Sigma \texttt{letfun } f(x_1, \ldots, x_k) = e_1 \texttt{ in } e_2\colon \tau'} \; \text{LETFUN}$$

$$\frac{\begin{array}{c} \Sigma(f) = \tau_1^\circ \times \ldots \times \tau_k^\circ \to \tau_{k+1} \\ D \vdash \tau = \tau_{k+1}[\tau_1^\circ := \tau_1', \ldots, \tau_k^\circ := \tau_k'] \qquad D \vdash C \end{array}}{D;\Gamma, x_1\colon \tau_1', \ldots, x_k\colon \tau_k' \vdash_\Sigma f(x_1, \ldots, x_k)\colon \tau} \; \text{FUNAPP}$$

FIGURE 3.1.   Typing rules excluding the ones for data types

$$\frac{D \vdash (e, n) = (1, 0)}{D;\Gamma \vdash_\Sigma \texttt{Empty}\colon \texttt{Tree}^{e,n}(\tau)} \; \text{EMPTY}$$

From $s_{\texttt{Tree}}$ we obtain that in a non-empty tree, the number of leaves is equal to the sum of the number of leaves in each subtree and that the number of nodes is one more than the sum of the number of nodes in each subtree. We use variables for the sizes of the subtrees and we relate them accordingly in the premise:

$$\frac{D \vdash (e, n) = (0, 1) + (e_1, n_1) + (e_2, n_2)}{D;\Gamma, v\colon \tau, l\colon \texttt{Tree}^{e_1,n_1}(\tau), r\colon \texttt{Tree}^{e_2,n_2}(\tau) \vdash_\Sigma \texttt{Node}(v, l, r)\colon \texttt{Tree}^{e,n}(\tau)} \; \text{NODE}$$

Similarly, in the typing rule for pattern matching a binary tree, we introduce fresh variables in the typing context of the premises for the unknown quantities and we add their relationship to the set of conditions.

$$\frac{\begin{array}{c} D, (e, n) = (1, 0); \Gamma, t\colon \texttt{Tree}^{e,n}(\tau) \vdash_\Sigma e_{\texttt{Empty}}\colon \tau' \\ D, (e, n) = (0, 1) + (e_1, n_1) + (e_2, n_2); \Gamma, \\ t\colon \texttt{Tree}^{e,n}(\tau), v\colon \tau, l\colon \texttt{Tree}^{e_1,n_1}(\tau), r\colon \texttt{Tree}^{e_2,n_2}(\tau) \vdash_\Sigma e_{\texttt{Node}}\colon \tau' \\ e_1, e_2, n_1\, n_2 \notin vars(D) \qquad v, l, r \notin dom(\Gamma) \end{array}}{D;\Gamma, t\colon \texttt{Tree}^{e,n}(\tau) \vdash_\Sigma \begin{array}{l} \texttt{match } t \texttt{ with} \mid \texttt{Empty} \Rightarrow e_{\texttt{Empty}} \\ \qquad\qquad\quad \mid \texttt{Node}(v, l, r) \Rightarrow e_{\texttt{Node}} \end{array}\colon \tau'} \; \text{MTREE}$$

To see how these rules work in practice, we apply them to a function to balance a (not necessarily ordered) binary tree. To simplify the example we add syntactic sugar to avoid `let` constructs. It is not our intention to explain the balancing algorithm, but just to show that there are many interesting functions that can be written in our language. We begin with a function for right-rotation of nodes. We use undefined to indicate a non-terminating expression with the required type.

$$r\_rot(v, l, r) : \alpha \times \mathsf{Tree}^{e_1, n_1}(\alpha) \times \mathsf{Tree}^{e_2, n_2}(\alpha) \to \mathsf{Tree}^{e_1 + e_2, n_1 + n_2 + 1}(\alpha) =$$
$$\mathtt{match}\ l\ \mathtt{with}\ |\ \mathsf{Empty} \Rightarrow \mathsf{undefined}$$
$$|\ \mathsf{Node}(v_1, l_1, r_1) \Rightarrow \mathsf{Node}(v_1, l_1, \mathsf{Node}(v, r_1, r))$$

By applying the rule MTREE we get two branches. The branch for the Empty case is undefined and thus we do not need to type check it. The other branch is

$$\cfrac{\cfrac{\begin{array}{l}(e_1, n_1) = \\ (e_{11} + e_{12}, n_{11} + n_{12} + 1)\end{array} \vdash \begin{array}{l}(e_1 + e_2, n_1 + n_2 + 1) = \\ (e_{11} + e_{12} + e_2, n_{11} + (n_{12} + n_2 + 1) + 1)\end{array}}{\begin{array}{l}(e_1, n_1) = \\ (e_{11} + e_{12}, n_{11} + n_{12} + 1); \\ v, v_1 : \alpha, l : \mathsf{Tree}^{e_1, n_1}(\alpha), \\ l_1 : \mathsf{Tree}^{e_{11}, n_{11}}(\alpha), \\ r_1 : \mathsf{Tree}^{e_{12}, n_{12}}(\alpha)\end{array} \vdash_{\Sigma} \begin{array}{l}\mathsf{Node}(v_1, l_1, \\ \mathsf{Node}(v, r_1, r))\end{array} : \mathsf{Tree}^{e_1 + e_2, n_1 + n_2 + 1}(\alpha)}\ \text{NODE}}{\begin{array}{l}v : \alpha, l : \mathsf{Tree}^{e_1, n_1}(\alpha), \\ r : \mathsf{Tree}^{e_2, n_2}(\alpha)\end{array} \vdash_{\Sigma} \mathtt{match}\ l \ldots : \mathsf{Tree}^{e_1 + e_2, n_1 + n_2 + 1}(\alpha)}\ \text{MTREE}$$

Similarly, we can type check the left-right rotation function. For simplicity we write it in a Haskell-like style of pattern matching.

$$lr\_rot : \alpha \times \mathsf{Tree}^{e_1, n_1}(\alpha) \times \mathsf{Tree}^{e_2, n_2}(\alpha) \to \mathsf{Tree}^{e_1 + e_2, n_1 + n_2 + 1}(\alpha)$$
$$lr\_rot(v, \mathsf{Node}(v_1, l_1, \mathsf{Node}(v_{12}, l_{12}, r_{12})), r) =$$
$$\mathsf{Node}(v_{12}, \mathsf{Node}(v_1, l_1, l_{12}), \mathsf{Node}(v, r_{12}, r))$$

Now we define the left balance function, which is easily type checked since both branches have the same type. The definitions of *balance* and RightWeight are omitted because they are not needed for our analysis.

$$l\_bal(v, l, r) : \alpha \times \mathsf{Tree}^{e_1, n_1}(\alpha) \times \mathsf{Tree}^{e_2, n_2}(\alpha) \to \mathsf{Tree}^{e_1 + e_2, n_1 + n_2 + 1}(\alpha) =$$
$$\mathtt{if}\ balance(l) == \mathsf{RightWeight}$$
$$\mathtt{then}\ lr\_rot(v, l, r)$$
$$\mathtt{else}\ r\_rot(v, l, r)$$

Then we type check a function that inserts an element into a balanced binary tree:

$$insert(a,t)\colon \alpha \times \mathsf{Tree}^{e,n}(\alpha) \to \mathsf{Tree}^{e+1,n+1}(\alpha) =$$

match t with | Empty $\Rightarrow$ Node(a, Empty, Empty)

| Node(v,l,r) $\Rightarrow$ let $l_2 = insert(a,l)$

in if $height(l_2) == height(r) + 2$

then $l\_bal(v, l_2, r)$

else Node(v, l_2, r)

Applying MTREE we get two branches. For the Empty branch we get the entailment $(e,n) = (1,0) \vdash (e+1, n+1) = (1+1, 0+0+1)$ and for the Node branch we have the judgement:

$$(e,n) = (e_1 + e_2, n_1 + n_2 + 1); \; t\colon \mathsf{Tree}^{e,n}(\alpha), \atop v\colon \alpha, l\colon \mathsf{Tree}^{e_1,n_1}(\alpha), r\colon \mathsf{Tree}^{e_2,n_2}(\alpha) \quad \vdash_\Sigma \mathsf{let}\; l_2 = \ldots \colon \mathsf{Tree}^{e+1,n+1}(\alpha)$$

Using LET we get $l_2\colon \mathsf{Tree}^{e_1+1,n_1+1}(\alpha)$. Both branches of the if have the same type, so we only need to check the entailment it generates:

$$(e,n) = (e_1 + e_2, n_1 + n_2 + 1) \vdash (e+1, n+1) = ((e_1+1)+e_2, (n_1+1)+n_2+1)$$

Then we define a function to build a balanced tree from a list:

$$build\_bal\_tree(xs)\colon \mathsf{List}^n(\alpha) \to \mathsf{Tree}^{n+1,n}(\alpha) =$$

match xs with | Nil $\Rightarrow$ Empty

| Cons(hd, tl) $\Rightarrow$ $insert(hd, build\_bal\_tree(tl))$

From the Nil branch we get the condition $n = 0 \vdash (n+1, n) = (1, 0)$, which is trivially true and for the Cons branch we have:

$$\frac{\vdash (n+1, n) = ((n-1)+1+1, (n-1)+1)}{hd\colon \alpha, tl\colon \mathsf{List}^{n-1}(\alpha) \vdash_\Sigma insert(hd, build\_bal\_tree(tl))\colon \mathsf{Tree}^{n+1,n}(\alpha)} \; \text{FUNAPP}$$

Finally, we define and type check a function that balances a binary tree:

$$balance\_tree(t)\colon \mathsf{Tree}^{e,n}(\alpha) \to \mathsf{Tree}^{n+1,n}(\alpha) = build\_bal\_tree(flatten(t))$$

where *flatten* is a function with type $\mathsf{Tree}^{e,n}(\alpha) \to \mathsf{List}^n(\alpha)$ that returns a list with the elements of a binary tree. By applying the typing rule for function application twice, we get the trivial entailment $\vdash (n+1, n) = (n+1, n)$. When the tree is flattened, we lose the information about e, thus e does not appear in the resulting type of *balance_tree*.

3.2.3 Typing Rules for Algebraic Data Types

Below, we give a procedure for obtaining typing rules for an arbitrary algebraic data type. Let $T(\overline{\alpha})$ be an algebraic data type defined as

$$\texttt{data } T(\overline{\alpha}) = C_1(\overline{\tau}_1(\overline{\alpha})) \mid \ldots \mid C_r(\overline{\tau}_r(\overline{\alpha}))$$

and let $size_T$ be the size function of $T(\overline{\alpha})$. For each constructor C_i we add a typing rule of the form

$$\frac{D \vdash \mathsf{p} = \mathsf{c}_i + \sum_{j=1}^{k_i} \mathsf{p}_{ij}}{D;\ \Gamma,\ x_{ij} \colon \gamma'_{ij}(T(\overline{\tau}))\ \text{for } j = 1..k_i \vdash_\Sigma C_i(x_{i1}, \ldots, x_{ik_i}) \colon T^{\mathsf{p}}(\overline{\tau})}\ C_i \ \text{for } i = 1..r$$

where c_i and the a_{ij} are taken from the definition of $size_T$, and γ'_{ij} is defined as

$$\gamma'_{ij}(T(\overline{\tau})) = \begin{cases} T^{\mathsf{p}_{ij}}(\overline{\tau}) & \text{if } \tau_{ij}(\overline{\tau}) = T(\overline{\tau}) \\ \tau_{ij}(\overline{\tau}) & \text{otherwise} \end{cases}$$

The idea is that if the type of x_{ij} is $T(\overline{\tau})$, the one we are defining the typing rules for, then it must have a size annotation that we call p_{ij}, otherwise its type is just $\tau_{ij}(\overline{\tau})$. There is a clear correspondence between γ and γ'.

We also add a typing rule for pattern matching an element of type $T(\overline{\alpha})$:

$$\frac{\begin{array}{c} D,\ \mathsf{p} = \mathsf{c}_i + \sum_{j=1}^{k_i} \mathsf{n}_{ij};\ \Gamma,\ x \colon T^{\mathsf{p}}(\overline{\tau}), \\ x_{ij} \colon \gamma'_{ij}(T(\overline{\tau}))\ \text{for } j = 1..k_i \end{array} \vdash_\Sigma e_i \colon \tau' \ \text{for } i = 1..r \qquad \mathsf{n}_{ij} \notin vars(D),\ x_{ij} \notin dom(\Gamma)\ \text{for } i = 1..r, j = 1..k_i}{D;\ \Gamma,\ x \colon T^{\mathsf{p}}(\overline{\tau}) \vdash_\Sigma \begin{array}{l} \texttt{match } x \texttt{ with } \mid C_1(x_{11}, \ldots, x_{1k_1}) \Rightarrow e_1 \\ \qquad\qquad\qquad\qquad\ \vdots \\ \qquad\qquad\qquad \mid C_r(x_{r1}, \ldots, x_{rk_r}) \Rightarrow e_r \end{array} \colon \tau'}\ \textsc{MatchT}$$

Each of the size variables of n_{ij} and the formal parameters of the constructors are assumed to be fresh. Notice that there is one premise per constructor. When $\gamma_{ij}(T(\overline{\tau}))$ is $\tau_{ij}(\overline{\tau})$ we regard n_{ij} as 0, that is, we omit that variable from the sum.

3.3 SOUNDNESS, DECIDABILITY AND COMPLETENESS

This section is devoted to soundness and completeness of the type system and decidability of type checking, extending previous results on these topics to a language with algebraic data types.

3.3.1 Soundness

Set-theoretic heap-aware semantics of a ground algebraic data type (i.e., a type where all size and type variables are instantiated) is an obvious extension of the semantics of lists that can be found, for instance, in [9]. Intuitively, an instance of a ground type is presented in a heap as a directed tree-like structure, that may overlap with other structures. The only restriction is that it must be acyclic.

Since our type system is not linear, that is, a program variable may be used more than once, a data structure in a heap may consist of overlapping substructures. This is the case, for instance, for a heap representation of $\text{Node}(1, t, t)$, where t is a non-empty tree. In general, in a calculation of the *size* of a structure, a node is counted as many times as it is referenced. Hence, a sensible size function gives an upper bound for the actual amount of constructor cells allocated by the structure. If there is no internal sharing, the sensible size function is equal to the amount of cells actually allocated.

A location is the address of some constructor-cell of a ground type. A *program value* is either an integer or boolean constant, or a location. A *heap* is a finite partial mapping from locations and fields to program values, and an *object heap* is a finite partial map from locations to *Constructor*, the set of (the names of) constructors. Below, we assume that for any heap h, there is an object heap oh such that $dom(h) = dom(oh)$.

Let τ be a type defined by a set of constructors C_i, where $1 \leq i \leq r$. With a constructor C_i of arity $k_i > 0$, we associate a collection of field names $C_i\_field_j$, where $1 \leq j \leq k_i$. Let *Field* be the set of all field names in a given program. We also assume that any null-ary constructor is placed in a location with 1 empty integer field. With a 0-arity constructor C_i we associate the field name $C_i\_field_1$. The reason for introducing a 'fake' field for null-ary constructors is to make the proofs more uniform. Formally:

$$Val\ v ::= \iota \mid b \mid \ell \qquad \ell \in Loc \qquad \iota \in \text{Int} \qquad b \in \text{Bool}$$
$$Heap\ h\ :\ Loc \rightharpoonup Field \rightharpoonup Val \qquad ObjHeap\ oh\ :\ Loc \rightharpoonup Constructor$$

We will write $h[\ell.field := v]$ for the heap equal to h everywhere but in ℓ, which at the field of ℓ named *field* gets the value v.

The semantics w of a program value v is a set-theoretic interpretation with respect to a specific heap h, its object heap oh and a ground type $\tau^\bullet$, via a five-place relation $v \models^{h;oh}_{\tau^\bullet} w$. Integer and boolean constants interpret themselves, and locations are interpreted as non-cyclic structures:

$$\iota \models^{h;oh}_{\text{Int}} \iota \qquad\qquad b \models^{h;oh}_{\text{Bool}} b$$

$\ell \models^{h;oh}_{T^c(\tau^\bullet)} C \qquad$ if C is a null-ary constructor of T, $\ell \in dom(h)$, $oh(\ell) = C$
$\qquad\qquad\qquad$ and the constant vector c is the size of C

$\ell \models^{h;oh}_{\tau^\bullet} C(w_1, \ldots, w_k) \qquad$ if $\ell \in dom(h)$, $oh(\ell) = C$
$\qquad\qquad\qquad\qquad C \colon \tau_1^\bullet \times \ldots \times \tau_k^\bullet \rightarrow \tau^\bullet$ (i.e. it is a ground instance),
$\qquad\qquad\qquad\qquad \tau^\bullet = T^{n^0}(\overline{\tau^{\bullet\prime}})$ for some $\overline{\tau^{\bullet\prime}}$, $n^0 = size_T(C(w_1, \ldots, w_k))$,
$\qquad\qquad\qquad\qquad$ and for all $1 \leq j \leq k \colon h.\ell.C\_field_j \models^{h|_{dom(h)\setminus\{\ell\}};oh|_{dom(oh)\setminus\{\ell\}}}_{\tau_j^\bullet} w_j$

where $h|_{dom(h)\setminus\{\ell\}}$ denotes the heap equal to h everywhere except for ℓ, where it is undefined.

When a function body is evaluated, a frame store maintains the mapping from program variables to values. At the beginning it contains only the actual function parameters, thus preventing access beyond the caller's frame. Formally, a frame store is a finite partial map from variables to values: *Store s: ExpVar* $\rightharpoonup$ *Val*.

An operational semantics judgement $s; h; oh, \mathscr{C} \vdash e \rightsquigarrow v; h'; oh'$ informally means that at a store s, a heap h, its object heap oh and with the set $\mathscr{C}$ of function closures (bodies), the evaluation of an expression e terminates with value v in the heap h' and object heap oh'.

Using heaps and frame stores, and maintaining a mapping $\mathscr{C}$ from function names to bodies for the function definitions encountered, the operational semantics of expressions is defined in a usual way. Here we give the rules for constructors and (non null-ary) pattern-matching. The other rules may be found in [10].

$$\frac{s(x_1) = v_1, \ldots, s(x_k) = v_k \qquad \ell \notin dom(h)}{s; h; oh, \mathscr{C} \vdash C(x_1, \ldots, x_k) \rightsquigarrow \ell; h[\ell.C\_field_1 := v_1, \ldots, \ell.C\_field_k := v_k]; oh[\ell := C]}$$

OSCons

$$oh(s(x)) = C_i \qquad h.s(x).C_i\_field_1 = v_1, \ldots, h.s(x).C_i\_field_{k_i} = v_{k_i}$$
$$s[x_1 := v_1, \ldots, x_{k_i} := v_{k_i}]; h; oh, \mathscr{C} \vdash e_i \rightsquigarrow v; h'; oh'$$

OSMATCH $- C_i$

$$s; h; oh, \mathscr{C} \vdash \quad \begin{matrix} \texttt{match } x \texttt{ with } | \ C_1(x_{11}, \ldots, x_{1k_1}) \Rightarrow e_1 \\ \vdots \\ | \ C_r(x_{r1}, \ldots, x_{rk_r}) \Rightarrow e_r \end{matrix} \quad \rightsquigarrow v; h'; oh'$$

Let a valuation $\varepsilon : SizeVar \rightarrow \mathscr{Z}$ map size variables to concrete sizes (integer numbers) and an instantiation $\eta : TypeVar \rightarrow \tau^{\bullet}$ map type variables to ground types. Applied to a type, context, or size expression, valuation and instantiation map all variables occurring in it to their valuation and instantiation images: $\varepsilon(p[+, -, *]p) = \varepsilon(p)[+, -, *]\varepsilon(p)$ and $\eta(\varepsilon(T^{\mathsf{p}}(\tau))) = T^{\varepsilon(\mathsf{p})}(\eta(\tau))$.

The soundness statement is defined by means of the following two predicates. One indicates whether a program value is meaningful with respect to a certain heap and ground type. The other does the same for sets of values and types, taken from a frame store and ground context:

$$Valid_{\mathsf{val}}(v, \tau^{\bullet}, h; oh) \quad = \quad \exists w. v \models_{\tau^{\bullet}}^{h, oh} w$$
$$Valid_{\mathsf{store}}(vars, \Gamma, s, h; oh) \quad = \quad \forall x \in vars. \ Valid_{\mathsf{val}}(s(x), \Gamma(x), h, oh)$$

Now, stating soundness of the type system is straightforward:

Theorem 3.1. *Let $s; h; oh, [\ ] \vdash e \rightsquigarrow v; h'; oh'$. Then for any context Γ, signature Σ, and type τ, such that* True; $\Gamma \vdash_{\Sigma} e : \tau$ *is derivable in the type system, and any size valuation ε and type instantiation η, it holds that if the store is meaningful w.r.t. the context $\eta(\varepsilon(\Gamma))$ then the output value is meaningful w.r.t the type $\eta(\varepsilon(\tau))$:*

$$\forall \eta, \varepsilon. \ Valid_{\mathsf{store}}(FV(e), \eta(\varepsilon(\Gamma)), s, h, oh) \implies Valid_{\mathsf{val}}(v, \eta(\varepsilon(\tau)), h', oh')$$

The proof is a routine done by induction on the operational-semantics tree. It can be found in the technical report [10].

3.3.2 Decidability

Type checking using the type system studied in this work seems to be straightforward because for every syntactic construction of the language there is only one applicable typing rule. The procedure ultimately reduces to proving equations involving rational polynomials.

Lemma 3.2. *The type checking problem $D; \Gamma \vdash_\Sigma e : \tau$ can be reduced to checking a finite number of entailments of the form $D' \vdash \mathsf{p} = \mathsf{q}$, where the variables in D', p and q are either free size variables of Γ or size variables introduced during the type checking procedure.*

Proof. By induction on the structure of the language.

But consider the following expression, where $f_i \colon \mathsf{List}^{n_1}(\alpha_1) \times \ldots \times \mathsf{List}^{n_k}(\alpha_k) \to \mathsf{List}^{p_i(n_1,\ldots,n_k)}(\alpha)$ for $i = 0, 1, 2$, (assuming we count only the number of elements).

```
let x = f₀(x₁,...,xₖ) in match x with | Nil ⇒ f₁(x₁,...,xₖ)
                                       | Cons(hd, tl) ⇒ f₂(x₁,...,xₖ)
```

When checking whether this expression has type $\mathsf{List}^{n_1}(\alpha_1) \times \ldots \times \mathsf{List}^{n_k}(\alpha_k) \to \mathsf{List}^{p(n_1,\ldots,n_k)}(\alpha)$, in the Nil branch we will get the entailment

$$p_0(n_1,\ldots,n_k) = 0 \vdash p(n_1,\ldots,n_k) = p_1(n_1,\ldots,n_k)$$

To validate this entailment we must know whether p_0 has roots or not (that is, whether the Nil branch can be entered at all). In [9] it is shown that for *any* given polynomial q, it is possible to construct a function f_0 whose result has as size annotation the polynomial $p_0 = q^2$, whose roots are exactly the ones of q. Hence, type checking reduces to solving Hilbert's tenth problem and thus it is undecidable.

The source of the problem in the previous example was that the pattern match was done over a variable bound by a let. We can avoid these cases with a syntactical restriction that we call *no-let-before-match*: given a function body, allow pattern matching only on the function parameters or variables bound by other pattern matchings. Even with this restriction, one can write all shapely primitive recursive functions for our data types because they induce a (polynomial) functor. For instance, the operator for primitive recursion on lists is defined as follows:

$$f(x, \bar{y}) = \mathtt{match}\ x\ \mathtt{with} \mid \mathsf{Nil} \Rightarrow g(\bar{y})$$
$$\mid \mathsf{Cons}(hd, tl) \Rightarrow h(hd, tl, \bar{y}, f(tl, \bar{y}))$$

where g and h are functions already defined, and $\bar{y}$ is a sequence of parameters. It is obvious that f satisfies the syntactic restriction. However, we want to emphasize that this condition is sufficient, but not necessary for decidability.

For the proof of decidability we refer the reader to the technical report [10]. The key step in the proof is to show that type checking can be reduced to a set of entailments of the form $D \vdash p = q$, where each set of constraints D determines *tree-decompositions* of the size variables, i.e. trees of size variables where a father is a linear combination of its children. Then we replace the variables in breadth-first order to obtain two polynomials in terms of the leaves of these trees. Checking the equality of the polynomials is then just a matter of comparing the coefficient of the variables with the same degree.

3.3.3 Completeness

The type system is not complete: there are shapely functions for which shapeliness cannot be proved by means of the typing rules and arithmetic. This comes as no surprise if we consider that the type system subsumes Peano arithmetic. Another reason for incompleteness is that the typing rule for if does not keep any size information obtainable from the condition. Consider, for instance, the following schema of expressions, where $f(x)$ is a list of integers:

$$\texttt{let}\, z = f(x) \,\texttt{in}\, \texttt{if}\, \textit{length}(z) == 0 \,\texttt{then}\, z \,\texttt{else}\, \mathsf{Nil}$$

These expressions have type $\mathsf{List}^0(\texttt{Int})$, however, the type checker fails to acknowledge it.

3.4 DISCUSSION AND FUTURE WORK

In this section we discuss a variation of our type system, a possible extension and future work.

First we note that instead of generating one typing rule for each constructor it is possible to derive a size-annotated type for each of them, add these types to the set of signatures Σ and then use the function application rule. This approach is preferred since it results in a type system with fewer rules, however, for presentation purposes, we have chosen to generate typing rules for them because it makes clearer the role that the set of constraints D plays. A typing rule for pattern matching each algebraic data type is still needed.

One possible extension to the language and the type system is to add *size-parametric data types*, i.e. types that are parameterized by a tuple of size variables that can be used as size annotations in the definition of the type.

An *m*-ary tree is a tree where each node has m subtrees. We say that a tree of height h is *h-full* if all the leaves are at height h. When the height is not relevant, we say that it is *full*. We can define *m*-ary full trees as a size-parametric data type.

$$\texttt{spdata}\, \mathsf{MFullTree}_m(\alpha) = \mathsf{Empty} \mid \mathsf{Node}(\alpha, \mathsf{List}^m(\mathsf{MFullTree}_m(\alpha)))$$

It is clear that this defines *m*-ary trees. They are also full because the subtrees at the same level must all have the same size. Assuming that we are counting the occurrences of each constructor,[2] it is not hard to come up with typing rules for

---

[2]Since the number of nodes in an *m*-ary full tree depends on its height, any function that re-shapes one of these trees will have size annotations involving logarithms. Therefore, for this data structure it would be better to define its size as its height.

MFullTree.

$$\frac{D \vdash (e, n) = (1, 0)}{D; \Gamma \vdash_{\Sigma} \mathsf{Empty} \colon \mathsf{MFullTree}_m^{e,n}(\tau)} \; \text{Empty}$$

$$\frac{D \vdash (e, n) = (0, 1) + m * (e', n')}{D; \Gamma, v \colon \tau, ts \colon \mathsf{List}^m(\mathsf{MFullTree}_m^{e',n'}(\tau)) \vdash_{\Sigma} \mathsf{Node}(v, ts) \colon \mathsf{MFullTree}_m^{e,n}(\tau)} \; \text{Node}$$

$$\frac{\begin{array}{c} D, (e, n) = (1, 0); \Gamma, t \colon \mathsf{MFullTree}_m^{e,n}(\tau) \vdash_{\Sigma} e_{\mathsf{Empty}} \colon \tau' \\ D, (e, n) = (0,1) + m * (e', n'); \Gamma, t \colon \mathsf{MFullTree}_m^{e,n}(\tau), \\ v \colon \tau, ts \colon \mathsf{List}^m(\mathsf{MFullTree}_m^{e',n'}(\tau)) \\ e', n' \notin vars(D) \qquad v, ts \notin dom(\Gamma) \end{array}}{D; \Gamma, t \colon \mathsf{MFullTree}_m^{e,n}(\tau) \vdash_{\Sigma} \begin{array}{l} \mathtt{match}\, t\, \mathtt{with} \mid \mathsf{Empty} \Rightarrow e_{\mathsf{Empty}} \\ \mid \mathsf{Node}(v, ts) \Rightarrow e_{\mathsf{Node}} \end{array} \colon \tau'} \; \text{MMFTree}$$

A size function for MFullTree counting both constructors is defined below:

$$
\begin{array}{ll}
size & \colon \mathsf{MFullTree}_m(\alpha) \to \mathcal{N} \times \mathcal{N} \\
size(\mathsf{Empty}) & = (1, 0) \\
size(\mathsf{Node}(v, ts)) & = (0, 1) + m * \mathtt{match}\, ts\, \mathtt{with} \mid \mathsf{Nil} \Rightarrow (0, 0) \\
& \qquad\qquad\qquad\qquad\qquad\quad \mid \mathsf{Cons}(hd, tl) \Rightarrow size(hd)
\end{array}
$$

But there is no direct relationship between this size function and the previous typing rules. The size function used in the typing rules is simpler because the size of the subtrees can be obtained from the typing context. In order to restore the relationship, we can add a parameter to the size function representing the size of the subtrees.

$$
\begin{array}{ll}
size & \colon \mathsf{MFullTree}_m(\alpha) \times (\mathcal{N} \times \mathcal{N}) \to \mathcal{N} \times \mathcal{N} \\
size(\mathsf{Empty}, (e', n')) & = (1, 0) \\
size(\mathsf{Node}(v, ts), (e', n')) & = (0, 1) + m * (e', n')
\end{array}
$$

This procedure can be applied to other data types, but the generalization is not elegant. Although this extension would add some expressiveness to the language, its usefulness is not clear since the added types are quite restricted (note, e.g. that a node at the bottom of an m-ary full tree has a list of m Empty subtrees).

We believe that our recent results on *type inference* for size-annotated lists [12] can be easily extrapolated to ordinary inductive types. Furthermore, we want to extend our current implementation to deal with data types both in the canonical way and by allowing user–defined size function. Our long–term goals are to study type systems annotated with upper and lower bound sizes and to investigate shapeliness in the context of imperative languages.

3.5 RELATED WORK

Amortized heap space analysis has been developed for linear bounds by Hofmann and Jost [5]. Precise knowledge of sizes is required to extend this approach to non-linear bounds [11]. Brian Campbell [4] extended this approach to infer bounds on *stack* space usage.

Other work on size analysis has been restricted to monotonic dependencies. In *type-based termination* analysis e.g. it is enough to assure that the size (more precisely, an upper bound of it) of a data structure decreases in a recursive call. Research by Pareto has yielded an algorithm to automatically check sized types where linear size expression are upper bounds [8]. In the thesis of Abel [1] ordinals above ω are considered as well (they are used, e.g. for types like streams). The language of (ordinal) size expressions for zero-order types in this work is rather simple: it consists of ordinal variables, ordinal successor, and an ordinal limit (see also [2]). This is enough for termination analysis, however for heap consumption analysis more sophisticated size expressions are needed. Construction of non-linear upper bounds using a traditional type system approach has been presented by Hammond and Vasconcelos [14], but this work leaves recurrence equations unsolved and is limited to monotonic dependencies. The work on quasi-interpretations by Bonfante et al. [3] also requires monotonic dependencies.

The EmBounded project aims to identify and certify resource-bounded code in *Hume*, a domain-specific high-level programming language for real-time embedded systems. In his thesis, Pedro Vasconcelos [13] uses abstract interpretation to automatically infer linear approximations of the sizes of recursive data types and the stack and heap of recursive functions written in a subset of *Hume*.

Exact input-output size dependencies have been explored by Jay and Sekanina [7]. In this work, a shapely program is translated into a program involving sizes. Thus, the relation between sizes is given as a program. However, deriving an arithmetic function from it is beyond the scope of the paper. In a closely related work [6], Jay and Cockett study shapely types, i.e., those whose data can be separated in a categorical setting. A notable difference is that we do not consider a type shapely per se, instead its size function determines whether it is shapely.

3.6 CONCLUSIONS

We studied an effect type system with size annotations for a first-order functional language. We provided generic typing rules for algebraic data types based on user–defined size functions and we proved soundness of the type system with respect to the operational semantics. Our choice to allow (not necessarily monotonic) polynomials as size annotations brings undecidability to type checking, however, it was shown that for a wide range of programs, decidability of type checking functions with algebraic data types can be ensured. Our experience is that in practice, the entailments obtained while type checking are easily solvable.

Although the practical applicability of this work is limited, it explores the current limits of the field. It is also a step towards our goal of providing a practical resource analysis. Its main limitation is that it requires size dependencies to be exact. We are working on an extension of the type system that allows to express lower and upper bounds by specifying a family of indexed polynomials.

REFERENCES

[1] A. Abel. *A Polymorphic Lambda-Calculus with Sized Higher-Order Types*. PhD thesis, LFE Theoretische Informatik, Ludwig-Maximilians-Universitt Mnchen, 2006.

[2] A. Abel. Implementing a Normalizer Using Sized Heterogeneous Types. *Journal of Functional Programming, MSFP'06 special issue*, 2008. To appear.

[3] G. Bonfante, J.-Y. Marion, and J.-Y. Moyen. Quasi-interpretations, a way to control resources. *Theoretical Computer Science*, 2009. To appear.

[4] B. Campbell. *Space Cost Analysis Using Sized Types*. PhD thesis, School of Informatics, University of Edinburgh, 2008.

[5] M. Hofmann and S. Jost. Static prediction of heap space usage for first-order functional programs. *SIGPLAN Not.*, 38(1):185–197, 2003.

[6] B. C. Jay and J. R. B. Cockett. Shapely Types and Shape Polymorphism. In *Programming Languages and Systems - ESOP '94*, pages 302–316. Springer–Verlag, 1994.

[7] B. C. Jay and M. Sekanina. Shape checking of array programs. In *Computing: the Australasian Theory Seminar, Australian Computer Science Communications*, volume 19, pages 113–121, 1997.

[8] L. Pareto. *Sized Types*. Chalmers University of Technology, Göteborg, 1998. Dissertation for the Licentiate Degree in Computing Science.

[9] O. Shkaravska, R. van Kesteren, and M. van Eekelen. Polynomial Size Analysis for First-Order Functions. In S. R. D. Rocca, editor, *Typed Lambda Calculi and Applications (TLCA'2007), Paris, France*, volume 4583 of *LNCS*, pages 351–366. Springer, 2007.

[10] A. Tamalet, O. Shkaravska, and M. van Eekelen. A Size-Aware Type System with Algebraic Data Types. Technical Report ICIS-R08006, Radboud University Nijmegen.

[11] M. van Eekelen, O. Shkaravska, R. van Kesteren, B. Jacobs, E. Poll, and S. Smetsers. AHA: Amortized Heap Space Usage Analysis. In M. Morazán, editor, *Selected Papers of the 8th International Symposium on Trends in Functional Programming (TFP'07), New York, USA*, pages 36–53. Intellect Publishers, 2007.

[12] R. van Kesteren, O. Shkaravska, and M. van Eekelen. Inferring static non-monotonically sized types through testing. In *Proceedings of 16th International Workshop on Functional and (Constraint) Logic Programming (WFLP'07), Paris, France*, volume 216C of *ENTCS*, pages 45–63, 2007.

[13] P. B. Vasconcelos. *Space Cost Analysis Using Sized Types*. PhD thesis, School of Computer Science, University of St. Andrews, August 2008.

[14] P. B. Vasconcelos and K. Hammond. Inferring Cost Equations for Recursive, Polymorphic and Higher-Order Functional Programs. In P. Trinder, G. Michaelson, and R. Peña, editors, *Implementation of Functional Languages: 15th International Workshop, IFL 2003, Edinburgh, UK, September 8–11, 2003. Revised Papers*, volume 3145 of *LNCS*, pages 86–101. Springer-Verlag, 2004.

Chapter 4

Confluence for Non-Full Functional Dependencies

Tom Schrijvers[1], Martin Sulzmann[2]
Category: Research Paper

Abstract: Previous work on type inference for functional dependencies demands that the dependency must fully cover all parameters of a type class to guarantee that the constraint solver is confluent. However, several interesting programs rely on non-full functional dependencies. For these, the underlying constraint is non-confluent, and hence type inference for these programs is possibly ill-behaved.

We investigate two approaches to restore confluence for non-full FDs. In the first approach, we characterize a class of transformable non-full to full FD programs where the resulting full FD program is confluent. This approach has some inherent limitations due to the use of constraint simplification during type inference. In the second approach, we show how to achieve confluence in general by applying a radically different type-inference approach which favours constraint propagation over simplification.

Our results provide new insights in type-inference issues behind functional dependencies and help to clarify some of the on-going discussions about the possible adoption of functional dependencies in a future Haskell standard.

4.1 INTRODUCTION

Haskell-style functional dependencies [4] provide a relational specification of user-programmable type improvement [3] connected to type-class instances. Functional dependencies are supported by both GHC and Hugs, and they are employed in numerous Haskell programs. The current state of the art on type inference for functional dependencies employs Constraint Handling Rules (CHRs) [2]. CHRs serve as a meta-language to describe the constraint solver underlying the type in-

---

[1]K.U.Leuven, Belgium; `tom.schrijvers@cs.kuleuven.be`.
[2]IT University of Copenhagen, Denmark; `martin.sulzmann@gmail.com`.

ferencer. Confluence of CHRs is important to ensure that the type inferencer is well-behaved. Unfortunately, the CHR encoding of FDs proposed in [9] cannot guarantee confluence for non-full FDs.

In this paper, we attack the challenging problem of restoring confluence for non-full functional dependencies. In summary, we make the following contributions:

- We revisit the non-confluence issue of Constraint Handling Rules (CHRs) resulting from non-full FDs and provide realistic examples which show that non-full FD programs represent an interesting and useful class of FD programs (Section 4.3).

- We establish a confluence result for non-full FDs by transformation to full FDs. Full FD programs are generally confluent. Hence, by transformation to full FDs we obtain confluence for non-full FDs. However, only a restricted class of non-full FD programs are transformable. (Section 4.4).

- We achieve a less restrictive confluence result for non-full FD programs by applying a radically different type-inference approach which exclusively uses constraint propagation (Section 4.5).

The idea of the propagation encoding is due to Claus Reinke but to the best of our knowledge we are the first to formally investigate the implications of his encoding scheme.

The upcoming section gives an overview of type inference with functional dependencies based on CHRs. Related work is discussed in Section 4.6. We conclude in Section 4.7.

4.2   TYPE INFERENCE WITH FUNCTIONAL DEPENDENCIES

This section gives an overview of the necessary concepts and previous results that are needed for a good understanding of the technical results of this paper.

Functional Dependencies   Functional dependencies [4] allow the programmer to influence the type-inference process. They improve types [3], and help to resolve ambiguities when translating type classes. We illustrate both points using the parameterized collections example from [4].

```
class Collects ce e | ce -> e where
  insert :: e->ce->ce
  delete :: e->ce->ce
  member :: e->ce->Bool
  empty  :: ce
```

Type classes are compiled by turning them into dictionaries (records holding member functions). Method `empty` yields an empty collection but the element type is not mentioned. Hence, it's not immediately clear which dictionary to choose. For example, we could encounter the situation of having to choose between `Collects [Integer] Integer` and `Collects [Integer] Int` but an arbitrary choice leads to ambiguities. By imposing the functional dependency `| ce -> e` such situations do not happen because the functional dependency guarantees that fixing the collection type `ce` uniquely determines the element type `e`. So `Collects [Integer] Integer` and `Collects [Integer] Int` cannot exist at the same time. Hence, there is no ambiguity.

Type Inference In terms of type inference, functional dependencies help the programmer to *improve* types.

```
inserttwo x y ce = insert x (insert y ce)
```

The program text of `inserttwo` yields type-class constraints `Collects ce e1` and `Collects ce e2`. Each constraints results from one of the two occurrences of `insert`. Thanks to the functional dependency we can infer that `e1` and `e2` must be equal. Hence, type inference yields the improved type

```
inserttwo :: Collects ce e => e -> e -> ce -> ce
```

Instance Improvement Type improvement provided by functional dependencies depends also on the set of available instances.

```
instance Eq e => Collects [e] e where ...
```

For brevity, we omit the instance body. Thanks to the functional dependency and the above instance, type inference for

```
insert3 x xs = insert x (tail xs)
```

yields

```
insert3 :: Eq e => e -> [e] -> [e]
```

Here is why. The program text of `insert3` gives rise to `Collects [e1] e2`. The functional dependency says that the collection type `[e1]` uniquely determines the element type `e2`. The programmer has narrowed down the possible choices for `e2` by specifying `instance ... => Collects [e] e`. Hence, `e2` and `e1` must be equivalent. But then we can reduce `Collects [e1] e1` to `Eq e1`.

The CHR Encoding In general, the type-improvement conditions implied by functional dependencies can be fairly complex and are often hard to understand. Previous work makes use of Constraint Handling Rules (CHRs) [2] to give a precise and systematic description of context reduction and type improvement. According to [9], the above class and instance declarations translate to the following CHRs.

- For each functional dependency fd_i of the form $a_{i_1},...,a_{i_k} \rightarrow a_{i_0}$, in a class declaration class $TC\ a_1\ ...\ a_n\ |\ fd_1,...,fd_m$, we generate

$$TC\ a_1...a_n,\ TC\ \theta(b_1)...\theta(b_n) ==> a_{i_0} = b_{i_0}$$

where $a_1...a_n, b_1...b_n$ are distinct type variables,
and $\theta(b_j) = \begin{cases} a_j & \text{if } j \in \{i_1,...,i_k\} \\ b_j & \text{otherwise} \end{cases}$

- Each instance declaration instance $C => TC\ t_1...t_n$ generates

$$TC\ t_1...t_n <==> C$$

If the context C is empty, we introduce the always-satisfiable constraint *True* on the right-hand side of generated CHRs.

- In addition, for each functional dependency fd_i in the class declaration, of the form $a_{i_1},...,a_{i_k} \rightarrow a_{i_0}$, we generate

$$TC\ \theta(b_1)...\theta(b_n) ==> t_{i_0} = b_{i_0}$$

where $b_1...b_n$ are distinct type variables,
and $\theta(b_j) = \begin{cases} t_j & \text{if } j \in \{i_1,...,i_k\} \\ b_j & \text{otherwise} \end{cases}$

FIGURE 4.1.   Translation of FD programs to CHRs

```
Collects ce e1, Collects ce e2 ==> e1 = e2    (FD)
Collects [e1] e2 ==> e1 = e2                  (Imp)
Collects [e] e <==> Eq e                      (Inst)
```

CHR solving is an extension of Herbrand unification over a user-programmable constraint domain. This is exactly what we need to describe type-class constraint solving. The first CHR rule (FD) captures the functional dependency. Each time the solver sees the two constraints (or instantiations of it) Collects ce e1 and Collects ce e2, the solver will add (propagate) the information that e1 and e2 are equivalent. In CHR syntax, constraint propagation is represented via ==>. Rule (Imp) therefore captures the improvement resulting from the type instance. The last rule (Inst) expresses context reduction. That is, whenever we see the constraint Collects [e] e (or instantiations of it), we reduce (simplify) this constraint to Eq e. Constraint simplification is represented via <==> in CHR syntax.

Figure 4.1 summarizes the translation to CHRs. We omit the treatment of superclasses for brevity. We write *FDToCHR(p)* to denote the set of all CHRs generated from an FD program p.

CHR-Based Type Inference   The benefit of translating functional-dependency programs to CHRs is that we obtain a systematic type-inference method based on CHR solving. Earlier we have seen that type inference (without type annotations) simply boils down to generating appropriate constraints out of the program text and then solving them with respect to the set of available CHR rules.

Type inference in the presence of type annotations is a bit more involved. Consider the earlier example where we have added some type annotation.

```
insert3 :: Eq e => [e] -> e -> [e]
insert3 xs x = insert (tail xs) x
```

To verify the correctness of the annotation, the type inferencer needs to check that the *given* constraints C_g from the annotation entail the *wanted* constraints C_w from the program text. The entailment check $C_g \supset C_w$ is logically equivalent to the equivalence check $C_g \Longleftrightarrow C_g \wedge C_w$. We can test for equivalence by normalizing (exhaustive CHR solving) the left and right–hand–side of $\Longleftrightarrow$ and checking the resulting constraints for syntactic equivalence. In case of the above type-annotated function, we effectively need to check for $\text{Eq } e \supset \text{Collects } [e] \ e$. Normalization yields

$$\begin{array}{l} \text{Eq e, Collects [e] e} \\ \rightarrowtail_{Inst} \quad \text{Eq e} \end{array}$$

We assume set semantics and the constraint $\text{Eq } e$ is in normal form. We find that the equivalence holds and therefore the function is type correct.

The Role of Confluence   For the equivalence-testing method (and therefore type inference) to be decidable and complete, we critically rely on termination and confluence of CHRs [7]. Termination of CHRs ensures that we can build normal forms in a finite number of steps. Confluence guarantees canonical normal forms: different derivations starting from the same point can always be brought together again.

Termination is notoriously hard to achieve [5] unless we impose rather harsh conditions on the set of allowable programs [9]. We therefore assume that guaranteeing termination is the user's responsibility. Possibly using some heuristics by for example limiting the number of solving steps to some number k. Any solving beyond k leads to the 'don't know' answer.

But we wish that confluence is guaranteed by some simple conditions which are satisfied by a reasonably large class of programs. The conditions identified in [9] to guarantee confluence of CHRs resulting from full functional-dependency programs are:

Definition 4.1 (Full Functional Dependencies). *We say the functional dependency* $\text{class } TC \ a_1 \dots \ a_n | a_{i_1}, \dots, a_{i_k} \to a_{i_0}$ *for a type class* TC *is* full *iff* $k = n - 1$.

A functional dependency is full if all type parameters of a type class are covered by the functional-dependency relation.

Definition 4.2 (Weak Consistency Condition). *Consider a declaration for class TC and any pair of instance declarations for that class:*

$$class\ C => \ TC\ a_1 \ ... \ a_n \ | \ fd_1, ..., fd_m$$
$$instance\ D_1 => \ TC\ t_1...t_n$$
$$instance\ D_2 => \ TC\ s_1...s_n$$

Then, for each functional dependency fd_i, of form $a_{i_1}, ..., a_{i_k} \to a_{i_0}$, the following condition must hold: for any substitution ϕ such that

$$\phi(t_{i_1}, ..., t_{i_k}) = \phi(s_{i_1}, ..., s_{i_k})$$

we must have that $\phi(t_{i_0})$ and $\phi(s_{i_0})$ are unifiable.

The Weak Consistency Condition says that the improvement conditions derived from instances must be non-conflicting. For example, the above program is inconsistent

```
class F a b | a -> b
instance F Int Float
instance F Int Bool
```

Consider the resulting CHR rules, in particular, the two last rules which conflict.

```
F a b, F a c ==> b = c
F Int Float   <=> True
F Int Bool    <=> True
F Int a       ==> a = Float
F Int a       ==> a = Bool
```

Inconsistency immediately implies non-confluence. Therefore, consistency is an essential condition.

The above condition is weaker than the (stronger) consistency condition in [9] which instead of '$\phi(t_{i_0})$ and $\phi(s_{i_0})$ are unifiable' requires that '$\phi(t_{i_0}) = \phi(s_{i_0})$'. Both conditions are equivalent in case we apply the Coverage Condition [9].

Definition 4.3 (Coverage Condition). *Consider a declaration for class TC, and any instance declaration for that class:*

$$class\ TC\ a_1 \ ... \ a_n \ | \ fd_1, ..., fd_m$$
$$instance\ C => TC\ t_1...t_n$$

Then, for each functional dependency $fd_i = a_{i_1}, ..., a_{i_k} \to a_{i_0}$, we require that

$$fv(t_{i_0}) \subseteq fv(t_{i_1}, ..., t_{i_k})$$

In the above, we assume that function fv computes the set of free variables.

For many FD programs the Coverage Condition is overly restrictive. See [9] for more details. However, we can weaken the Coverage Condition as follows.

Definition 4.4 (Weak Coverage Condition[3]). *For each functional dependency* $a_{i_1}, \ldots, a_{i_k} \rightarrow a_{i_0}$ *of class TC and*

$$\mathtt{instance}\, C \Rightarrow\, TC\, t_1 \ldots t_n$$

we must have that $fv(t_{i_0}) \subseteq closure(C, fv(t_{i_1}, \ldots, t_{i_k}))$, *where* $closure(C, vs)$ *is the least fix-point of the following equation:*

$$F(X) \quad = \quad vs \cup \left\{ fv(t_{i_0}) \;\middle|\; \begin{array}{l} TC\, t_1 \ldots t_n \in C, \\ TC \text{ has functional dependency } a_{i_1}, \ldots, a_{i_k} \rightarrow a_{i_0}, \\ fv(t_{i_1}, \ldots, t_{i_k}) \subseteq X \end{array} \right\}$$

In the above, we treat the instance context C as a set of (type class) constraints.

The Weak Coverage Condition says that all variables in the domain of the FD are uniquely determined by FDs in the instance context (plus building the transitive closure of those uniquely determined variables). In essence, the Weak Coverage Condition says that functional dependencies must behave 'functionally'.

```
class H a b c | a -> b
instance H a b Int => H [a] [b] Int
instance H b a Bool => H [a] [b] Bool
```

Both instances satisfy the Weak Consistency Condition. But they do not satisfy the (stronger) Consistency Condition from [9]. This situation is possible, because the Coverage Condition is violated. For example, in `H [a] [b] Int` variable b is not covered by the first parameter `[a]`. However, the Weak Coverage Condition holds because b is covered by `H a b Int` from the instance context. The second instance violates the Weak Coverage Condition because the parameters of the H type class have been swapped. Breaking the Weak Coverage Condition immediately results in non-confluence of the resulting CHRs. See [9] for details.

The upcoming section examines what role (non-)fullness plays for (non-) confluence. Later Sections 4.4 and 4.5 investigate methods how to achieve confluence for non-full FDs.

4.3 THE CONFLUENCE PROBLEM OF NON-FULL FDS

Non-Full FDs The `Stream` type class from the `parsec` package[4] provides a generic interface for streams:

```
class (Monad m) => Stream s m t | s -> t where
    uncons :: s -> m (Maybe (t,s))
```

Here s is the stream, t is the type of tokens and m is the monad in which the stream can be read. The functional dependency `s -> t` expresses that the token type can be derived from the stream type. The above FD is *non-full* because the type-class parameter m plays no part in the FD `s -> t`.

Lists are a simple instance of streams:

---

[3]Referred to as Refined Weak Coverage in [9].
[4]Available at http://hackage.haskell.org.

```
instance (Monad m) => Stream [t] m t where
    uncons []        = return Nothing
    uncons (x:xs) = return $ Just (x,xs)
```

The token type is the element type of the list. The monad type is independent of the two others: we can read from a list in any monad and the element type does not depend on the monad type.

A file cursor (the combination of a file handle and position) would be another kind of stream, one that is only usable inside the IO monad.

```
data Cursor = Cursor Handle Int
instance Stream Cursor IO Char where
    uncons (Cursor h p)
        = do hSeek AbsoluteSeek p h
             eof <- hIsEOF h
             if eof then return Nothing
             else do c  <- hGetChar h
                     p' <- hGetPosn h
                     return $ Just (c,Cursor h p')
```

A recursive example, is the pairing of two streams (without methods for brevity):

```
instance (Stream s1 m t1, Stream s2 m t2) =>
        Stream (s1,s2) m (t1,t2)
```

An advanced example is the BlockStream, which chops the output of a stream in blocks of a certain size. If the underlying stream runs out of tokens in the middle of a block, the block is padded with tokens from a default source, which depends on the monad. In the case of the IO monad, the padding is taken from standard input. In the case of the state transformer monad StateT, the padding is taken from the state. The code looks looks like:

```
data BlockStream s = BS { block_stream ::  s,
                          block_size ::  Int }
instance (Stream s IO t, Read t) =>
        Stream (BlockStream s) IO [t]
instance Stream s m t =>
        Stream (BlockStream s) (StateT [t] m) [t]
```

Other examples of non-full FDs can be found on HackageDB in the ArrayRef and StrategyLib packages.

Confluence Problem   Consider this type-class program with a non-full FD:

```
class F a b c | a -> b
instance F a b Bool => F [a] [b] Bool
```

The consequence of non-fullness is that the CHRs resulting from the above program are non-confluent. We show non-confluence by giving two non-joinable derivations. Here are the CHRs resulting from the above program according to [9]:

```
F a b1 c, F a b2 d ==> b1 = b2                    (FD)
F [a] [b] Bool <=> F a b Bool                     (Inst)
F [a] b c ==> b = [b1]                             (Imp)
```

These two distinct derivations from the same set of constraints illustrate the non-confluence:

$$F\ [a]\ [b]\ Bool,\ F\ [a]\ b2\ d \qquad\qquad (1)$$

$$
\begin{array}{ll}
\rightarrowtail_{FD} & F\ [a]\ [b]\ Bool,\ F\ [a]\ [b]\ d,\ b2\ =\ [b] \\
\rightarrowtail_{Inst} & F\ a\ b\ Bool,\ F\ [a]\ [b]\ d,\ b2\ =\ [b] \qquad (2)
\end{array}
$$

$$
\begin{array}{ll}
\rightarrowtail_{Inst} & F\ a\ b\ Bool,\ F\ [a]\ b2\ d \\
\rightarrowtail_{Imp} & F\ a\ b\ Bool,\ F\ [a]\ [c]\ d,\ b2\ =\ [c] \qquad (3)
\end{array}
$$

In the first derivation, we first apply the (FD) rule and propagate b2 = [b], followed by an application of rule (Inst). The other derivation immediately applies rule (Inst) and then rule (Imp). No further rule applications are possible and we can see that both derivations yield a different result. We say that the CHRs are non-confluent which means that our CHR-based type inference is potentially incomplete.

For example, suppose that type inference needs to verify that constraint (1) entails constraint (2) (which clearly holds see the first derivation). CHRs are non-confluent and therefore we possibly reduce (1) to (3) using the second derivation. Constraints (2) and (3) differ and therefore we falsely report that the entailment does not hold.

4.4 THE FULL FD ENCODING OF NON-FULL FDS

4.4.1 Transformable Non-Full FDs

The above non-confluence is not inherent in the non-full FDs themselves; it is an artefact of the CHR encoding of [9]. In [9], already a class of *transformable* non-full FD is identified. A transformation is given to transform these non-full FDs into full FDs.

Rather than to copy the formal definition of the transformation, we illustrate the transformation by applying it to our program:

```
class FD a b | a -> b
instance FD a b => FD [a] [b]

class FD a b => F a b c
instance F a b Bool => F [a] [b] Bool
```

The transformation factors out the (non-full) FD a -> b into a separate type class FD a b with a full FD a -> b.

Unfortunately, the transformation of [9] is restricted to instances that do not overlap in the domain of the functional dependency. In the following, we will see a more general transformation.

4.4.2   Extended Transformation of Non-Full FDs

In general, the above transformation leads to problems. Consider the program:

```
class H a b | a -> b
class F a b c | a -> b
instance F a b Bool => F [a] [b] Bool
instance H a b       => F [a] [b] Char
```

After the transformation, we get:

```
class H a b | a -> b
class FD a b => F a b c
instance F a b Bool => F [a] [b] Bool
instance H a b       => F [a] [b] Char

class FD a b | a -> b
instance FD a b => FD [a] [b]
instance H  a b => FD [a] [b]
```

The problem in this encoding is that the two instances of the type class FD overlap, and are non-confluent. We say that the FD is an *improper* non-full FD. Superficially, it seems that the b parameter is functionally determined by the a parameter alone. However, the above overlap bears out that this is incorrect. Only the top-level type constructor [] is determined by a alone. The remainder of b also depends on the particular instance that is matched. In other words, it also depends on c. Hence, an *improper* non-full FD is situated somewhere in-between a full and a proper non-full FD.

The improper non-full FD can be captured with an additional *instance selector* type class Sel as follows.[5]

```
class H a b | a -> b
class F a b c | a c -> b
instance Sel [a] [b] c => F [a] [b] c

class Sel a b c | a c -> b
instance F a b Bool => Sel [a] [b] Bool
instance H a b       => Sel [a] [b] Char
```

While the F type class's functional dependency has both a and c in its domain, it only matches on a in the instance. The latter instantiates the b parameter with the top-level type constructor [], and delegates to the selector type class Sel. Now Sel is allowed to match on c to choose the appropriate instance.

Formally, the class of programs our transformation addresses is:

Definition 4.5 (Extended Transformable Non-Full FDs). *Consider a class declaration*

$$class\, C => TC\, a_1\, \ldots\, a_n \mid a_1,\ldots,a_k\; ->\; a_{k+1}$$

---

[5]In general we have one selector function for each set of overlapping instances.

where $k+1 < n$. We say that TC is extended transformable to full FDs iff for every two declarations instance C => TC $t_1 \ldots t_n$ *and* instance C' => TC $t'_1 \ldots t'_n$ *and such that $\phi(t_1) = \phi(t'_1), \ldots, \phi(t_k) = \phi(t'_k)$ for some substitution ϕ, there exist two alpha-renamings α_1 and α_2 such that $\alpha_1(t_1) = t'_1, \ldots, \alpha_1(t_k) = t'_k$ and $t_1 = \alpha_2(t'_1), \ldots, t_k = \alpha_2(t'_k)$.*

The extended transformation is then:

Definition 4.6 (Extended Non-Full to Full FD Transformation). *Consider an FD program p with a class declaration*

$$\text{class } C \Rightarrow TC \, a_1 \ldots a_n \mid a_1, \ldots, a_k \rightarrow a_{k+1}$$

where $k+1 < n$. If TC is extended transformable, then the transformation, denoted xNFToF(p), consists of:

- *One class declaration:*

$$\text{class } C \Rightarrow TC \, a_1 \ldots a_n \mid a_1, \ldots, a_k, a_{k+2}, \ldots, a_n \rightarrow a_{k+1}$$

- *For each sequence $t_1, \ldots, t_k, t_{k+1}$ of a TC instance head that is unique modulo variable renaming, we get one new instance of TC:*

$$\text{instance } Sel_j \, t_1 \ldots t_{k+1} \, a_{k+2} \ldots a_n \Rightarrow TC \, t_1 \ldots t_{k+1} \, a_{k+2} \ldots a_n$$

and a class declaration for Sel_j, which is a fresh type class name:

$$\text{class } Sel_j \, a_1 \ldots a_n \mid a_1, \ldots, a_k, a_{k+2}, \ldots, a_n \rightarrow a_{k+1}$$

- *For each original* instance C => TC $t_1 \ldots t_n$ *a new instance of the corresponding Sel_j type class:*

$$\text{instance } C \Rightarrow Sel_j \, t_1 \ldots t_n$$

The transformation establishes confluence, because it yields only full FDs and the original program's instance heads in their entirety were non-overlapping.

Theorem 4.7 (Confluence). *Let p be an extended transformable non-full FD program. Then, FDToCHR(xNFToF(p)) is confluent iff p satisfies the Weak Consistency Condition.*

It is interesting to compare the relative strengths of the original and transformed program with the standard translation $FDToCHR(\cdot)$. We measure the strength in terms of the logical (first-order) meaning of CHRs [2].

Definition 4.8 (CHR Logical Meaning). *The translation function $[\![\cdot]\!]$ from CHR rules to first-order formulas is:*

$$
\begin{aligned}
[\![c \mathrel{<==>} d_1, \ldots, d_m]\!] &= \forall \bar{a}'(c \leftrightarrow (\exists \bar{\beta} \, d_1 \wedge \cdots \wedge d_m)) \\
[\![c_1, \ldots, c_n \mathrel{==>} d_1, \ldots, d_m]\!] &= \forall \bar{a}(c_1 \wedge \cdots \wedge c_n \supset (\exists \bar{\beta} \, d_1 \wedge \cdots \wedge d_m))
\end{aligned}
$$

where $\bar{a}' = fv(c)$, $\bar{a} = fv(c_1 \wedge \cdots \wedge c_n)$ and $\bar{\beta} = fv(d_1 \wedge \cdots \wedge d_m) - \bar{a}$. In the above, we assume that $\leftrightarrow$ and $\supset$ denote Boolean equivalence and implication.

It turns out that the transformed program's theory is weaker than that of the original program.

Theorem 4.9 (Soundness). *Let p be an extended transformable non-full FD program. Then, $[\![FDToCHR(p)]\!], \mathcal{T} \models [\![FDToCHR(xNFToF(p))]\!]$, where $\mathcal{T}$ relates the intermediate type-class symbols* Sel_j *to the main type-class symbols* TC*. For each*

$$\texttt{instance } Sel_j \, t_1 \, \ldots \, t_{k+1} \, a_{k+2} \, \ldots \, a_n \;\texttt{=>}\; TC \, t_1 \, \ldots \, t_{k+1} \, a_{k+2} \, \ldots \, a_n$$

in xNFToF(p), $\mathcal{T}$ *contains an axiom:*

$$\forall \overline{a}.Sel_j \, t_1 \, \ldots \, t_{k+1} \, a_{k+2} \, \ldots \, a_n \leftrightarrow TC \, t_1 \, \ldots \, t_{k+1} \, a_{k+2} \, \ldots \, a_n$$

where $\overline{a} = fv(t_1, \ldots, t_{k+1}, a_{k+2}, \ldots, a_n)$

Of course, we want the transformed program's theory to be weaker, because the original program's theory may be inconsistent, equating too many types. For instance, if we extend our running example with some additional instances:

```
instance F Int Foo Bool
instance H Int Bar
```

Then from `F [Int] b1 Bool` and `F [Int] b2 Char`, we could conclude `b1 = b2 = Foo = Bar` for the original program, which is clearly inconsistent. As it should be, this is not the case for the transformed program.

Our attempts to further relax the class of transformable non-full FDs based on the *FDToCHR*(·) translation have failed. Even with increasingly complex non-full to full transformations, we could not establish confluence.

4.5 PROPAGATION TRANSLATION OF NON-FULL FDS

A different encoding of FDs, in terms of propagation CHRs only, was suggested by Claus Reinke on the Haskell-Prime mailing list. Below we formalize his idea and state important results.

The basic idea of Claus Reinke's translation scheme is to replace <=> (simplification) in the (Inst) rule with ==> (propagation). Under this propagation-only translation scheme, the earlier 'problematic' non-full FD example

```
class F a b c | a -> b
instance F a b Bool => F [a] [b] Bool
```

translates to

```
F a b1 c, F a b2 d ==> b1 = b2          (FD)
F [a] [b] Bool ==> F a b Bool           (Inst)
F [a] b c ==> b = [b1]                   (Imp)
```

The propagation translation of FDs is short and elegant. Moreover, it directly supports improper FDs. Recall the earlier improper FD programs

```
class H a b | a -> b
class F a b c | a -> b
instance F a b Bool => F [a] [b] Bool    -- (1)
instance H a b => F [a] [b] Char
```

and its propagation encoding[6]

```
H a b, H a c ==> b = c          (FDH)
F a b c, F a d e ==> c = e      (FDF)
F [a] [b] Bool ==> F a b Bool   (Inst1)
F [a] [b] Char ==> H a b        (Inst2)
F [a] c d ==> c = [b1]          (Imp1)
F [a] c d ==> c = [b2]          (Imp2)
```

Definition 4.10 (Propagation Translation). *The propagation translation of an FD program p, denoted FDToPropCHR(p), is FDToCHR(p) where all <==> arrows are substituted by ==>.*

We easily obtain the desired confluence result for non-full FDs. A CHR program with only propagation rules is trivially confluent; there are no critical pairs.

Theorem 4.11 (Confluence of Propagation Translation). *Let p be an FD program. Then, the set FDToPropCHR(p) of CHRs is confluent.*

We also compare the relative strengths of *FDToPropCHR*($\cdot$), the propagation translation, with *FDToCHR*($\cdot$), the standard translation. We refer to the latter as the *standard theory* and to the former as the *propagation theory*. It straightforwardly follows that the propagation theory is weaker than the standard theory.

Theorem 4.12 (Standard Entails Propagation Translation). *Let p be a FD program. Then, $[\![FDToCHR(p)]\!] \models [\![FDToPropCHR(p)]\!]$.*

An immediate consequence is that any improvement in the propagation theory also holds in the standard theory.

Corollary 4.13 (Soundness of Propagation Improvement). *Let p be a FD program, C be a set of type-class constraints and t_1 and t_2 two types. If $[\![FDToPropCHR(p)]\!] \models C \supset t_1 = t_2$ then $[\![FDToCHR(p)]\!] \models C \supset t_1 = t_2$.*

However, the other direction does not hold in general as shown by the program

```
class F a b | a -> b
instance G a b => F a b
```

In the standard theory, the constraint set G a b, F a c implies b = c which is not the case in the propagation theory because from G a b we cannot conclude F a b.

---

[6]One of the two improvement rules is redundant.

This is not surprising because while the set *FDToPropCHR(p)* is confluent in general, hence, the propagation theory is consistent in the logical sense, the set *FDToCHR(p)* is non-confluent unless we impose fullness of FDs and the Weak Consistency and Coverage Conditions. The above program violates the Weak Coverage Condition and the standard theory becomes even inconsistent if we include

```
instance G Int Int
instance G Int Bool
```

From `G Int Int`, `G Int Bool` we derive `G Int Int`, `F Int Bool` which implies `Int=Bool`.

However, we can establish that the propagation theory entails the same amount of improvement as the standard theory if the standard translation yields a terminating and confluent set of CHRs.

Theorem 4.14 (Completeness of Propagation Improvement). *Let p be a FD program, C be a set of type-class constraints and t_1 and t_2 two types such that FDToCHR(p) is terminating and confluent. If $[\![FDToCHR(p)]\!] \models C \supset t_1 = t_2$ then $[\![FDToPropCHR(p)]\!] \models C \supset t_1 = t_2$.*

Proof. (Sketch) Under assumptions $[\![FDToCHR(p)]\!] \models C \supset t_1 = t_2$ and termination and confluence we can apply the completeness of entailment result stated in [7] which yields $C \rightarrowtail^*_{FDToCHR(p)} C', t_1 = t_2$ for some appropriate C'. Any derivation step in *FDToCHR(p)* is also possible in *FDToPropCHR(p)*, the only difference being that derivations in *FDToPropCHR(p)* never delete constraints. Hence, we can conclude that $C \rightarrowtail^*_{FDToPropCHR(p)} C'', t_1 = t_2$ for some appropriate C''. The logical soundness of CHR results in [2] then immediately yields $[\![FDToPropCHR(p)]\!] \models C \supset t_1 = t_2$ which concludes the proof.

The above results show that the propagation encoding is the superior translation scheme. If the standard translation is well-behaved, i.e. terminating and confluent, then the propagation translation behaves similarly. If the standard translation is ill-behaved, then the propagation translation is still well-behaved. Below, we discuss further the practical consequences of using the propagation encoding.

Time vs Space Trade-Off   The propagation encoding potentially uses more space than the standard encoding. However, it can put this space to good use in the form of memoing, which comes naturally.

Consider the type-level Fibonacci relation `Fib n f` which denotes that f is the nth Fibonacci number:

```
data Z      -- type-level
data S n    -- natural numbers

class Fib n f | n -> f
instance Fib Z     (S Z)
```

```
instance Fib (S Z) (S Z)
instance (Fib (S n) f1, Fib n f2, Add f1 f2 f)
         => Fib (S (S n)) f

class Add a b c | a b -> c
instance Add Z b b
instance Add a b c => Add (S a) b (S c)
```

Using the standard evaluation strategy for CHRs, i.e. the refined operational semantics [1], exhibits $\mathcal{O}(2^n)$ time complexity and $\mathcal{O}(1)$ space complexity.

The propagation encoding, however, stores all intermediate calls and avoids repeated calls with the (FD) rule:

```
Fib n f1, Fib n f2 ==> f1 = f2              (FD)
```

This results in a linear time complexity ($\mathcal{O}(n)$) at the cost of storing the n intermediate calls ($\mathcal{O}(n)$ space complexity).

The memoing effect comes naturally in the propagation encoding, also for other evaluation strategies, as long as we give precedence to the FD rule over instance reductions. The memoing effect can also be achieved with the other encoding, but requires a specific evaluation strategy that gives precedence to (1) the FD rule and (2) instance reduction of *bigger* constraints.

4.6 RELATED WORK

The original paper on functional dependencies [4] introduced two conditions (Consistency and Coverage) and conjectured that these conditions are sufficient to guarantee termination and confluence of the constraint solver underlying the type inferencer. This conjecture was formally verified in [9]. However, in practice, the Termination and Coverage Conditions are too limiting and rule out a large class of interesting programs.

The Weak Coverage Condition developed in [9] covers a much wider class of programs while guaranteeing confluence. However, the CHR-based encoding scheme could not deal properly with non-full FDs (and therefore a large class of interesting programs are ruled out again). In this paper, we have shown how to restore confluence for a large class of non-full FDs based on a transformation scheme to confluent full FDs.

The propagation encoding (suggested by Claus Reinke) even guarantees confluence for FD programs without imposing any restrictions. The current implementation of checking type classes in GHC is already fairly close to the propagation encoding: it implements a similar memoing technique.

4.7 CONCLUSION AND FUTURE WORK

We have shown that the non-confluence of non-full FDs is not inherent. Confluence for non-full FDs can be restored based on alternative encoding schemes.

The precise results we have stated relate the alternative encoding schemes to the original FD to CHR scheme introduced in [9].

The evidence translation of functional dependencies is still an open issue. We believe that the non-full to full FD transformation scheme in combination with results reported in [6] make it possible to translate a significant set of FD programs to type families (also known as type functions) [6, 5]. Type families are the 'functional' equivalent of FDs. Their evidence translation is well-studied [8] and already implemented in GHC.

Acknowledgments

We are grateful to Claus Reinke for explaining to us his idea of using propagation rules for not forgetting improvement opportunities. Thanks to Ross Paterson and Bulat Ziganshin for kindly pointing out several practical examples of non-full FDs. The feedback of Claus Reinke, Mark Jones and the anonymous reviewers on this paper is greatly appreciated.

Tom Schrijvers is a post-doctoral researcher of the Fund for Scientific Research, Flanders (Belgium).

REFERENCES

[1] G. J. Duck, P. J. Stuckey, M. J. García de la Banda, and C. Holzbaur. The refined operational semantics of Constraint Handling Rules. In *Proc of ICLP'04*, volume 3132 of *LNCS*, pages 90–104. Springer-Verlag, 2004.

[2] T. Frühwirth. Theory and practice of constraint handling rules. *Journal of Logic Programming, Special Issue on Constraint Logic Programming*, 37(1-3):95–138, 1998.

[3] M. P. Jones. Simplifying and improving qualified types. In *FPCA '95: Conference on Functional Programming Languages and Computer Architecture*. ACM Press, 1995.

[4] M. P. Jones. Type classes with functional dependencies. In *Proc. of ESOP'00*, volume 1782 of *LNCS*. Springer-Verlag, 2000.

[5] T. Schrijvers, S. Peyton Jones, M. Chakravarty, and M. Sulzmann. Type Checking with Open Type Functions. In Peter Thiemann, editor, *International Conference on Functional Programming*, pages 51–62. ACM Press, 2008.

[6] T. Schrijvers, M. Sulzmann, M. M. T. Chakravarty, and S. Peyton Jones. Towards open type functions for Haskell. In Olaf Chitil, editor, *Implementation and Application of Functional Languages*, pages 233–251, 2007. Published as Tech. Report No. 12-97, Computing Laboratory, University of Kent.

[7] P. J. Stuckey and M. Sulzmann. A theory of overloading. *ACM Transactions on Programming Languages and Systems (TOPLAS)*, 27(6):1–54, 2005.

[8] M. Sulzmann, M. M. T. Chakravarty, S. Peyton Jones, and K. Donnelly. System F with type equality coercions. In *Proc. of ACM SIGPLAN Workshop on Types in Language Design and Implementation (TLDI'07)*, pages 53–66. ACM Press, 2007.

[9] M. Sulzmann, G. J. Duck, S. Peyton Jones, and P. J. Stuckey. Understanding functional dependencies via constraint handling rules. *J. Funct. Program.*, 17(1):83–129, 2007.

Chapter 5

A Leaner Specification for Generalized Algebraic Data Types

Arie Middelkoop,[1] Atze Dijkstra,[1] S. Doaitse Swierstra[1]
Category: Research

Abstract: The type systems of current approaches for dealing with Generalized Algebraic Data Types (GADTs) tend to be more algorithmic than declarative in nature, and are incomplete in the sense that they deal with specific issues only. When implementing GADTs, this raises the question whether complex type system infrastructure is needed, and secondly, if all requirements were taken into account during implementation. We answer these questions by giving a declarative specification with less demands on infrastructure, and which deals with the key issues related to a GADT implementation.

5.1 INTRODUCTION

Generalized Algebraic Data Types (GADTs for short) allow for additional equalities to hold between type variables, witnessed by pattern matching on GADT constructors. These equalities are then used to coerce the type of an expression to an equivalent type. We give a more extensive introduction to GADTs in Section 5.3.

There are many applications that show that GADTs are a useful addition to languages. For example when dealing with transformations on typed abstract syntax for the implementation of domain-specific languages [2]. Therefore, we added support for GADTs in EHC, the Haskell compiler that we are developing at Utrecht University. We describe our implementation in terms of some specification. However, we were unable to find a specification that is sufficiently simple

---

[1]Universiteit Utrecht, The Netherlands; {ariem,atze,doaitse}@cs.uu.nl.

to match our implementation, because of two reasons. We sketch these reasons here, and defer a more thorough discussion to Section 5.2.

The first reason is that the type systems given by most approaches are complex. A reason for this is that algorithmic type systems are given, which rely on advanced type system infrastructures for the implementation. This makes it harder to incorporate ideas when the infrastructures differ.

Secondly, the GADT-aspect of an approach is often not discussed in isolation, but alongside other language features. This makes it difficult to determine if one requirement of an approach relates to the GADT-aspect, or is a requirement related to another language feature.

Therefore, we conclude that a specification is needed that is less complex and only takes the key issues of GADTs into account. The techniques we use are not novel: we take the constraint-based approach of Sulzmann et al. [11] and combine this with the unification-based approach of Peyton Jones et al. [6]. However, the resulting type system is easier and less tied to a particular implementation.

More concretely, we give:

- A declarative type system (Section 5.4) for an explicitly typed System F-like language extended with GADTs, using qualified types with equalities as qualifiers. Type conversions are restricted without having to resort to rigid types [6] or type shapes [8].

- A denotational semantics (Section 5.5) by giving a translation to a subset of System F_C, which is a System F-like language with explicit type coercions, defined by Sulzmann et al. [10].

5.2   RELATED WORK

An approach for GADTs consists of two components: a type information propagation component and a type conversion component. A type information propagation strategy determines what is known type information based on user-supplied type signatures, and what is inferred type information. A type conversion strategy deals with the construction of coercion terms.

5.2.1   Type information propagation strategies

Pottier et al. [8] use shape inference, where a shape represents known type information based on user-supplied signatures. These shapes are spread throughout the syntax tree in order to locate possible coercions. Their approach uses complex algorithms to spread the shapes as far as possible (depending on some quality versus performance trade-off parameter). The essential part concerning GADTs is that incompatible shapes are normalized with respect to some equation system, which is not made explicit in their work. From an implementer's point of view, this description is a concrete description of the equation system, and it requires infrastructure for spreading shapes.

Similarly, Peyton Jones et al. [6, 7] define a notion of wobbly types to combine type checking and type inference, which is based on earlier work on boxy types [12]. A rigid type represents known type information based on user-supplied type information, whereas a wobbly type is based on inferred information. The idea is then that type conversions are only applied on rigid types, for reasons of predictability and most-general typing. Aside from wobbly types, the authors use concepts such as 'fresh most general unifiers' and lexically scoped type variables in their presentation. It is hard to distinguish which of these concepts are really required, and which of these concepts are actually related to other language features that are covered by their approach (such as type families).

We incorporated an equivalent notion of wobbly and rigid types in our specification: in an explicitly typed System F-variant, the skolemnized type constants are rigid types, and we only allow type conversions on those.

The exact choice of propagation strategy is an orthogonal issue. By allowing type conversions only on known type information, a better propagation strategy just means that less explicit types have to be given by the programmer. This is the reason why we have chosen an explicitly typed source language in the first place. In fact, for our own implementation of this specification, we piggy backed on the infrastructure of the implementation of a higher-ranked impredicate type system. It has two propagation strategies, of which the advanced one has a concept of hard- and soft-type context, which can be compared to rigid and boxy types [4].

5.2.2 Type conversion strategies

Peyton Jones et al. [6, 7] use a unification-based strategy, where type conversion is called type refinement. A fixpoint substitution is constructed that, for each type equation introduced by pattern matching, contains a mapping for each (non-wobbly) type component of the left-hand side of an equation, to the corresponding type component on the right-hand side of an equation. The substitution is then used to normalize the types under consideration. The presentation is intertwined with the type propagation strategy, which makes it hard to separate these concepts. More recent continuation of this work by Sulzmann et al. [10] puts the GADT aspect in relative isolation.

Wazny [13] uses a constraint-based strategy. The GADT aspect of this strategy is covered separately by Sulzmann et al. [11, 9]. They also formulate the typing problems in terms of solving constraints with CHRs. The difference is that we restrict ourselves to equality constraints, and do not need the machinery required to solve implication constraints. Furthermore, their typing/translation rules do not mention how to deal with existential data types, which may be transparent to the given approach, but is of interest to a reader because GADT examples [2] often use them. Finally, in contrast to Peyton Jones et al., restrictions on type conversions are not mentioned.

We rely on their encoding for GADTs as qualified types in our approach (i.e. data constructors take a list of equality constraints). This encoding makes explicit which type variables are equated to what types, which gives slightly more information than an encoding with type signature notation (although these encodings can be mapped to each other).

As an overall observation concerning the related work, we use a constraint-based strategy similar to that of Wazny, but use the unification-based strategy of Peyton Jones et al. for the specific part of the implementation that deals with the decomposition of equality constraints.

5.3 MOTIVATION AND EXAMPLES

A typical implementation of an embedded domain specific language consists of some combinators to construct an abstract syntax tree, and some functionality in the host language to manipulate this abstract syntax tree. After analysis and transformation, the abstract syntax tree is translated to some denotation in the host language in order to use it.

For example, assume that we use Haskell as a host language and embed an expression language containing only tuples and numbers, using the following abstract syntax:

> **data** *Expr*
>   = *Num Int*
> | *Tup Expr Expr*

However, the following straightforward translation of the expression to a tuple in the host language does not type check, because the inferred types for the case alternatives are not the same:

> *eval e* = **case** *e* **of**
>   *Num i* → *i*
>   *Tup p q* → (*eval p, eval q*)

We can bypass this restriction imposed by the Haskell type system by using a typed abstract syntax and encode a proof that the generated tuples are type correct. For that, we add a type parameter t to the abstract syntax, which represents the type of the expression, and embed in the constructors a proof (with type *Equal t t′*) that states that this t is equal to the real type $t′$ of this specific expression (an *Int* for a *Num* and some tuple type for a *Tup*):

> **data** *Expr t*
>   =   *Num* (*Equal t Int*)   *Int*
> | ∀ *a b* . *Tup* (*Equal t* (*a,b*)) (*Expr a*) (*Expr b*)

Baars et al. [1] give a definition of this *Equal* data type and some operations, including a function *coerce* that converts the type to a proved equivalent type, and some combinators to construct equality proofs:

> *coerce* :: *Equal a b* → *a* → *b*
> sym   :: *Equal a b* → *Equal b a*
> *refl*   :: *Equal a a*

Now, we can modify the *eval* function in such a way that the case alternatives have the same type (namely the *t* in *Expr t*):

$$eval :: Expr\ t \rightarrow t$$
$$eval\ e = \textbf{case}\ e\ \textbf{of}$$
$$\qquad Num\ ass\ i \quad \rightarrow coerce\ (sym\ ass)\ i$$
$$\qquad Tup\ \ ass\ p\ q \rightarrow coerce\ (sym\ ass)\ (eval\ p, eval\ q)$$

The assumptions used by *eval* need to be proved when constructing values of type *Expr t*, which we achieve by using *refl*:

$$Tup\ refl\ (Num\ refl\ 4)\ (Num\ refl\ 2) \qquad :: Expr\ (Int, Int)$$

The important observation to make at this point is that the proofs are a *static* property of the program. Hence, the goal is to construct these proofs automatically, at those places explicitly indicated by the programmer using type signatures. In the case of the example, at those places where the type *t* shows up.

In order not to tie ourselves to Haskell or to a specific implementation of a type system, we use as source language an explicitly typed lambda calculus, called System F_A [10], where the equalities are not encoded as values, but with qualified type notation similar to Stuckey et al. [9]:

```
data Expr t =
   |        (t ≐ Int)     ⇒ Val Int
   | ∃a b . (t ≐ (a,b)) ⇒ Tuple (Expr a) (Expr b)
; let (eval :: ∀t . Expr t → t)
    = Λt → λ (e :: Expr t) →
      (case e of
         Num (x :: Int) → x
         (Tup p q) a b  → (,) (eval a p) (eval b q)
      ) :: t
  in eval (Tup (Num 4) (Num 2))
```

Similarly, instead of translating to Haskell, we translate to an explicitly typed lambda calculus with native support for equality proofs, called System F_C [10]:

```
data Expr t =
   |        Num (t~Int)    Int
   | ∃a b . Tup  (t~(a,b)) (Expr a) (Expr b)
; let (eval :: ∀t . Expr t → t)
    = Λt → λ (e :: Expr t) →
      (case e of
         Num eqInt (x :: Int)  → x                         ▷ sym eqInt
         (Tup eqTup p q) a b → (,) (eval a p) (eval b q) ▷ sym eqTup
      ) :: t
  in eval (Tup (Int, Int) (Num Int 4) (Num Int 2))
```

Each constructor contains equality proofs of type *t1*~*t2* (a proof that *t1* and *t2* are equal), called *coercions*, which can be used after pattern matching on them. The ▷ operator corresponds with the *coerce* function given above. Note that sym in this case is not a function, but a construction in the target language that operates on coercions, and that a type *t* as coercion represents the reflexivity *t*~*t*.

A specification for GADTs consists of two parts: a type system for the source language (Section 5.4), and a translation that constructs the equality proofs and inserts the coercions (Section 5.5).

5.4   TYPE SYSTEM

Source language   We use an explicitly typed source language extended with GADTs . This source language is a minor variation on System F_A [10], which we call System F_A'. The key difference is support for existential quantification and a slightly more uniform representation of pattern matches. The syntax of System F_A' is given in Figure 5.1.

A *v* is an identifier of which the denotation is a unique type constant. Although these identifiers can appear where a type or type variable is expected, they play an important role later. They are introduced at two places: when opening an existential using a pattern match (P.APP.EXIST) and with a universal abstraction (E.UNIV.ABS).

Each equality is encoded as a qualified type. The LHS is – without loss of generality – syntactically restricted to be a (bound) type variable. Existentials for a data constructor are introduced with an ∃ instead of the ∀ that is written in Haskell there.

The pattern language is similar to the expression language. Identifiers are bound to fields of a constructor using applications of variables. Likewise, universally quantified variables are instantiated by applying a type, and existentials are opened by applying a unique type constant.

Notation   First some notation before we give a type system for the source language. The semicolon in the rules for patterns acts as a separator to indicate that Γ and Δ are separate environments. Juxtaposition of environments (i.e. $\Delta\,\Gamma$) represents environment concatenation. $\Gamma\,(x) = t$ states that *x* is bound to *t* in Γ. Furthermore, we use an overbar to indicate a list. A single value at the position where a list is expected is implicitly assumed to be a singleton list. Juxtaposition of lists represents list concatenation. The components of the list are accessible with a subscript *i*. A type $\tau\,[\overline{\tau}]$ is obtained by replacing some components of τ in some fixed way with types $\overline{\tau}$. With $\tau^a = \tau\,[\overline{\tau^a}]$ and $\tau^b = \tau\,[\overline{\tau^b}]$, we express that τ^a and τ^b have a common structure τ, with corresponding differences in τ_i^a and τ_i^b respectively.

Type System   The type rules for expressions are given in Figure 5.3, with the meaning that in environment Γ, the expression *e* has type τ. The type rules for a

$e \in Expr$
$\rightarrow \quad C$ (E.CON)
$\mid \quad x$ (E.VAR)
$\mid \quad e\,e$ (E.APP.EXPR)
$\mid \quad e\,\tau$ (E.APP.UNIV)
$\mid \quad \lambda p\,.\,e$ (E.LAM.ABS)
$\mid \quad \Lambda v\,.\,e$ (E.UNIV.ABS)
$\mid \quad$ **let** $\overline{p = e}$ **in** e (E.LET)
$\mid \quad$ **case** e **of** $\overline{p \rightarrow e} :: \tau$ (E.CASE)

$d \in Decl$
$\rightarrow \quad$ **data** $D\,\overline{\alpha} = \overline{\mid \exists\overline{\beta}\,.\,x \doteq \tau \Rightarrow C\,\overline{\tau}}$

$t \in Program$
$\rightarrow \quad \overline{d};e$ (TOPLEVEL)

$x, \alpha, \beta \in Var$ $D \in TyCon$
$v \quad \in TyConst$ $C \in ValCon$
$TyConst \subseteq Var$

$p \in Pattern$
$\rightarrow \quad C$ (P.CON)
$\mid \quad x :: \tau$ (P.VAR)
$\mid \quad p\,p$ (P.APP.PAT)
$\mid \quad p\,\tau$ (P.APP.UNIV)
$\mid \quad p\,v$ (P.APP.EXIST)

$\tau \in Type$
$\rightarrow \quad C$ (T.CON)
$\mid \quad x$ (T.VAR)
$\mid \quad \tau\,\tau$ (T.APP)
$\mid \quad \forall x\,.\,\tau$ (T.FORALL)
$\mid \quad \exists x\,.\,\tau$ (T.EXISTS)
$\mid \quad \overline{\tau \doteq \tau} \Rightarrow \tau$ (T.EQS)

$\Gamma, \Delta \in Env$
$\rightarrow \quad x :: \tau,\, \Gamma$
$\mid \quad x,\, \Gamma$
$\mid \quad \tau \doteq \tau,\, \Gamma$

Figure 5.1. **Syntax of System** F_A'

pattern given in Figure 5.4 denote that in environment Γ, the pattern p has type τ, with bindings for variables in Δ.

When we ignore the special rules E.APP.EQS, E.COERCE, and P.APP.EQS for the moment, the rules are a minor variation on a type system for System F. The differences are:

- Scoping is made explicit by collecting bindings for a pattern in a local environment Δ.

- An existential is opened with a pattern match using P.APP.EXIST by instantiation to a fresh fixed type variable v (a type constant). Such a v may not escape the scope of the pattern match, which is enforced by demanding that the only variables that may escape are those that are bound in the global environment Γ in rules E.LAM.ABS, E.LET, and E.CASE.

- There are two type signatures in the environment for a constructor: a constructor signature $\Gamma\,(C)$ and a deconstructor signature $\Gamma\,(C^\circ)$. The constructor signature defines which which equalities need to be proved and which values have to be supplied. The deconstructor signature gives the dual definition: which values can be extracted when pattern matching against this constructor and which equalities can be assumed to be proved. Finally, Figure 5.2 defines how these signatures are derived from a data type declaration.

$$\boxed{\Gamma \vdash_d d}$$

$$\frac{\begin{array}{c} \Gamma\,(C_i^\circ) = \forall\overline{\alpha}\;\exists\overline{\overline{\beta}}_i\,.\,\overline{(x^l \doteq \tau^r)} \Rightarrow \tau_{i,0} \to \ldots \to \tau_{i,n_i} \to D\,\overline{\alpha}_i \\ \Gamma\,(C_i) = \forall\overline{\alpha}\forall\overline{\beta}_i\,.\,\overline{(x^l \doteq \tau^r)} \Rightarrow \tau_{i,0} \to \ldots \to \tau_{i,n_i} \to D\,\overline{\alpha}_i \\ D \in \Gamma \end{array}}{\Gamma \vdash_d \textbf{data}\ D\,\overline{\alpha} = |\ \overline{\exists\overline{\beta}}.\,\overline{(x^l \doteq \tau^r)} \Rightarrow C\,\overline{\tau}}\ \text{ADT}_G$$

Figure 5.2.   Data definition type rules (G)

Type Conversions   Without the three special rules, typing the example of Section 5.3 fails. We demand that the right-hand sides of the case alternatives are of type t, but the first case alternative is of type *Int*. The pattern match against the *Num* constructor gives us the proof that the *Int* is actually equal to the t. We exploit this knowledge using rule E.COERCE, by substituting the t for *Int* when typing the case alternative. Only those type constants (like t) may be substituted; we discuss this later. This rule uses the entailment relation $\Vdash$, which states that in environment Γ, the two types are proved to be equal.

$$\boxed{\Gamma \vdash_e e : \tau}$$

$$\frac{\begin{array}{c} \Gamma \vdash_e e : \overline{[v := \tau]}\, \tau' \\ \Gamma \Vdash \tau_i \doteq v_i \end{array}}{\Gamma \vdash_e e : \tau'}\ \text{E.COERCE}_G$$

$$\frac{\Gamma \Vdash \tau_i^l \doteq \tau_i^r \quad \Gamma \vdash_e e : (\overline{\tau^l \doteq \tau^r}) \Rightarrow \tau}{\Gamma \vdash_e e : \tau}\ \text{E.APP.EQS}_G \qquad \frac{\Gamma\,(C) = \tau}{\Gamma \vdash_e C : \tau}\ \text{E.CON}_G$$

$$\frac{\Gamma\,(x) = \tau}{\Gamma \vdash_e x : \tau}\ \text{E.VAR}_G \qquad \frac{\begin{array}{c} \Gamma \vdash_e a : \tau^a \\ \Gamma \vdash_e f : \tau^a \to \tau \end{array}}{\Gamma \vdash_e f\, a : \tau}\ \text{E.APP.EXPR}_G$$

$$\frac{\Gamma \vdash_e f : \forall \alpha.\ \tau}{\Gamma \vdash_e f\ \tau^a : [\alpha := \tau^a]\ \tau}\ \text{E.APP.UNIV}_G$$

$$\frac{\begin{array}{c} \Gamma;\Delta \vdash_p p : \tau^a \\ \Delta\,\Gamma \vdash_e e : \tau \\ \mathrm{ftv}\,(\tau) \cap \mathrm{ftv}\,(\Delta) \subseteq \mathrm{ftv}\,(\Gamma) \end{array}}{\Gamma \vdash_e \lambda p\,.\,e : \tau^a \to \tau}\ \text{E.LAM.ABS}_G$$

$$\frac{\begin{array}{c} v,\Gamma \vdash_e e : \tau \\ v \notin \mathrm{ftv}\,(\Gamma) \end{array}}{\Gamma \vdash_e \Lambda v\,.\,e : \forall v.\ \tau}\ \text{E.UNIV.ABS}_G \qquad \frac{\begin{array}{c} \Gamma;\Delta \vdash_p p_i : \tau_i \\ \Delta\,\Gamma \vdash_e e : \tau \\ \Delta\,\Gamma \vdash_e e_i : \tau_i \\ \mathrm{ftv}\,(\tau) \cap \mathrm{ftv}\,(\Delta) \subseteq \mathrm{ftv}\,(\Gamma) \end{array}}{\Gamma \vdash_e \mathbf{let}\ \overline{p = e}\ \mathbf{in}\ e : \tau}\ \text{E.LET}_G$$

$$\frac{\begin{array}{c} \Gamma;\Delta_i \vdash_p p_i : \tau^p \\ \Delta_i \Gamma \vdash_e e_i : \tau \\ \Gamma \vdash_e e^s : \tau^p \\ \mathrm{ftv}\,(\tau^p) \cap \mathrm{ftv}\,(\Delta_i) \subseteq \mathrm{ftv}\,(\Gamma) \end{array}}{\Gamma \vdash_e (\mathbf{case}\ e^s\ \mathbf{of}\ \overline{p \to e}) :: \tau : \tau}\ \text{E.CASE}_G$$

Figure 5.3.   Expression type rules (G)

$$\boxed{\Gamma;\Delta \vdash_p p : \tau}$$

$$\frac{\Gamma\ (C^\circ) = \tau}{\Gamma;\Delta \vdash_p C : \tau}\ \text{P.CON}_G \qquad \frac{\Delta\ (x) = \tau}{\Gamma;\Delta \vdash_p x :: \tau : \tau}\ \text{P.VAR}_G$$

$$\frac{\begin{array}{c}\Gamma;\Delta \vdash_p a : \tau^a \\ \Gamma;\Delta \vdash_p f : \tau^a \to \tau\end{array}}{\Gamma;\Delta \vdash_p f\, a : \tau}\ \text{P.APP.PAT}_G \qquad \frac{\Gamma;\Delta \vdash_p f : \forall \alpha.\ \tau}{\Gamma;\Delta \vdash_p f\ \tau^a : [\alpha := \tau^a]\ \tau}\ \text{P.APP.UNIV}_G$$

$$\frac{\begin{array}{c}\Gamma;\Delta \vdash_p f : \exists \alpha.\ \tau \\ v \in \Delta \quad v \notin \texttt{ftv}\ (\Gamma)\end{array}}{\Gamma;\Delta \vdash_p f\, v : [\alpha := v]\ \tau}\ \text{P.APP.EXIST}_G$$

$$\frac{\Gamma;\Delta \vdash_p f : (\overline{\tau^l \doteq \tau^r}) \Rightarrow \tau \quad \tau_i^l \doteq \tau_i^r \in \Delta}{\Gamma;\Delta \vdash_p f : \tau}\ \text{P.APP.EQS}_G$$

Figure 5.4.   Pattern type rules (G)

The rule E.APP.EQS is used to actually prove that *t* is equal to *Int* when we construct a value with the constructor *Num*, and rule P.APP.EQS allow us to extract this proof from the *Num* constructor and introduce it as an assumption in the environment.

Entailment   Figure 5.5 gives the entailment rules. A derivation of these rules is a proof of equality between two types. The first two rules represent symmetry and transitivity of an equality relation. Rule E.ASSUME uses an assumption from the environment. The subsumption rule decomposes an equality proof in proofs for components of type types. The congruence rules allows for proving an equality with subcomponents converted if there is an equality proof for it. Again, only type constants *v* need to be converted. The decomposition and subsumption rules are often needed when a type conversion has to be applied deep inside a type. Transitivity is not used often, but there are examples [2] with matches on more than one constructor where transitivity is needed to combine equality proofs.

Discussion   The explicitly typed source language allows us to abstract from a particular choice of type checking and type inference strategy, which (although important) is a separate issue. There is, however, a concept we have to take into account. A successful GADT pattern match results in additional assumptions between the equality of types, allowing types to be converted. Not all types are allowed to be converted for reasons of predictability and most general typing (when

$$\boxed{\Gamma \Vdash \tau^l \doteq \tau^r}$$

$$\frac{\Gamma \Vdash \tau^r \doteq \tau^l}{\Gamma \Vdash \tau^l \doteq \tau^r} \text{ E.SYM}_G \qquad \frac{\Gamma \Vdash \tau^l \doteq \tau^a \quad \Gamma \Vdash \tau^a \doteq \tau^r}{\Gamma \Vdash \tau^l \doteq \tau^r} \text{ E.TRANS}_G$$

$$\frac{\tau^l \doteq \tau^r \in \Gamma}{\Gamma \Vdash \tau^l \doteq \tau^r} \text{ E.ASSUME}_G \qquad \frac{\Gamma \Vdash v_i \doteq \tau_i \quad \Gamma \Vdash [\overline{v := \tau}] \, \tau^a \doteq \tau^b}{\Gamma \Vdash \tau^a \doteq \tau^b} \text{ E.CONGR}_G$$

$$\frac{\Gamma \Vdash \tau \, [\overline{\tau^a}] \doteq \tau \, [\overline{\tau^b}]}{\Gamma \Vdash \tau_i^a \doteq \tau_i^b} \text{ E.SUBSUME}_G$$

Figure 5.5. Entailment rules (G)

dealing with type inference). This is the reason why Peyton Jones et al. distinguish rigid types [6]. In our explicitly typed system, the concept of rigid types relates to type constants v introduced by universal abstraction and existential pattern matching. By allowing conversions only to such a constant, we obtain a specification that takes into account which types are allowed to be converted, while leaving the choice of type inference or propagation strategy up to the implementation.

So, the type constants v determine the positions where types can be converted. In the example of Section 5.3, the requirement that the case alternatives all need to be of type t (coming from *Expr t*), dictates that there needs to be a conversion from the actual type of the case alternative to this type t.

Furthermore, note that the three special rules are not syntax directed. An implementation decides where to apply these rules. For example, assuming that the target language is extended with some additional syntax, and that the example of Section 5.3 is lifted to some evaluation monad m:

```
data Expr t
    = Val (t~Int) t
    | ∀a b . Tuple (t~(a,b)) (Expr a) (Expr b)
;let (eval :: ∀t m . Monad m ⇒ Expr t → m t)
    = Λt m → λ(e :: Expr t) →
    (case e of
        Val    eqInt (x :: t)   → return m (x ▷ sym eqInt)
        (Tuple eqTup p q) a b →
            do ep ← eval m a p
               eq ← eval m b q
               return m ((,) ep eq ▷ sym eqTup)) :: m t
```

In the above code, the type conversion is applied as deep as possible. Another possibility is to convert as shallow as possible. For example, by changing the first case alternative to *return m x* ▷ (*m* (sym *eqInt*)), where the coercion *m* (of type *m*∼*m*) represents reflexivity, and the application of the coercions represent a coercion of type *m Int*∼*m t*. Other possibilities are a mixture between shallow and deep. This choice should not have an effect on the outcome of the program, but since it affects the structure of the target expression, a particular choice may be more beneficial depending on a particular implementation.

5.5   TRANSLATION

We give a translation to System F_C in order to give a semantics to the GADTs in our source language.

Target Language   We limit our explanation to the fragment of System F_C that we need. This fragment is given in Figure 5.6. See Sulzmann et al. [10] for a full explanation. There are some essential differences with respect to the source language:

- A proof of equality is made explicit as a *coercion* value γ with the type $\tau^1 \sim \tau^2$, meaning that γ is a witness that the type τ^1 is equal to type τ^2. Constructors store coercions as additional fields, and require them to be passed (E.APP.COE) when constructing values with such a constructor. Pattern matching against such a constructor bind an identifier to the coercion, allowing referencing to this coercion (C.VAR).

- The *cast* operator ▷ takes an expression $\hat{e}$ of type τ^1, and a coercion of type $\tau^1 \sim \tau^2$, and converts the type of $\hat{e}$ to τ^2.

- There are several language constructs to operate on coercions. Transitivity ($\gamma^1 \circ \gamma^2$) and symmetry (sym) have the usual interpretation. The left construct decomposes a coercion on type applications to a coercion of only the function part. Similarly, the right construct decomposes a coercion to the argument part. Coercion application $\gamma^1 \gamma^2$ creates a coercion that applies γ^1 to the function part of a type application and γ^2 to the argument part. Reflexivity of type $\tau \sim \tau$ is encoded as the coercion (not type!) τ. The other two constructs deal with quantors in types.

See Sulzmann et al. [10] for a type system of the target language.

Coercion Construction   In environment Γ, the source expression *e* with type τ is translated to the same expression $\hat{e}$ in the target language, with two exceptions (Figure 5.7). The key idea here is that a derivation of entailment is an equality proof out of which a coercion is constructed. The entailment relation expresses here that in environment Γ, τ^l is equal to τ^r, witnessed by the coercion γ (of type $\tau^l \sim \tau^r$).

$$
\begin{array}{ll}
\hat{e} \rightarrow & e \\
\quad | & \hat{e} \triangleright \gamma \qquad \text{(E.CAST)} \\
\quad | & \hat{e}\,\gamma \qquad \text{(E.APP.COE)} \\[1em]
\hat{d} \rightarrow & \textbf{data}\; D\,\overline{\alpha} = \overline{\,|\; \overline{\exists \overline{\beta}}\,.\, C\,\overline{\gamma}\,\overline{\hat{\tau}}\,} \\[1em]
\hat{\tau} \rightarrow & \tau \setminus \{\dot{=} \Rightarrow\} \\
\quad | & \gamma \rightarrow \hat{\tau} \\[1em]
\hat{p} \rightarrow & p \\
\quad | & \hat{p}\,\gamma \qquad \text{(P.APP.COE)}
\end{array}
\qquad
\begin{array}{ll}
\gamma \in Coercion \\
\quad \rightarrow & x \qquad \text{(C.VAR)} \\
\quad | & \gamma\,\gamma \qquad \text{(C.APP)} \\
\quad | & \hat{\tau} \qquad \text{(C.REFL)} \\
\quad | & \textsf{sym}\;\gamma \qquad \text{(C.SYM)} \\
\quad | & \gamma \circ \gamma \qquad \text{(C.TRANS)} \\
\quad | & \textsf{left}\;\gamma \qquad \text{(C.LEFT)} \\
\quad | & \textsf{right}\;\gamma \qquad \text{(C.RIGHT)} \\
\quad | & \forall \alpha\,.\, \gamma \qquad \text{(C.UNIV)} \\
\quad | & \gamma @ \hat{\tau} \qquad \text{(C.INST)} \\[1em]
\Gamma \quad | & x \mapsto \tau \dot{=} \tau, \Gamma
\end{array}
$$

Figure 5.6. **Syntax of the target language**

$$\boxed{\Gamma \vdash_e e : \tau \rightsquigarrow \hat{e}}$$

$$
\frac{
\begin{array}{c}
\Gamma \Vdash \tau^l_i \dot{=} \tau^r_i \rightsquigarrow \gamma \\
\Gamma \vdash_e e : \overline{(\tau^l \dot{=} \tau^r)} \Rightarrow \tau \rightsquigarrow \hat{e}
\end{array}
}{
\Gamma \vdash_e e : \tau \rightsquigarrow \hat{e}\,\gamma
}\; \text{E.APP.EQS}_T
$$

$$
\frac{
\begin{array}{c}
\Gamma \vdash_e e : \overline{[v := \tau]}\,\tau' \rightsquigarrow \hat{e} \\
\Gamma \Vdash \tau_i \dot{=} v_i \rightsquigarrow \gamma_i \\
\gamma = \textbf{lift}\;\overline{\gamma}
\end{array}
}{
\Gamma \vdash_e e : \tau' \rightsquigarrow \hat{e} \triangleright \gamma
}\; \text{E.COERCE}_T
$$

Figure 5.7. **Expression type rules (T)**

Rule E.APP.EQS states that if a proof of equality is expected for the source language, that this proof as coercion γ is passed explicitly as parameter in the target language.

With Rule E.COERCE, type constants v deep inside τ' are converted. The small coercions $\bar{\gamma}$ for these type constants need to be combined into one coercion that operates on the entire τ', by adding the appropriate amount of coercion applications, universal abstractions and instantiations, and reflexive-coercions. For reasons of space, we hide this triviality behind the function **lift**.

$$\boxed{\Gamma \Vdash \tau^l \doteq \tau^r \leadsto \gamma}$$

$$\frac{\Gamma \Vdash \tau^r \doteq \tau^l \leadsto \gamma}{\Gamma \Vdash \tau^l \doteq \tau^r \leadsto \text{sym } \gamma}\ \text{E.SYM}_T \qquad \frac{\Gamma \Vdash \tau^l \doteq \tau^a \leadsto \gamma^1 \quad \Gamma \Vdash \tau^a \doteq \tau^r \leadsto \gamma^2}{\Gamma \Vdash \tau^l \doteq \tau^r \leadsto \gamma^2 \circ \gamma^1}\ \text{E.TRANS}_T$$

$$\frac{\Gamma(x) = (\tau^l \doteq \tau^r)}{\Gamma \Vdash \tau^l \doteq \tau^r \leadsto x}\ \text{E.ASSUME}_T \qquad \frac{\Gamma \Vdash v_i \doteq \tau_i \leadsto \gamma_i \quad \gamma = \textbf{lift } \bar{\gamma} \quad \Gamma \Vdash [\overline{v := \tau}]\ \tau^a \doteq \tau^b \leadsto \gamma^{il}}{\Gamma \Vdash \tau^a \doteq \tau^b \leadsto \gamma^{il} \circ \gamma}\ \text{E.CONGR}_T$$

$$\frac{\Gamma \Vdash \tau\,[\overline{\tau^a}] \doteq \tau\,[\overline{\tau^b}] \leadsto \gamma \quad \bar{\gamma} = \textbf{decompose } \gamma}{\Gamma \Vdash \tau_i^a \doteq \tau_i^b \leadsto \gamma_i}\ \text{E.SUBSUME}_T$$

Figure 5.8. Entailment rules (T)

The actual construction of the coercion is a side effect of using the entailment rules of Figure 5.8 to proof an equality.

- The translation for pattern matches translates each assumption $\tau^l \doteq \tau^r$ of a constructor to an explicit match on a coercion of type $\tau^l \sim \tau^r$, binding this coercion to some unique identifier x and adding this binding to the environment. Then, entailment rule E.ASSUME lookups this binding in the environment and refers to it as the coercion x.

- The coercion for the congruence rule may only replace some type constants somewhere deep inside the type structure. Again, **lift** is used for the construction of the full coercion.

- The subsumption rule decomposes a coercion in small coercions, by adding the appropriate amount of `left` and `right` coercions in front of them. We omit rules for this decomposition and hide this triviality behind the **decompose** function.

5.6 CONCLUSION

We described a translation of GADTs to an explicitly typed system with qualified types (Section 5.5) with equality constraints as qualifiers. The type system comes basically for free, since dealing with assumptions and insertion of evidence is already done by the system for qualified types. Adding GADTs to such a language boils down to implementing an entailment relation on equality constraints. To prevent having entailment rules for each construct in the type language, we used an auxiliary relation to construct coercions based on the structure of types.

To validate our work, we added support for GADTs to the Essential Haskell compiler [3], using Constraint Handling Rules [5] to implement the entailment rules. The EH language has a rich type system (higher ranked types, impredicative types, existential types, many type class extensions, scoped instances, polymorphic kinds, extensible records). The implementation is orthogonal to all these extensions.

5.6.1 Future work

The obvious future work is to describe our implementation in terms of this specification. Second to that, we can now describe implementation issues separately, such as the propagation of type information, and the implementation of entailment. For example, the following issues can now be described without having to give an implementation for other aspects of a GADT implementation:

The construction of equality proofs can be expensive, especially when big types with many variables are involved. There are two potential directions for optimization. The solver uses a trie-structure to select candidate CHRs and is optimized to deal with a great number of very specific CHR rules. By generating many but specialized versions of the CHR rules based on the GADT declarations, we hope to reduce the time it takes to select the next applicable rule. Furthermore, there can be several applicable rules to choose from during a solve step. At the moment, the choice is non-deterministic, but more advanced heuristics are definable in the CHR framework (for example, to make the symmetry rule the least attractive choice). These optimizations can speed up the time it takes to construct an equality proof considerably.

A succeeding pattern match witnesses that the type equalities hold. However, in the presence of irrefutable patterns, the pattern match may not have taken place. One way to deal with this is to only assume the additional type equalities when the pattern match is not inside an irrefutable pattern. This approach is taken by the Haskell compiler GHC for example. However, since we formulated GADTs in terms of qualified types and have the facilities for evidence generation at our disposal, we can do better: generate coercion functions that force evaluation of the irrefutable pattern when a coerced value is evaluated which needed the corresponding assumption. Proper heuristics need to be defined to minimize the forcing of evaluations.

Acknowledgements   We thank the anonymous referees for their comments; the student paper feedback report in particular. Special thanks to Lucília Camarao from Universidade Federal de Ouro Preto, Brazil, for her support just before the first submission deadline.

This work was supported in part by Microsoft Research through its European PhD Scholarship Programme.

REFERENCES

[1] A. I. Baars and S. D. Swierstra. Typing dynamic typing. In *ICFP '02: Proceedings of the seventh ACM SIGPLAN International Conference on Functional Programming*, volume 37, pages 157–166. ACM Press, September 2002.

[2] A. I. Baars and S. D. Swierstra. Typed transformations of typed abstract syntax. http://www.cs.uu.nl/wiki/Center/TTTAS, 4 2008.

[3] A. Dijkstra. EHC Web. `http://www.cs.uu.nl/wiki/Ehc/WebHome`, 2004.

[4] A. Dijkstra. *Stepping through Haskell*. PhD thesis, Utrecht University, Department of Information and Computing Sciences, 2005.

[5] T. Frühwirth. Theory and practice of constraint handling rules. *Journal of Logic Programming, Special Issue on Constraint Logic Programming*, 37(1-3):95–138, October 1998.

[6] S. L. Peyton Jones, D. Vytiniotis, S. Weirich, and G. Washburn. Simple unification-based type inference for gadts. In *ICFP*, pages 50–61, 2006.

[7] S. L. Peyton Jones, G. Washburn, and S. Weirich. Wobbly types: type inference for generalised algebraic data types. Technical Report MS-CIS-05-26, University of Pennsylvania, Computer and Information Science Department, Levine Hall, 3330 Walnut Street, Philadelphia, Pennsylvania, 19104-6389, July 2004.

[8] F. Pottier and Y. Régis-Gianas. Stratified type inference for generalized algebraic data types. In *POPL*, pages 232–244, 2006.

[9] P. J. Stuckey and M. Sulzmann. Type inference for guarded recursive data types. *CoRR*, abs/cs/0507037, 2005.

[10] M. Sulzmann, M. M. T. Chakravarty, S. L. Peyton Jones, and K. Donnelly. System F with type equality coercions. In *TLDI*, pages 53–66, 2007.

[11] M. Sulzmann, J. Wazny, and P. J. Stuckey. A framework for extended algebraic data types. In *FLOPS*, pages 47–64, 2006.

[12] D. Vytiniotis, S. Weirich, and S. L. Peyton Jones. Boxy types: inference for higher-rank types and impredicativity. In J. H. Reppy and J. L. Lawall, editors, *ICFP*, pages 251–262. ACM, 2006.

[13] J. R. Wazny. *Type inference and type error diagnosis for Hindley/Milner with extensions*. PhD thesis, The university of Melbourne, January 2006.

Chapter 6

One Vote for Type Families in Haskell!

Louis-Julien Guillemette,* Stefan Monnier*
Category: Position

Abstract: Generalized Algebraic Data Types (GADTs) allow programmers to capture invariants of their data structures through type annotations on data constructors. However, when working with GADTs, it is often difficult to concisely and precisely express the way data manipulations maintain those invariants. One can use GADTs or multi-parameter type classes to model relations on types, but the results are not always satisfactory. The recent introduction of open type families in GHC offers an attractive alternative. They are a type system extension by which functions over types can be defined directly, much like term-level functions, and appear in type signatures.

We illustrate the use of type families in the context of a type-preserving compiler written in Haskell. We compare the results with an *ad hoc* solution that uses GADTs to encode functions on types. We argue that type families promote a more direct programming style that eliminates much code bloat and translates into increased run-time performance. They offer better modularity and require fewer type annotations than type classes, which require that class constraints be propagated between compilation phases.

We also describe a use of type families to capture more complex data structure invariants. We mention current limitations that we face with these more advanced uses, in which we need to convince the type checker that the type families we define satisfy certain properties. We sketch a proposal of a language extension to directly support such properties.

*Université de Montréal, C.P. 6128, succ. Centre-Ville, Montréal, Québec, Canada.
++1 (514) 343-6111 x3545; {guillelj,monnier}@iro.umontreal.ca.

6.1 INTRODUCTION

There is a definite trend in richly typed functional languages to incorporate features from dependently typed languages and proof assistants. In the world of Haskell, an important step in this direction has been the introduction of Generalized Algebraic Data Types (GADTs) in GHC. GADTs can be seen as a restricted form of dependent types, where the stage distinction between terms and types is not lost. They allow data constructors to bear extra type annotations that can describe the shape, size, content, or other properties of the data. These annotations can be used to express key invariants of the data structures, and thus rule out invalid uses of the data.

Even before GADTs were around, the rich type system of Haskell and its proposed extensions lent itself to simulating dependent typing. Typically this could be done with sophisticated uses of type classes (as in [4]), or even plain old parametric polymorphism (as in [12]). But as GADTs extend the basic notion of data declaration at the core of the language, they promise to support a sort of dependent programming in a more direct manner. But while GADTs constrain the data that can be constructed, they do not naturally lend themselves to impose some relationship between different chunks of data, e.g. to state that the list returned by a *filter* function is shorter than its argument. Multi-parameter type classes can sometimes serve that purpose, although the results are often contrived and difficult to understand. Alternatively, as GADTs can essentially encode relations on types, they can be used as runtime proofs of relations on the types of the inputs and outputs of a function. While this approach is flexible, it tends to be rather verbose and incurs run-time overhead.

There has recently been a proposal to extend Haskell with functions over types, or so-called *type families* [17, 16]. They allow the programmer to define functions over types by case analysis, and refer to these functions in the signatures of functions (or data constructors). This development had been introduced in GHC and we could thus experiment with those new tools. Our experience has generally been that precise relationships between types can be expressed succinctly and precisely, while achieving the same effect using other techniques requires rather more indirect and elaborate encodings.

Type families are a generalization of associated types [3], in the sense that they can be defined independently of type classes. The question whether associated types or the alternative approach of multi-parameter type classes with functional dependencies [10], should make it to the next Haskell standard [15], is one of the most hotly debated issues in the standardization effort. This motivated us to document our experience and take a position in favour of type families.

6.1.1 Context

We have been using GADTs extensively in the context of a type-preserving compiler for a functional language [7, 8]. The primary use we make of GADTs is to encode program representations of our source and intermediate languages, in

data *ValK t* **where**
    LamK :: (*ValK t* → *ExpK*) → *ValK* (*t* → *Void*)
    PairK :: *ValK s* → *ValK t* → *ValK* (*s*,*t*)

data *ExpK* **where**
    AppK :: *ValK* (*t* → *Void*) → *ValK t* → *ExpK*

data *Void*

FIGURE 6.1. **Encoding of the CPS language**

a way that enforces each language's type system. As a starting point, the simply
typed λ-calculus can be encoded as:

data *Exp t* **where**
    Lam :: (*Exp s* → *Exp t*) → *Exp* (*s* → *t*)
    App :: *Exp* (*s* → *t*) → *Exp s* → *Exp t*

In contrast to an ordinary algebraic data type, a GADT definition can have data
constructors of varying type. Here, the type *Exp* has a type parameter *t* that reflects the source type of the expression: a Haskell term of type *Exp t* encodes an
expression of source type τ, where *t* is the Haskell type we use to reflect τ. We
can also view *Exp* as an encoding of type derivations rather than just expressions,
as type derivations are in one-to-one correspondence with well-typed expressions.

The tricky part is to give a type to a function that implements a transformation
over *Exp*. We will take the example of the CPS conversion, as its theory is well
understood (see e.g. [2, 14]). At first approximation, its type would be:

$$cps :: Exp\ t \rightarrow (ValK\ t' \rightarrow ExpK) \rightarrow ExpK$$

where *ValK t* is a value in CPS of type *t* and *ExpK* is a well-formed CPS expression; the two data types are defined in Fig. 6.1. The second argument to *cps*
is an expression parameterized by a value of object type t', consistent with the
source type *t*; it abstracts the context which will consume the value produced by
the evaluation of the original expression.

The relationship between *t* and t' is captured by a function mapping source
types to types in CPS:

$$\mathscr{K}\llbracket \tau_1 \rightarrow \tau_2 \rrbracket = (\mathscr{K}\llbracket \tau_1 \rrbracket, \mathscr{K}\llbracket \tau_2 \rrbracket \rightarrow \textbf{void}) \rightarrow \textbf{void}$$

In CPS, functions do not return to the caller, so they do not have a return type,
and they are called *continuations*. The type of a continuation expecting type τ is
denoted $\tau \rightarrow$ **void**. As an example, the identity function on integers, $\lambda x\,.\,x$ of type
int → **int**, is converted to a function $\lambda \langle x, k \rangle\,.\,k\,x$ of type $\langle \textbf{int}, \textbf{int} \rightarrow \textbf{void} \rangle \rightarrow \textbf{void}$.

In the sections that follow, we will see different implementations of *cps* using
different types. We will focus on the rule that CPS-converts a function application:

$$\mathscr{K}_{\exp}\llbracket e_1\ e_2 \rrbracket\,k = \mathscr{K}_{\exp}\llbracket e_1 \rrbracket\,(\lambda v_1.\ \mathscr{K}_{\exp}\llbracket e_2 \rrbracket\,(\lambda v_2.\ v_1\,\langle v_2, k \rangle))$$

Restricting to the case of function application rather than function abstraction relieves us from the intricacies of dealing with binders, so as to better focus on type issues.

Outline   The rest of this paper is structured as follows. We first introduce type families and implement the function *cps* using these (Section 6.2). We then consider an alternative solution that uses only GADTs (Section 6.3), and one that uses type classes (Section 6.4). We describe a more advanced use of type families for encoding more sophisticated typed languages and some limitations thereof (Section 6.5), and sketch a proposal to address these limitations (Section 6.6).

6.2   TYPE FAMILIES

Type families allow us to directly define functions over types by case analysis, in a way that resembles term-level function definitions with pattern matching. For example, we can define a type function *Add* that computes (statically) the sum of two Peano numbers:

> **data** *Z*; **data** *S i*   — natural numbers encoded as types

> **type family** *Add n m*
> **type instance** *Add Z m* = *m*
> **type instance** *Add (S n) m* = *S (Add n m)*

We can then use this type family to express the fact that an *append* function over length-annotated lists produces a list of the expected length:

> **data** *List elem len* **where**
>   *Cons* :: *elem* → *List elem n* → *List elem (S n)*
>   *Nil* :: *List elem Z*

> *append* :: *List elem n* → *List elem m* → *List elem (Add n m)*
> *append Nil l* = *l*
> *append (Cons h t) l* = *Cons h (append t l)*

To see how the first clause of *append* type-checks: by the type signature of *append*, the right-hand side should have type *List elem (Add Z m)*; *l* actually has type *List elem m*, which is the same, since *Add Z m* reduces to *m* by the definition of *Add*. For the second clause, the type signature of append requires that the right-hand side have type *List elem (Add (S n) m)*; actually *Cons h (append t l)* has type *List elem (S (Add n m))*, which is the same after the second clause of *Add* is applied, in reverse.
   We can define $\mathscr{K}[\![-]\!]$ similarly:

> **type family** *CPS t*
> **type instance** *CPS (s → t)* = *((CPS s, CPS t → Void) → Void)*

and we can refer to it in the type of *cps*:

data *CPS t t'* **where**
    CpsFun :: *CPS s s'* → *CPS t t'*
               → *CPS* $(s → t)$ $((s', t' → Void) → Void)$

data *CPSterm t* **where**
    CPSterm :: *CPS t t'* → $((ValK\ t' → ExpK) → ExpK)$ → *CPSterm t*

cps :: *Exp t* → *CPSterm t*
cps $(App\ e_1\ e_2)$ =
  case *cps* e_1 **of**
    CPSterm $(CpsFun\ ss'\ tt')\ e_1'$ →
      case *cps* e_2 **of**
        CPSterm $ss_2'\ e_2'$ →
          case *cpsUnique ss' ss*$_2'$ **of**
            EqRefl → *CPSterm tt'* $(\lambda k → e_1\ (\lambda v_1 → e_2\ (\lambda v_2 →$
                             $AppK\ v_1\ (PairK\ v_2\ (LamK\ k)))))$

data *Equal a b* **where**
    EqRefl :: *Equal a a*

cpsUnique :: *CPS t t'* → *CPS t t''* → *Equal t' t''*
cpsUnique = ...

FIGURE 6.2. **All-GADT CPS conversion**

cps :: *Exp t* → $(ValK\ (CPS\ t) → ExpK) → ExpK$

We can then implement *cps* in the most straightforward way and have the type-checker verify that the constraints on object types are respected:

cps $(App\ e_1\ e_2)\ k$ =
  cps e_1 $(\lambda v_1 →$
    cps e_2 $(\lambda v_2 →$
      $AppK\ v_1\ (PairK\ v_2\ (LamK\ k))))$

In this example we get GHC's type checker to verify that our CPS conversion is type preserving, *for free*: were we to use a plain algebraic data type instead of a GADT and not bother to enforce type preservation, the code of *cps* would be identical.

6.3 MORE GADTS

In the days when type families were not available, a workable solution (which we did use extensively) was to encode the type function $\mathscr{K}[\![-]\!]$ as relation using a GADT, and have *cps* produce an existential package containing a proof that the output term expected a continuation of suitable type. The type of *cps* then looks like:

$$cps :: Exp\ t \rightarrow (\exists t'.\ (CPS\ t\ t', (ValK\ t' \rightarrow ExpK) \rightarrow ExpK))$$

A term of type $CPS\ t\ t'$ encodes a proof that $\mathscr{K}\,[\![\tau]\!] = \tau'$, where t encodes τ and t' encodes τ'. The above signature for cps actually abuses Haskell notation: in reality we need to introduce another GADT ($CPSterm\ t$) to bind an existential type and couple the term with the proof that it is of the expected type. The actual implementation is shown in Fig. 6.2.

As $\mathscr{K}\,[\![-]\!]$ is encoded as a relation, we need a separate proof that this relation is a function. This is accomplished by the $cpsUnique$ function, which produces a witness that $\tau' = \tau''$, given proofs that $\mathscr{K}\,[\![\tau]\!] = \tau'$ and $\mathscr{K}\,[\![\tau]\!] = \tau''$; such witnesses are encoded with the type equality GADT, $Equal$. We call this function when converting a function application to ensure that the function and its argument are of compatible type.

In comparison to our initial solution with type families, the one shown here is unsatisfactory:

- It is cluttered with manipulations of existential packages. As a result, the code doing the translation roughly doubles in size.

- It requires a number of additional artifacts, such as the type $CPSterm$ and the function $cpsUnique$.

- Constructing and inspecting the existential packages incurs run-time overhead.

- The 'proofs' that the types match are encoded in an unsound logic: a proof term could be set to *undefined*, or its evaluation could run into an infinite loop. The type system guarantees that the constructed proof terms are well-formed, but Haskell does not provide a way to statically verify that the proof terms are properly constructed. Such proofs can be checked at runtime instead, with the obvious runtime cost, but even then, it can be difficult to convince oneself that the runtime checks are complete.

6.4   TYPE CLASSES

Type classes are meant to support *ad hoc* polymorphism: they allow the programmer to define functions that behave differently at different types. It is not immediately clear that this feature can be useful in our case: after all, cps proceeds by case analysis over the syntactic constructs, not the types. But there may be some indirect use of type classes by which we can express the way our syntax-directed translation produces terms of the expected type.

Multi-parameter type classes with functional dependencies allow us to define some form of intentional type functions. For example, we can express the type function $\mathscr{K}\,[\![-]\!]$ as follows:

```
class CPS t t' | t → t'
instance (CPS s s', CPS t t') ⇒ CPS (s → t) ((s',t' → Void) → Void)
```

The first line declares a type class *CPS* as a relation between two parameters t and t', and states that t' is uniquely determined by t, so in effect we have a function from t to t'. The second line defines the function at $s \to t$. For type classes to be useful, they are normally equipped with member functions. We might try to define *cps* in this way:

> **class** *CPS t t'* $\mid t \to t'$
> **where** *cps* :: *Exp t* $\to$ *(ValK t'* $\to$ *ExpK)* $\to$ *ExpK*

Individual instance declarations are required to implement the member functions for the types they cover, for example:

> **instance** *(CPS s s', CPS t t')* $\Rightarrow$ *CPS (s* $\to$ *t) ((s',t'* $\to$ *Void)* $\to$ *Void)*
> **where** *cps* = ...

This example would give the translation for λ-abstractions. We would define other instances and implement *cps* for other introduction forms if we had any. But we cannot do the same for elimination forms, as they are not identified with source types of a particular form. For example, we cannot say in general of what form the type of a function application $e_1\ e_2$ will be, as it depends on the return type of e_1.

One thing we can do is define the function *cps* separately from the class *CPS* and have it handle all the syntactic forms:

> *cps* :: *CPS t t'* $\Rightarrow$ *Exp t* $\to$ *(ValK t'* $\to$ *ExpK)* $\to$ *ExpK*
> *cps (App e_1 e_2) k* =
>   *cps e_1 (λv_1* $\to$
>   *cps e_2 (λv_2* $\to$
>   *AppK v_1 (PairK v_2 (LamK k))))*

For this this to work, the compiler must know that there are instances of *CPS* that cover the types of e_1 and e_2. This forces us to add a class context to the constructor *App*:

> *App* :: *CPS s s'* $\Rightarrow$ *Exp (s* $\to$ *t)* $\to$ *Exp s* $\to$ *Exp t*

Note that we do not need to mention *CPS t t'* in this context, because the return type of *App* is *Exp t*, and we already have *CPS t t'* in the context of *cps*.

The problem with these class constraints is that they embed knowledge about the CPS translation into the source language. So earlier phases get polluted by constraints that are specific to the later CPS phases. In general these class constraints propagate from the CPS conversion phase all the way up to the type checking or type inference phase, which is the only phase where the types are sufficiently ground to make it possible to create the corresponding proofs. Of course, other compilation phases such as closure conversion or hoisting would require similar class constraints on their data constructors, which would propagate to the front-end as well. Class inheritance might sometimes be used to combine or synthesize these. But there is an inherent lack of modularity in this scheme, which amounts to pre-computing in some previous phase the type-level translation of a subsequent phase.

6.5   FURTHER USES OF TYPE FAMILIES

Type families are also useful to capture more complex invariants of data structures. We constructed an encoding of System F, where a set of type families implement substitution over System F types. In this section we describe this encoding as well as the difficulties we encountered when implementing code transformations over it.

Our representation of System F types encodes type variables (bound by $\forall$) as de Bruijn indices. For instance, the type of the swap function for pairs:

$$\forall \alpha, \beta. \langle \alpha, \beta \rangle \rightarrow \langle \beta, \alpha \rangle$$

would be represented as:

$$All\ (All\ ((Var\ (S\ Z), Var\ Z) \rightarrow (Var\ Z, Var\ (S\ Z))))$$

The data constructor for the intermediate language's representation of type application ($e[\tau]$) is defined as:

data *Exp t* **where**

   ...

  TpApp :: *Exp* (*All s*) $\rightarrow$ *Exp* (*Subst s t Z*)

where *Subst* is the type family that implements substitution over types, defined below. Note that the type t is implicit in this definition. The type of *TpApp* encodes the usual typing rule for type application:

$$\frac{\Gamma \vdash e : \forall \alpha.\ \tau_1}{\Gamma \vdash e[\tau_2] : \tau_1[\tau_2/\alpha]}$$

With de Bruijn indices, we omit type variables in universal types, and substitution eliminates an index rather than a type variable, so the above rule would read:

$$\frac{\Gamma \vdash e : \forall \tau_1}{\Gamma \vdash e[\tau_2] : \tau_1[\tau_2/0]}$$

where 0 is the smallest de Bruijn index. The form $\tau[\tau'/i]$ yields the type τ where the index i has been eliminated, and τ' has been substituted in place of it. This capture-avoiding substitution is formally defined in Figure 6.3. It is a conventional substitution over de Bruijn terms (as in, e.g. [11]). When substituting τ in place of the index i, the free variables of τ must be incremented in order to avoid capture; this is accomplished by the 'update' function $U_k^i(\tau)$ (sometimes also called 'shift') whose effect is to adjust all indices no smaller than k (those are the free variables) by incrementing them by i.

The substitution and update functions encode directly as Haskell type families. As their definition involves arithmetic over indices, we also need to define type functions accordingly. The complete list of type functions, with their meaning, is

$$(\forall \tau_0)[\tau/i] \;=\; \forall(\tau_0[\tau/i+1])$$

$$j[\tau/i] \;=\; \begin{cases} j-1 & \text{if } j>i \\ U_0^i(\tau) & \text{if } j=i \\ j & \text{if } j<i \end{cases}$$

$$(\tau_1 \to \tau_2)[\tau/i] \;=\; \tau_1[\tau/i] \to \tau_2[\tau/i]$$

$$\mathbf{int}[\tau/i] \;=\; \mathbf{int}$$

$$U_k^i(\forall \tau) \;=\; \forall(U_{k+1}^i(\tau))$$

$$U_k^i(j) \;=\; \begin{cases} j+i & \text{if } j \geq k \\ j & \text{if } j<k \end{cases}$$

$$U_k^i(\tau_1 \to \tau_2) \;=\; U_k^i(\tau_1) \to U_k^i(\tau_2)$$

$$U_k^i(\mathbf{int}) \;=\; \mathbf{int}$$

FIGURE 6.3. Substitution over System *F* types

as follows:

type family *Subst* t_1 t_2 i — $\tau_1[\tau_2/i]$ Substitute t_2 for i in t_1

type family *U* k i t — $U_k^i(\tau)$ Add i to indices in t no smaller than k

type family *Pred* i — $i-1$ Predecessor of i

type family *Add* i j — $i+j$ Sum of i and j

type family *CMP* i j t_1 t_2 t_3 — $\begin{cases} \tau_1 & \text{if } i<j; \\ \tau_2 & \text{if } i=j; \\ \tau_3 & \text{if } i>j. \end{cases}$

The definition of individual type families is straightforward:

type instance *Subst* $(All\ s)$ t $i = All$ $(Subst\ s\ t\ (S\ i))$

type instance *Subst* $(Var\ j)$ t $i = CMP$ i j $(Var\ (Pred\ j))$ $(U\ Z\ i\ t)$ $(Var\ j)$

...

type instance *U* k i $(All\ t) = All$ $(U\ (S\ k)\ i\ t)$

type instance *U* k i $(Var\ j) = Var$ $(CMP\ j\ k\ j\ (Add\ j\ i)\ (Add\ j\ i))$

...

6.5.1 Limitations

We were able to extend our CPS conversion (and subsequently the other phases as well) to work with this representation of polymorphism using type families. The technical difficulty it introduces is that some work is needed to convince the type checker that we obtain a well-typed term when converting a type application (or abstraction), as it involves reconstructing a term whose type is defined by a substitution. For instance, the translation of a type application is defined as:

$$\mathscr{K}_{\exp}[\![e[\tau]]\!]\ k = \mathscr{K}_{\exp}[\![e]\!]\ (\lambda x\,.\,x[\mathscr{K}[\![\tau]\!]]\ (\lambda y\,.\,k\ y))$$

The type safety of this rule relies on the fact that our notion of substitution commutes with the type translation:

Lemma 6.1. *(subst-$\mathscr{K}[\![-]\!]$ commute) For all source types τ_1, τ_2 and index i,*

$$\mathscr{K}[\![\tau_1[\tau_2/i]]\!] = \mathscr{K}[\![\tau_1]\!][\mathscr{K}[\![\tau_2]\!]/i].$$

To put this in context, it means that we need to make a coercion between the types:

$ValK\ (Subst\ (CPS\ s)\ (CPS\ t)\ Z)$

and

$ValK\ (CPS\ (Subst\ s\ t\ Z))$

for the supplied continuation (k) to be of a type compatible with the translated term. To provide this coercion, we have two options: we can add it to the context as a required type predicate, or implement the lemma as a term-level function.

Lemma in the context   We can annotate the data constructor *TpApp* with a constraint stating that the lemma holds for the types in question.

> **data** *Exp t* **where**
>> . . .
>> $TpApp :: CPS\ (Subst\ s\ t\ Z) \sim Subst\ (CPS\ s)\ (CPS\ t)\ Z \Rightarrow$
>>> $Exp\ (All\ s) \rightarrow Exp\ (Subst\ s\ t\ Z)$

A constraint of the form $s \sim t$ means that the types s and t, although possibly syntactically different, are equivalent after applying a process of normalization (which in particular eliminates applications of type functions). These *type equality coercions* [23] are another feature introduced in GHC along with type families.

We can then implement *cps* as follows[1]:

$cps\ (TpApp\ e)\ k\ = cps\ e\ (\lambda x \rightarrow TpAppK\ x\ (LamK\ k))$

This scheme basically moves the burden of proving the property to the point where the property is trivial to prove because s is known. This means it is propagated just like type class constraints in Section 6.4, and suffers from the same problems: the proof that *Subst* and *CPS* commute ends up being constructed in the front end and propagated through the compiler pipeline until reaching the CPS phase. Also this has to be done for every such property we need, and it appears that we generally cannot combine or synthesize those proofs from each other using something like class inheritance, so we end up with very large type annotations throughout the compiler.

Lemma as a function   An alternative solution is to implement the lemma as a term-level function, which produces a witness that the coercion is valid. Its type is:

> $substCpsCommute ::$
>> $TypeRep\ s \rightarrow TypeRep\ t \rightarrow NatRep\ i$
>> $\rightarrow Equiv\ (CPS\ (Subst\ s\ t\ i))\ (Subst\ (CPS\ s)\ (CPS\ t)\ i)$

> **data** *Equiv s t* **where**
>> $Equiv\ ::\ s \sim t \Rightarrow Equiv\ s\ t$

---

[1] Note that type application is implicit in Haskell syntax, hence the difference from the definition of $\mathcal{K}_{exp}[\![-]\!]$.

The type *Equiv* reifies a type equality coercion at the term level, and generalizes the type *Equal* from Section 6.3. The lemma itself (*substCpsCommute*) can be defined by case analysis over runtime type representations (*TypeRep*) of the types *s* and *t*. Alternatively, it can do a dynamic test: it can construct a representation of the two types to prove equal and perform a comparison over them to supply evidence that they match.

Of course, in order to apply the lemma, we now need type annotations on the data constructor:

data *Exp t* **where**
  . . .
  TpApp :: *TypeRep s* → *TypeRep t* → *Exp (All s)* → *Exp (Subst s t Z)*

The implementation of *cps* is then:

cps (TpApp sr tr e) k =
  case *substCpsCommute sr tr* **of**
    Equiv → *cps e* (λx → *TpAppK x (LamK k)*)

In addition to the type annotations on the syntax, implementing the coercions such as Lemma 6.1 at the term level has the disadvantage that the lemma itself is implemented in an unsound logic, and executing the lemma incurs run-time overhead.

6.5.2 The view from the other sides

Note that if we did not want to use type families, we could still encode type functions such as *CPS* and *Subst* as relations, using either GADTs or type classes, as we did in Section 6.3 and 6.4. For instance, using GADTs to encode substitutions, the constructor for type application would look like:

data *Exp t* **where**
  . . .
  TpApp :: *Subst s t Z t'* → *Exp (All s)* → *Exp t'*

or, using type classes:

data *Exp t* **where**
  . . .
  TpApp :: *Subst s t Z t'* ⇒ *Exp (All s)* → *Exp t'*

where *Subst s t i t'* would be the relation such as $s[t/i] = t'$. This can make for potentially large type annotations, and suffers from the same inconveniences as discussed earlier. Especially, a GADT-based encoding would require proofs that the five relations defined are indeed functions.

In such a situation, the lemma we would need to prove would look like the following:

CPS s cps_s ∧ *CPS t cps_t* ∧ *Subst cps_s cps_t Z cpssubst*
⇔ *Subst s t Z subst* ∧ *CPS subst cpssubst*

If the relations are encoded as GADTs, this lemma can be proved straightforwardly by writing the corresponding Haskell function. But it would of course incur a runtime cost, would need one function for each direction, and would still suffer from the fact that those proofs are written in an inconsistent logic.

If the relations are encoded as type classes, we apparently just need to move the constraint into the context for Haskell to prove it for us. Of course, this suffers as before from the fact that those constraints will spread very far and pollute a lot of the code, but this is the least of our problem: the constraints we need to encode can not always be expressed in the appropriate form, because type class constraints can only be first order, i.e. we could state a constraint such as *Subst* (*CPS s*) (*CPS t*) *Z* = *CPS* (*Subst s t Z*) for particular type parameters *s* and *t*, whereas we sometimes need the constraint to hold for all *t*.

The lemmas proposed in the next section for type families could probably be extended to apply to type classes as well, in which case they could probably be used here as well.

6.6 LEMMAS OVER TYPE FAMILIES

The previous section motivates the need for a facility by which some form of reasoning about type families could be carried out at the type level, so as to avoid the pitfalls of run-time checks without having type annotations encumber the whole compiler.

One difficulty with type families is that they are by definition *open*, i.e. nothing prevents a type family from being extended with instances for unforeseen types. This problem was already recognized in [17] where they point out that they cannot rely on properties such as *Add n Z* = *n* since a new instance of *Add* may define *Add Int i* = *Z*.

Thus we cannot complete proofs of lemmas that holds for *all* possible types. There are two ways to work around this difficulty: close the world, or leave it open but only to new instances that satisfy the lemma.

Closed world   One possible solution is to introduce what we would call *data kinds*, which introduce new kinds, along with associated type constructors, much like *data types* introduce new types with associated data constructors. This is the approach taken in Omega [21] as well as in most proof assistants such as Coq [6] and Agda [1]. This would work well for our type-preserving compiler, but would be a significant departure from GHC's current type families.

Open world   If the world is wide open, our lemma simply does not hold in general, so we have no hope of proving it. We have to close the world to some extent but we can leave it ajar: rather than disallow extending the type family with new instances altogether, we will simply constrain new instances to obey the lemma(s) that apply to the type family.

This idea is somewhat similar to type class inheritance or to functional dependencies of multi-parameter type classes: functional dependencies also restrict the set of possible instances, so as to make sure that a property is preserved, and type class inheritance requires every instance to obey the constraints imposed by the parent.

6.6.1 Syntax

Ideally, we would like to state properties such as Lemma 6.1, and have the type checker verify that all instances of the relevant families satisfy the property. The syntax for introducing such lemmas could be as follows:

lemma *substCpsCommute* : *Subst* (*CPS s*) (*CPS t*) *i* ∼ *CPS* (*Subst s t i*)

This declaration would have the effect of introducing a function (of the same name) which can be used to discharge the constraint expressed by the lemma:

substCpsCommute :: (*Subst* (*CPS s*) (*CPS t*) *i* ∼ *CPS* (*Subst s t i*) ⇒ *a*) → *a*

That is, the function *substCpsCommute* can be applied to turn a piece of code which needs the lemma in its context in order to type-check, into one that does not need it. Of course, this sort of identity function should be optimized out so as to have no run-time cost. Resuming our example from Section 6.5.1, we could write *cps* as:

cps (*TpApp e*) *k* = *substCpsCommute e'*
   where *e'* :: *Subst* (*CPS s*) (*CPS t*) *Z* ∼ *CPS* (*Subst s t Z*) ⇒ *ExpK*
        e' = *cps e* (λ*x* → *TpAppK x* (*LamK k*))

or better yet:

cps (*TpApp e*) *k* = *substCpsCommute cpsTpApp e k*
   where *cpsTpApp* :: *Subst* (*CPS s*) (*CPS t*) *Z* ∼ *CPS* (*Subst s t Z*) ⇒
             Exp (*All s*) → (*ValK* (*CPS* (*All s*))) → *ExpK*) → *ExpK*
     cpsTpApp e k = *cps e* (λ*x* → *TpAppK x* (*LamK k*))

where the coercion *substCpsCommute cpsTpApp* can be lifted outside of the recursion, should it have a run-time cost.

Explicit proofs If fully automatic checking of the lemmas turns out to be impractical, we will need to provide explicit proofs along with instance declarations. If for example we extend *CPS* and *Subst* to handle product types, the syntax for proving that the new instances satisfy the lemma could look as follows:

type instance *CPS* (*a*, *b*) = (*CPS a*, *CPS b*)
type instance *Subst* (*a*, *b*) *t i* = (*Subst a t i*, *Subst b t i*)
proof *substCpsCommute* : *CPS* (*Subst* (*a*, *b*) *t i*)
   {- reduce -}   ∼ (*CPS* (*Subst a t i*), *CPS* (*Subst b t i*))
   {- induction -}   ∼ (*Subst* (*CPS a*) (*CPS t*) *i*, *Subst* (*CPS a*) (*CPS t*) *i*)
   {- reduce -}   ∼ *Subst* (*CPS* (*a*, *b*)) (*CPS t*) *i*

The proof consists of a series of coercions that begins with the left-hand side of the coercion to prove valid and ends with its right-hand side. Each step of the proof is justified by either applying a known lemma, or simply because the two types reduce to the same canonical form.

As shown here, a particular lemma may depend on more than one type family. Also they will often need to resort to induction. Additionally to checking that the proof steps are correct, the system will need to verify that the induction, if any, is well founded, that the various proof chunks provided do cover all (currently) possible cases. This last problem can be difficult in the presence of dependent types [19], but as long as Haskell's type system remains itself simply typed, this should not be a major hurdle.

6.7   RELATED WORK

Type classes were proposed in [24] and extended to multiple parameters with functional dependencies in [10]. GADTs have been proposed several times in one form or another and under a variety of names, see for example [5, 22, 25]. Some of those systems, such as Omega [21] provide type level functions similar to type families except that they are closed. In our case, such type level functions would work as well as type families. Type families were proposed in [17, 16] and are related to associated types [3].

Taming the open world assumption has already been done several times in different contexts. We have already mentioned that the inheritance hierarchy of type classes imposes constraints on the possible new instances [24]. And similarly functional dependencies [10], used to restrict the set of instances of some multi-parameter type classes, to make sure that although the world is open, the unknown part is constrained to obey the property described by the functional dependencies.

In a different context, Carsten Schürmann [18] uses a *regular world assumption* to constrain the type environments in LF judgments, so as to circumvent the difficulties inherent to the non-inductive nature of *higher-order abstract syntax*.

[20] shows what a CPS translation would look like with the equivalent of type families in a closed world. [13] presents a more sophisticated set of coercions where the coercions can be computed by type-level functions, thus allowing to write proofs of type-equivalence lemmas at the level of types.

The details of our experience writing a type preserving compiler in Haskell can be found in [7, 8, 9].

6.8   CONCLUSION

Results   We have updated every phase of the compiler (CPS conversion, closure conversion, a function hoisting phase, and a conversion from higher-order abstract syntax to de Bruijn indices) to use type families instead of GADTs in the way illustrated here, and the results have been largely positive, cutting down on code size drastically and improving performance significantly. The shift to using type families in place of type functions encoded with GADTs did not introduce any new difficulties.

For the purpose of the comparison, we assembled two versions of the CPS conversion over a simply typed language (with integers, pairs and recursion), one using proof witnesses encoded as GADTs, and one using type functions. The use of type functions resulted in a speed-up of an order of magnitude, in fact speeding up by a factor of 30 when compiled with GHC version 6.8.2. Although this comparison is anecdotal in nature, it clearly shows that the run-time cost of checking proofs is significant. The size of the code implementing the transformation also dropped by roughly 40%.

Acknowledgments We'd like to thank Tom Schrijvers and Martin Sulzmann for fruitful discussions.

Source code The source code used for the comparison is available from the author's web page:

```
http://www-etud.iro.umontreal.ca/~guillelj/cps-tf/
```

REFERENCES

[1] The Agda programming language.
http://appserv.cs.chalmers.se/users/ulfn/wiki/agda.php.

[2] A. Appel. *Compiling with Continuations*. Cambridge University Press, 1992.

[3] M. M. T. Chakravarty, G. Keller, S. P. Jones, and S. Marlow. Associated types with class. In *POPL '05: Proceedings of the 32nd ACM SIGPLAN-SIGACT Symposium on Principles of Programming Languages*, pages 1–13, New York, NY, USA, 2005. ACM Press.

[4] C. Chen, D. Zhu, and H. Xi. Implementing Cut Elimination: A Case Study of Simulating Dependent Types in Haskell. In *Proceedings of the 6th International Symposium on Practical Aspects of Declarative Languages*, pages 239–254, Dallas, TX, June 2004. Springer-Verlag LNCS vol. 3057.

[5] J. Cheney and R. Hinze. First-class phantom types. Technical Report CUCIS TR2003-1901, Cornell University, 2003.

[6] The Coq proof assistant. http://coq.inria.fr.

[7] L.-J. Guillemette and S. Monnier. Type-safe code transformations in Haskell. In *Programming Languages meets Program Verification*, volume 174(7) of *Electronic Notes in Theoretical Computer Science*, pages 23–39, Aug. 2006.

[8] L.-J. Guillemette and S. Monnier. A type-preserving closure conversion in Haskell. In *Haskell Workshop*. ACM Press, Sept. 2007.

[9] L.-J. Guillemette and S. Monnier. A type-preserving compiler in Haskell. In *International Conference on Functional Programming*, Victoria, BC, Sept. 2008.

[10] M. P. Jones. Type classes with functional dependencies. In *European Symposium on Programming*, volume 1782 of *LNCS*, pages 230–244, 2000.

[11] F. Kamareddine. Reviewing the classical and the de Bruijn notation for λ-calculus and pure type systems. *Journal of Logic and Computation*, 11, 2001.

[12] C. McBride. Faking it: Simulating dependent types in Haskell. *Journal of Functional Programming*, 12(5):375–392, 2002.

[13] S. Monnier. The Swiss coercion. In *Programming Languages meets Program Verification*, pages 33–40, Freiburg, Germany, Sept. 2007. ACM Press.

[14] G. Morrisett, D. Walker, K. Crary, and N. Glew. From System F to typed assembly language. In *Symposium on Principles of Programming Languages*, pages 85–97, Jan. 1998.

[15] S. Peyton-Jones et al. The Haskell Prime Report. Working Draft, 2007.

[16] T. Schrijvers, S. Peyton Jones, M. M. T. Chakravarty, and M. Sulzmann. Type checking with open type functions. In *International Conference on Functional Programming*, Victoria, BC, Sept. 2008.

[17] T. Schrijvers, M. Sulzmann, S. Peyton Jones, and M. M. T. Chakravarty. Towards open type functions for Haskell. Presented at IFL 2007, Technical Report No. 12-07, University of Kent, UK, 2007.

[18] C. Schürmann. A meta logical framework based on realizability. In *Logical Frameworks and Meta-Languages*, Santa Barbara, CA, June 2000, Inria.

[19] C. Schürmann and F. Pfenning. A coverage checking algorithm for LF. In *International Conference on Theorem Proving in Higher-Order Logics*, Sept. 2003, Springer.

[20] Z. Shao, B. Saha, V. Trifonov, and N. Papaspyrou. A type system for certified binaries. In *Symposium on Principles of Programming Languages*, pages 217–232, Jan. 2002.

[21] T. Sheard. Languages of the future. In *OOPSLA '04: Companion to the 19th Annual ACM SIGPLAN Conference on Object-Oriented Programming Systems, Languages, and Applications*, pages 116–119, New York, NY, USA, 2004. ACM Press.

[22] T. Sheard and E. Pašalić. Meta-programming with built-in type equality. In *Logical Frameworks and Meta-Languages*, Cork, July 2004, ENTCS.

[23] M. Sulzmann, M. M. T. Chakravarty, S. Peyton Jones, and K. Donnelly. System F with type equality coercions. In *Types in Language Design and Implementation*, Jan. 2007, ACM.

[24] P. Wadler and S. Blott. How to make ad hoc polymorphism less ad hoc. In *Symposium on Principles of Programming Languages*, Austin, TX, Jan. 1989.

[25] H. Xi, C. Chen, and G. Chen. Guarded recursive datatype constructors. In *Symposium on Principles of Programming Languages*, pages 224–235, New Orleans, LA, Jan. 2003.

Chapter 7

Optimization of Dynamic, Hybrid Signal Function Networks

Neil Sculthorpe,[1] Henrik Nilsson[2]
Category: Research

Abstract: Functional Reactive Programming (FRP) is an approach to reactive programming where systems are structured as networks of functions operating on signals. FRP is based on the synchronous data-flow paradigm and supports both continuous-time and discrete-time signals (hybrid systems). What sets FRP apart from most other languages for similar applications is its support for systems with dynamic structure and for higher-order data-flow constructs. This raises a range of implementation challenges. This paper contributes towards advancing the state of the art of FRP implementation by studying the notion of signal change and change propagation in a setting of hybrid signal function networks with dynamic structure. To sidestep some problems of certain previous FRP implementations that are structured using arrows, we suggest working with a notion of composable, multi-input and multi-output signal functions. A clear conceptual distinction is also made between continuous-time and discrete-time signals. We then show how establishing change-related properties of the signal functions in a network allows such networks to be simplified (static optimization) and can help reducing the amount of computation needed for executing the networks (dynamic optimization). Interestingly, distinguishing between continuous-time and discrete-time signals allows us to characterize the change-related properties of signal functions more precisely than what we otherwise would have been able to, which is helpful for optimization.

---

[1]School of Computer Science, University of Nottingham, United Kingdom;
nas@cs.nott.ac.uk.

[2]School of Computer Science, University of Nottingham, United Kingdom;
nhn@cs.nott.ac.uk.

7.1 INTRODUCTION

Functional Reactive Programming (FRP) grew out of Conal Elliott's and Paul Hudak's work on Functional Reactive Animation [13]. The idea of FRP is to allow the full power of modern functional programming to be used for implementing *reactive systems*: systems that interact with their environment in a *timely* manner. This is achieved by describing such systems in terms of functions mapping *signals* (time-varying values) to signals and combining such functions into signal-processing networks. The nature of the signals depends on the application domain. Examples include input from sensors in robotics applications [25], video streams in the context of graphical user interfaces [11] and games [12, 7], and synthesised sound signals [14].

A number of FRP variants exist. However, *the synchronous data-flow principle*, and support for both *continuous* and *discrete* time (*hybrid systems*), are common to most of them. There are thus close connections to synchronous data-flow languages like Esterel [4], Lustre [17], and Lucid Synchrone [6, 26], hybrid automata [18], and languages for hybrid modelling and simulation, like Simulink [1]. FRP, however, goes beyond most of these approaches by supporting higher-order data-flow (first-class reactive entities) and highly-dynamic system structure, all tightly integrated with a fully-fledged functional language. The Yampa implementation of FRP [23], a domain-specific embedding in Haskell, is a good example, and the starting point for this paper.

It is well-known how to implement synchronous data-flow networks with static structure efficiently [21, 17]. However, higher-order data-flow and dynamic system structure in combination with support for hybrid systems raise new implementation challenges. Specifically, Yampa, while demonstrably useful for fairly demanding applications [7, 14], has scalability issues.

One such issue is that Yampa implements discrete-time signals as continuous-time signals carrying an option type. Computations on discrete-time signals, which should only be carried out when those signals are defined, thus become computations on continuous-time signals, where computation takes place at every time step. Yampa regains some of the lost efficiency through dynamic optimization of the signal function network [22], but only up to a point.

Further, Yampa is structured using arrows [19, 24]. Signal functions thus map a single input signal to a single output signal. Multiple inputs and outputs must be encoded through signals carrying tuples of values. The 'true signals' (which serve as direct point-to-point communication channels) thus get hidden in an encoding layer, making it difficult to keep track of the signal flow and to exploit knowledge about network interdependencies for optimization purposes.

This paper is a step towards a more scalable and finally more efficient implementation approach for a Yampa-like reactive language. We first study signal change and how change propagates in a setting of a dynamic network of signal-processing functions and mixed continuous-time and discrete-time signals. To sidestep the second problem outlined above, we adopt a setting of composable, multi-input and multi-output signal functions. While not yet formalized, we have nevertheless found that this setting helps us to focus on the core issues.

As any digital implementation of a reactive system has to be sampled, one may wonder whether the continuous-time signals really are any different from the discrete-time signals at the implementation level. Interestingly, such a difference does emerge in our analysis of the notion of change, and it turns out to be possible to take advantage of this to characterize the properties of certain signal functions more precisely than what otherwise would have been the case.

Having studied the notion of change, we show how change-related properties of signal functions can be exploited to improve the implementation of a signal function network in two ways. The first is *static*. Here we provide a number of algebraic identities that can be used to simplify a network before signal processing starts and after each structural change of the network. The other is *dynamic*. This concerns *incremental evaluation* of a signal processing network, taking advantage of the fact that an output of a signal function often (but not always!) remains unchanged unless the input changes. Here, the multi-input and multi-output signal function setting is critical: representing multiple signals by a single signal carrying tuples, as in Yampa at present, makes the notion of change far too coarse grained as a change in one field of a tuple implies that the entire tuple has changed.

7.2 SIGNALS AND SIGNAL FUNCTIONS

7.2.1 Fundamentals

Signals are time-varying values. In FRP, they are conceptually modelled as functions from time to value. *Signal functions* are conceptually functions that operate on signals. We introduce the type constructor *SF* for signal functions. Thus, at a first approximation, we have:

$$Signal\ a \approx Time \to a$$
$$SF\ a\ b\ \ \approx Signal\ a \to Signal\ b$$

We reiterate that these are just conceptual definitions. In the FRP version presented here, only signal functions are first-class entities. Signals have no independent existence: they only exist indirectly through the signal functions.

To ensure that signal functions are realizable, we require them to be *causal* (the output must not depend on future inputs). We thus refine the conceptual definition of signal functions by imposing this additional requirement:

$$SF\ a\ b = \{\ sf :: Signal\ a \to Signal\ b \mid \forall\ t :: Time, \forall\ s, s' :: Signal\ a,$$
$$(\forall\ t' \leqslant t, s\ t' \equiv s'\ t') \Rightarrow (sf\ s\ t \equiv sf\ s'\ t)\ \}$$

Some signal functions are such that their output only depends on their input at the *current* point in time. We refer to these as *stateless* signal functions:

$$SF_{stateless}\ a\ b = \{\ sf :: Signal\ a \to Signal\ b \mid \forall\ t :: Time, \forall\ s, s' :: Signal\ a,$$
$$(s\ t \equiv s'\ t) \Rightarrow (sf\ s\ t \equiv sf\ s'\ t)\ \}$$

Clearly, $SF_{stateless}\ a\ b \subseteq SF\ a\ b$. Another way of characterizing the stateless signal functions is as those that can be defined by applying a function pointwise to an input signal. This is often referred to as *lifting* the function. Lifting functions is central to the arrows framework, and is achieved through the combinator *pure* (also called *arr*). In our setting, *pure* could be defined as:

$$pure \quad :: (a \rightarrow b) \rightarrow SF \ a \ b$$
$$pure \ f \ s = f \circ s$$

The remaining (causal) signal functions, those with output that may depend on past input, are called *stateful*. In an implementation, stateful signal functions would keep track of any requisite information pertaining to past input by storing it in an internal state. Hence the names stateful and stateless.

Two other subsets of the causal signal functions are of interest to us: *constant* signal functions and *decoupled* signal functions. Constant signal functions are those that produce the same output at all points in time, regardless of the input signal. Decoupled signal functions are those with output that does not depend on the *current* input, only on *past* inputs:

$$SF_{constant} \ a \ b \ = \{ sf :: SF \ a \ b \ | \ \forall \ t, t' :: Time, \forall \ s, s' :: Signal \ a,$$
$$sf \ s \ t \equiv sf \ s' \ t' \}$$

$$SF_{decoupled} \ a \ b = \{ sf :: SF \ a \ b \ | \ \forall \ t :: Time, \forall \ s, s' :: Signal \ a,$$
$$(\forall \ t' < t, s \ t' \equiv s' \ t') \Rightarrow (sf \ s \ t \equiv sf \ s' \ t) \}$$

7.2.2   Continuous-Time and Discrete-Time Signals

As previously discussed, FRP supports both continuous-time and discrete-time signals. Discrete-time signals are defined only at discrete points in time. They can be modelled as a signal carrying an option type (e.g. *Signal* (*Maybe a*)), with an additional requirement that such a signal only has *countably* many *occurrences* (points in time where the signal is not *Nothing*). This is how discrete-time signals are *implemented* in Yampa.

However, this particular implementation choice (which was necessitated by a desire to support both continuous-time and discrete-time signals in the arrows framework) is one reason why Yampa does not scale well. Thus, we want to make a clear distinction between continuous-time and discrete-time signals at the conceptual level in the following, so as to ultimately enable an implementation where discrete-time signals truly only 'exist' when the conceptual signal has an occurrence. We therefore refine the conceptual definition of signals:

$$\textbf{type } CSignal \ a \approx Time \rightarrow a \qquad \text{-- Continuous-time signals}$$
$$\textbf{type } ESignal \ a \approx Time \rightarrow Maybe \ a \quad \text{-- Discrete-time signals}$$
$$\textbf{data } Signal \ a \ = C \ (CSignal \ a)$$
$$| \ E \ (ESignal \ a)$$

We are using Haskell-like notation here and in the following. However, we go beyond Haskell in some ways, notably in terms of types. This is not too much of a concern as our main focus is the conceptual level: we are *not* suggesting that a reactive language should be literally *implemented* as described. That said, we have successfully prototyped the relevant parts of our conceptual framework in the dependently typed language Agda, and also in Haskell by exploiting type classes [20].

To illustrate, we give a refined conceptual definition of *pure*:

$$pure \qquad :: (a \rightarrow b) \rightarrow SF \, a \, b$$
$$pure \, f \, (C \, s) = C \, (f \circ s)$$
$$pure \, f \, (E \, s) = E \, (fmap \, f \circ s)$$

7.2.3 Higher-Arity Signal Functions

Next, we need to introduce higher-arity signal functions: signal functions having more than one input and output. To that end, we are going to use what we call signal vectors. Signal vectors are conceptually products of heterogeneous signals. However, they do *not* nest, but are always flat: there are never any signals of signals. Moreover, it is only a type-level construct, and it is intimately tied to the notion of signal functions, with no independent meaning of its own *outside the conceptual level*, just as signals only exist conceptually. Syntactically, the signal vector type is constructed as follows:

$$
\begin{aligned}
SigVec = \ &\langle\rangle & &\text{-- Empty signal vector} \\
\mid \ &\langle C \, t \rangle & &\text{-- Singleton, continuous-time, signal vector} \\
\mid \ &\langle E \, t \rangle & &\text{-- Singleton, discrete-time, signal vector} \\
\mid \ &SigVec \text{ :++: } SigVec & &\text{-- Signal-vector concatenation.}
\end{aligned}
$$

Note that concatenation of signal vectors is associative, and that the empty signal vector is the unit of concatenation, implying the following type equalities:

$$(as \text{ :++: } bs) \text{ :++: } cs \equiv as \text{ :++: } (bs \text{ :++: } cs)$$
$$as \text{ :++: } \langle\rangle \equiv as \equiv \langle\rangle \text{ :++: } as$$

In our *conceptual* definitions, we will nevertheless allow ourselves to use signal vectors as values, just as signals were used conceptually as values in the previous sections. When needed, we will reuse the above type-level notation for denoting signal vector values.

Signal functions are refined further to *always* work on signal vectors.

$$\textbf{type} \ (SigVec \, as, SigVec \, bs) \Rightarrow SF \, as \, bs = as \rightarrow bs$$

Thus, a type *SF as bs* implies that the type variables *as* and *bs* are signal vectors.

We will often use the angle bracket notation directly when writing down signal function types; for example:

$$SF \, \langle C \, Double, E \, Int \rangle \, \langle E \, Bool \rangle$$

We will also allow ourselves to quantify over the *time domain* (*C* or *E*) of signals, thus allowing signal functions to be polymorphic in the time domain; for example:

$$SF \, \langle td \, Double \rangle \, \langle td \, Double, td \, Double \rangle$$

To illustrate the ideas above, we give the final conceptual definition of *pure*:

$$pure \qquad :: (a \to b) \to SF \; \langle td \; a \rangle \; \langle td \; b \rangle$$
$$pure \, f \; \langle C \; s \rangle = \langle C \; (f \circ s) \rangle$$
$$pure \, f \; \langle E \; s \rangle = \langle E \; (fmap \, f \circ s) \rangle$$

7.3   SIGNAL FUNCTION NETWORKS

Systems are described by composing signal functions into signal function *networks*. Such networks are directed graphs, where the nodes are signal functions and the edges are signals. We limit ourselves to *acyclic* networks in the following.

7.3.1   Network Construction

Any acyclic network can be expressed in terms of sequential and parallel composition (and primitive signal functions for duplicating, eliminating, and combining signals). We reuse the names of the arrow combinators to express these compositions ($\ggg$ and $\ast\!\ast\!\ast$ respectively), with the following conceptual definitions:

$$(\ggg) \qquad :: SF \; as \; bs \to SF \; bs \; cs \to SF \; as \; cs$$
$$sf1 \ggg sf2 = sf2 \circ sf1$$
$$(\ast\!\ast\!\ast) \qquad :: SF \; as \; cs \to SF \; bs \; ds \to SF \; (as \mathbin{:\!\!+\!\!:} bs) \; (cs \mathbin{:\!\!+\!\!:} ds)$$
$$sf1 \ast\!\ast\!\ast sf2 \; = \lambda \, (as \mathbin{:\!\!+\!\!:} bs) \to sf1 \; as \mathbin{:\!\!+\!\!:} sf2 \; bs$$

7.3.2   Dynamic Network Structure

A network has a *dynamic structure* if the structure of the network can change during network execution. This is achieved by using *switch* constructs that replace signal functions in response to events. A basic switch has type:

$$switch :: SF \; as \; (\; \langle E \; e \rangle \mathbin{:\!\!+\!\!:} bs) \to (e \to SF \; as \; bs) \to SF \; as \; bs$$

The behaviour of the switch is to run the initial signal function (the first argument), emitting all but the head (the event) of the output vector as the overall output. When there is an event occurrence in the event signal, the value of that signal is fed into the function (the second argument) to generate a new signal function. The entire switch construct is then removed from the network and replaced with this new signal function. We will use *switch* as a third primitive combinator.

7.3.3   Network Examples

Figure 7.1 shows an example of a simple *static* network (one that contains no switches). This network can be expressed as:

$$sf1 \ggg (sf2 \ast\!\ast\!\ast sf3) \ggg sf4$$

Figure 7.2 shows a simple *dynamic* network, which can be expressed as:

$$sfA \ggg (sfB \ast\!\ast\!\ast switch \; sfC \; (\lambda \_ \to sfD)) \ggg sfE$$

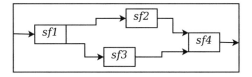

FIGURE 7.1.   An example of a static network

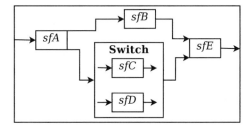

FIGURE 7.2.   An example of a dynamic network

7.4   CHANGE

A signal function network can be optimized by eliminating parts of the network that will never change. For example, a constant signal function always outputs the same value; the signal function itself is thus not needed, only the value it produces. However, we must first define precisely what we mean by *change*.

7.4.1   Change Definition

If a continuous-time signal has a continuous co-domain, we say that, at any given point in time, it is *changing* if it has a non-zero time derivative at that point in time. If a continuous-time signal has a discrete co-domain, then instead we say that, at any given point in time, the signal is changing if there is an abrupt change in the value of the signal at that point in time.

We will consider event (discrete-time) signals to be changing only at the instants of an event occurring. This coincides with the definition of change for continuous-time signals with discrete co-domains.

The above constitute a definition of change for our *conceptual* model of signals. In practice, however, a signal function network is executed over a discrete sequence of sample times, rather than treating time truly continuously. We will thus adapt the definitions in terms of the type of *sample time*, isomorphic to the natural numbers:

$$STime \cong \mathbb{N}$$

Thus, *STime* is the set of time points at which a system is sampled. We allow ourselves to use *pred t* and *succ t* to refer to the preceding and succeeding sample point, respectively (where $t :: STime$).

The discrete-time definition of change is as follows:

- A continuous-time signal (for both continuous and discrete co-domains) is changing *iff* its value at the current time sample differs from its value at the preceding time sample.

- An event signal is changing *iff* there is an event occurrence at the current time sample.

$$
\begin{array}{ll}
unchanging & :: SigVec\ as \Rightarrow as \to STime \to Bool \\
unchanging\ \langle\rangle & t = True \\
unchanging\ (as \mathbin{:\!\#\!\!:} bs)\ t = unchanging\ as\ t \wedge unchanging\ bs\ t \\
unchanging\ \langle C\ s\rangle & t = \textbf{if}\ t \equiv 0\ \textbf{then}\ True\ \textbf{else}\ s\ t \equiv s\ (pred\ t) \\
unchanging\ \langle E\ s\rangle & t = s\ t \equiv Nothing
\end{array}
$$

Notice that for continuous-time signals, the definition of change cannot be applied at the first sample time. In practice, the first sample time is a special case for the execution of signal function networks, when initialization of signal functions occurs. The details of this are unimportant for our present purposes; we simply define all continuous-time signals to be *unchanging* at the first sample time.

7.4.2   Change Classifications

We now classify our signal functions according to their change properties.

Some signal functions always yield unchanging output. We denote these signal functions with a *U* subscript for *Unchanging*.

These are not equivalent to the *constant* signal functions. An event source that outputs identical event occurrences at every sample time is *constant*, but not *unchanging* because of our definition of change on event signals.

$$SF_U\ as\ bs = \{\ sf :: SF\ as\ bs \mid \forall\ t :: STime, \forall\ ss :: as, unchanging\ (sf\ ss)\ t\ \}$$

Another group of signal functions are such that their output cannot change unless their input does. We denote these with an *I* subscript for *Input-dependent*. This includes all stateless functions, but, because of our definition of change on event signals, also some stateful signal functions.

$$
\begin{aligned}
SF_I\ as\ bs = \{\ sf :: SF\ as\ bs \mid \forall\ t :: STime, \forall\ ss :: as, \\
unchanging\ ss\ t \Rightarrow unchanging\ (sf\ ss)\ t\ \}
\end{aligned}
$$

Finally, the subscript *V* for *Varying* is adopted if there is no particular constraint on when the output can change (i.e. it could vary at any sample time). Note that the unchanging signal functions are a subset of the input-dependent signal functions, which are a subset of the varying signal functions.

$$SF_U\ as\ bs \subseteq SF_I\ as\ bs \subseteq SF_V\ as\ bs$$

Whenever we refer to a signal function which may be in any change class, we will either omit the subscript or use a variable.

7.4.3 Composite Change Classifications

The change class of a composite signal function can be computed from the change classes of the signal functions that it comprises. We annotate the type signatures of the primitive combinators to reflect this:

$$\textbf{data } ChangeClass = U \mid I \mid V \textbf{ deriving } (Eq, Ord)$$

$$(\ggg) \qquad :: SF_x \ as \ bs \rightarrow SF_y \ bs \ cs \rightarrow SF_{(x \ggg y)} \ as \ cs$$

$$(***) \qquad :: SF_x \ as \ cs \rightarrow SF_y \ bs \ ds \rightarrow SF_{(x \sqcup y)} \ (as \mathbin{:\!\!+\!\!:} bs) \ (cs \mathbin{:\!\!+\!\!:} ds)$$

$$switch \quad :: SF_x \ as \ (\ \langle E \ e \rangle \mathbin{:\!\!+\!\!:} bs) \rightarrow (e \rightarrow SF_y \ as \ bs) \rightarrow SF_x \ as \ bs$$

$$(\ggg) \qquad :: ChangeClass \rightarrow ChangeClass \rightarrow ChangeClass$$

$$x \ggg U = U$$
$$x \ggg V = V$$
$$x \ggg I \ = x$$

7.4.4 Example Signal Functions

We now consider some common primitive signal functions, and the change classes they fall into. Conceptual definitions are given for the simpler of these examples.

Two *unchanging* signal functions are *never* and *constant*: *never* is an event source that never produces an event occurrence; whereas *constant* emits the same value as output at every time sample.

$$constant \quad :: c \rightarrow SF_U \ as \ \langle C \ c \rangle$$
$$constant \ c = \lambda\_ \rightarrow \ \langle C \ (\lambda\_ \rightarrow c) \rangle$$

$$never \qquad :: SF_U \ as \ \langle E \ e \rangle$$
$$never \qquad = \lambda\_ \rightarrow \ \langle E \ (\lambda\_ \rightarrow Nothing) \rangle$$

The canonical *input-dependent* signal functions are the stateless ones created by *pure*.

$$pure :: (a \rightarrow b) \rightarrow SF_I \ \langle td \ a \rangle \ \langle td \ b \rangle$$

The *edge* and *hold* signal functions mediate between event signals and continuous-time signals: *edge* emits an event whenever its input changes from *False* to *True*; *hold* emits the value carried by its most recent input event.

$$edge \qquad :: SF_I \ \langle C \ Bool \rangle \ \langle E \ () \rangle$$
$$edge \ \langle C \ s \rangle \ = \ \langle E \ (\lambda t \rightarrow \textbf{if } s \ t \wedge \neg (s \ (pred \ t)) \textbf{ then } Just \ () \textbf{ else } Nothing) \rangle$$

$$hold \qquad :: a \rightarrow SF_I \ \langle E \ a \rangle \ \langle C \ a \rangle$$
$$hold \ a \ \langle C \ s \rangle \ = \ \langle C \ holdAux \rangle$$
$$\qquad\qquad\qquad \textbf{where } holdAux \ t = \textbf{case } s \ t \textbf{ of}$$
$$\qquad\qquad\qquad\qquad\qquad Nothing \rightarrow \textbf{if } t \equiv 0 \textbf{ then } a \textbf{ else } s \ (pred \ t)$$
$$\qquad\qquad\qquad\qquad\qquad Just \ b \ \ \rightarrow b$$

Because of the way change was defined for event signals, both *edge* and *hold* are classified as *input-dependent*. The extra precision thus gained, compared with a classification as *varying*, is very useful for optimization purposes.

Two *varying* signal functions are *integral* (which integrates the input signal over time) and *iPre* (which introduces a one time-sample-interval delay).

$$integral :: Num\ a \Rightarrow SF_V \langle C\ a \rangle\ \langle C\ a \rangle$$
$$iPre\quad :: a \rightarrow SF_V \langle C\ a \rangle\ \langle C\ a \rangle$$

7.5   NETWORK OPTIMIZATIONS

We are now in a position to state a number of algebraic identities for compositions of signal functions in terms of the change classes of the involved signal functions. These identities can be used to statically optimize a network. By *optimise*, we mean simplifying a network by eliminating or combining signal functions, such that we reduce the amount of computation required to execute the network. We thereby increase the potential scalability of our networks, though the actual efficiency gain from such optimizations will depend on the details of the implementation used.

Recall that parallel and sequential composition are associative, which can be exploited to maximize the applicability of these identities.

$$sf1 \ggg (sf2 \ggg sf3) \equiv (sf1 \ggg sf2) \ggg sf3$$
$$sf1 \lll\!\!\ast (sf2 \lll\!\!\ast sf3)\quad \equiv (sf1 \lll\!\!\ast sf2) \lll\!\!\ast sf3$$

Also of use are *identity* and *sfNil*, the units of sequential and parallel composition, respectively.

$$identity\quad :: SF_I\ as\ as$$
$$identity\ as = as$$
$$sfNil\qquad :: SF_U \langle \rangle\ \langle \rangle$$
$$sfNil \langle \rangle\quad = \langle \rangle$$
$$identity \ggg sf \equiv sf \equiv sf \ggg identity$$
$$sfNil\quad \lll\!\!\ast sf \equiv sf \equiv sf \lll\!\!\ast sfNil$$

Two sequential compositions in parallel can be rewritten as two parallel compositions in sequence (and conversely, provided the types match).

$$(sf1 \ggg sf2) \lll\!\!\ast (sf3 \ggg sf4) \equiv (sf1 \lll\!\!\ast sf3) \ggg (sf2 \lll\!\!\ast sf4)$$

Unchanging signal functions distribute into switches over sequential composition.

$$sf1_U \ggg switch\ sf2\ f \equiv switch\ (sf1_U \ggg sf2)\ (\lambda e \rightarrow sf1_U \ggg f\ e)$$

Signal functions with zero *output* signals can be reclassified as unchanging, as can *input-dependent* signal functions with zero *input* signals.

$$SF_x\ as\ \langle \rangle\ \equiv SF_U\ as\ \langle \rangle$$
$$SF_I \langle \rangle\ bs \equiv SF_U \langle \rangle\ bs$$

Any *unchanging* signal function (whether primitive or composite) can be eliminated from a network. To aid with this, we define a utility function, *extract*, that computes the output of any unchanging signal function. A function *vtail*, which computes the tail of a signal vector, is assumed.

$$
\begin{array}{ll}
extract & :: SF_U \; as \; bs \rightarrow bs \\
extract \; (constant \; c) & = \langle C \; (\lambda_- \rightarrow c) \rangle \\
extract \; never & = \langle E \; (\lambda_- \rightarrow Nothing) \rangle \\
extract \; (sf1_U *\!\!*\!\!* sf2_U) & = extract \; sf1_U \; :\!\!+\!\!: \; extract \; sf2_U \\
extract \; (sf1 \ggg sf2_U) & = extract \; sf2_U \\
extract \; (sf1_U \ggg sf2_I) & = sf2 \; (extract \; sf1_U) \\
extract \; (switch \; sf_U \; f) & = vtail \; (extract \; sf_U) \\
\\
sf_U & \equiv \lambda_- \rightarrow extract \; sf_U \\
\\
(sf1 *\!\!*\!\!* sf2_U *\!\!*\!\!* sf3) & \equiv (sf1 *\!\!*\!\!* (\lambda_- \rightarrow \langle \rangle) *\!\!*\!\!* sf3) \ggg \\
\quad \ggg switch \; sf4 \; f & \quad switch \; (\lambda(as :\!\!+\!\!: bs) \rightarrow sf4 \; (as :\!\!+\!\!: extract \; sf2_U :\!\!+\!\!: bs)) \\
& \quad (\lambda e \rightarrow (\lambda(as :\!\!+\!\!: bs) \rightarrow f \; e \; (as :\!\!+\!\!: extract \; sf2_U :\!\!+\!\!: bs))) \\
\\
(sf1 *\!\!*\!\!* sf2_U *\!\!*\!\!* sf3) & \equiv (sf1 *\!\!*\!\!* (\lambda_- \rightarrow \langle \rangle) *\!\!*\!\!* sf3) \ggg \\
\quad \ggg sf4 & \quad (\lambda(as :\!\!+\!\!: bs) \rightarrow sf4 \; (as :\!\!+\!\!: extract \; sf2_U :\!\!+\!\!: bs))
\end{array}
$$

7.5.1 Optimization Opportunites

These identities can be used to optimize a network before execution begins (e.g. at compile time). However, for a *dynamic* signal function network, the structure of the network can change at run-time. New subnetworks are being constructed, and existing networks may shift into an optimizable structure. Thus, there are opportunities for *dynamic* optimizations. Newly constructed networks can be optimized before they start running. Also, the entire network can be re-optimized whenever a switch occurs, so as to take advantage of any structural changes. However, the latter may be inefficient for large networks, unless we restrict optimization to the locality of the switch occurrence.

7.5.2 Example Optimization

As an example, consider the following network (where *f* is an arbitrary function):

$$(constant \; False) \ggg edge \ggg switch \; (pure \; id *\!\!*\!\!* constant \; 5) \; f$$

We can add change classifications to the signal functions within this network, allowing us to then reduce the network by applying the identities.

$$
\begin{array}{l}
((constant_U \; False \ggg edge_I)_U \ggg (switch \; (pure_I \; id *\!\!*\!\!* constant_U \; 5)_I) \; f)_I)_U \\
= \qquad \{ sf_U \equiv \lambda_- \rightarrow extract \; sf_U \} \\
(\lambda_- \rightarrow extract \; (constant_U \; False \ggg edge_I)) \ggg (switch \; (pure_I \; id *\!\!*\!\!* constant_U \; 5)_I \; f)_I \\
= \qquad \{ extract \; (sf1_U \ggg sf2_I) = sf2_I \; (extract \; sf1_U) \} \\
(\lambda_- \rightarrow edge \; (extract \; (constant \; False))) \ggg (switch \; (pure_I \; id *\!\!*\!\!* constant_U \; 5)_I \; f)_I \\
= \qquad \{ extract \; (constant \; c) = \langle C \; (\lambda_- \rightarrow c) \rangle \} \\
(\lambda_- \rightarrow edge \; \langle C \; (\lambda_- \rightarrow False) \rangle) \ggg (switch \; (pure_I \; id *\!\!*\!\!* constant_U \; 5)_I \; f)_I \\
= \qquad \{ edge \; \langle C \; s \rangle = \langle E \; (\lambda t \rightarrow \textbf{if} \; s \; t \wedge \neg (s \; (pred \; t)) \; \textbf{then} \; Just \; () \; \textbf{else} \; Nothing) \rangle \}
\end{array}
$$

$(\lambda \_ \rightarrow \langle E \ (\lambda t \rightarrow \textbf{if} \ (\lambda \_ \rightarrow \textit{False}) \ t \wedge \neg \ ((\lambda \_ \rightarrow \textit{False}) \ (\textit{pred } t)) \ \textbf{then} \ \textit{Just} \ ()$
$\textbf{else} \ \textit{Nothing}\rangle \ ) \ggg (\textit{switch} \ (\textit{pure}_I \ \textit{id} \ast\!\!\ast\!\!\ast \ \textit{constant}_U \ 5)_I f)_I$

$=$ \qquad $\{ \textit{Simplification} \}$

$(\lambda \_ \rightarrow \langle E \ (\lambda t \rightarrow \textit{Nothing}) \rangle \ ) \ggg (\textit{switch} \ (\textit{pure}_I \ \textit{id} \ast\!\!\ast\!\!\ast \ \textit{constant}_U \ 5)_I f)_I$

$=$ \qquad $\{ \textit{never} = \lambda \_ \rightarrow \ \langle E \ (\lambda \_ \rightarrow \textit{Nothing}) \rangle \ \}$

$(\textit{never}_U \ggg (\textit{switch} \ (\textit{pure}_I \ \textit{id} \ast\!\!\ast\!\!\ast \ \textit{constant}_U \ 5)_I f)_I)_U$

$=$ \qquad $\{ \textit{sf1}_U \ggg \textit{switch} \ \textit{sf2} \ f \equiv \textit{switch} \ (\textit{sf1}_U \ggg \textit{sf2}) \ (\lambda e \rightarrow \textit{sf1}_U \ggg f \ e) \}$

$(\textit{switch} \ (\textit{never}_U \ggg (\textit{pure}_I \ \textit{id} \ast\!\!\ast\!\!\ast \ \textit{constant}_U \ 5)_I)_U \ (\lambda e \rightarrow \textit{never}_U \ggg f \ e))_U$

$=$ \qquad $\{ \textit{sf}_U \equiv \lambda \_ \rightarrow \textit{extract } \textit{sf}_U \}$

$\lambda \_ \rightarrow \textit{extract} \ (\textit{switch} \ (\textit{never}_U \ggg (\textit{pure}_I \ \textit{id} \ast\!\!\ast\!\!\ast \ \textit{constant}_U \ 5)_I)_U \ (\lambda e \rightarrow \textit{never}_U \ggg f \ e))$

$=$ \qquad $\{ \textit{extract} \ (\textit{switch} \ \textit{sf}_U \ f) = \textit{vtail} \ (\textit{extract } \textit{sf}_U) \}$

$\lambda \_ \rightarrow \textit{vtail} \ (\textit{extract} \ (\textit{never}_U \ggg (\textit{pure}_I \ \textit{id} \ast\!\!\ast\!\!\ast \ \textit{constant}_U \ 5)_I))$

$=$ \qquad $\{ \textit{extract} \ (\textit{sf1}_U \ggg \textit{sf2}_I) = \textit{sf2}_I \ (\textit{extract } \textit{sf1}_U) \}$

$\lambda \_ \rightarrow \textit{vtail} \ ((\textit{pure}_I \ \textit{id} \ast\!\!\ast\!\!\ast \ \textit{constant}_U \ 5) \ (\textit{extract never}))$

$=$ \qquad $\{ \textit{extract never} = \langle E \ (\lambda \_ \rightarrow \textit{Nothing}) \rangle \ \}$

$\lambda \_ \rightarrow \textit{vtail} \ ((\textit{pure}_I \ \textit{id} \ast\!\!\ast\!\!\ast \ \textit{constant}_U \ 5) \ \langle E \ (\lambda \_ \rightarrow \textit{Nothing}) \rangle \ )$

$=$ \qquad $\{ \textit{sf1} \ast\!\!\ast\!\!\ast \ \textit{sf2} = \lambda \, (\textit{as} \ \text{:\!+\!:} \ \textit{bs}) \rightarrow \textit{sf1 as} \ \text{:\!+\!:} \ \textit{sf2 bs} \}$

$\lambda \_ \rightarrow \textit{vtail} \ ((\lambda \, (\textit{as} \ \text{:\!+\!:} \ \textit{bs}) \rightarrow \textit{pure id as} \ \text{:\!+\!:} \ \textit{constant 5 bs}) \ \langle E \ (\lambda \_ \rightarrow \textit{Nothing}) \rangle \ )$

$=$ \qquad $\{ \textit{as} \equiv \textit{as} \ \text{:\!+\!:} \ \langle \rangle \ \}$

$\lambda \_ \rightarrow \textit{vtail} \ ((\lambda \, (\textit{as} \ \text{:\!+\!:} \ \textit{bs}) \rightarrow \textit{pure id as} \ \text{:\!+\!:} \ \textit{constant 5 bs}) \ (\ \langle E \ (\lambda \_ \rightarrow \textit{Nothing}) \rangle \ \text{:\!+\!:} \ \langle \rangle \ ))$

$=$ \qquad $\{ \textit{Simplification} \}$

$\lambda \_ \rightarrow \textit{vtail} \ (\textit{pure id} \ \langle E \ (\lambda \_ \rightarrow \textit{Nothing}) \rangle \ \text{:\!+\!:} \ \textit{constant 5} \ \langle \rangle \ )$

$=$ \qquad $\{ \textit{constant } c = \lambda \_ \rightarrow \ \langle C \ (\lambda \_ \rightarrow c) \rangle \ \}$

$\lambda \_ \rightarrow \textit{vtail} \ (\textit{pure id} \ \langle E \ (\lambda \_ \rightarrow \textit{Nothing}) \rangle \ \text{:\!+\!:} \ (\lambda \_ \rightarrow \ \langle C \ (\lambda \_ \rightarrow 5) \rangle \ ) \ \langle \rangle \ )$

$=$ \qquad $\{ \textit{Simplification} \}$

$\lambda \_ \rightarrow \textit{vtail} \ (\textit{pure id} \ \langle E \ (\lambda \_ \rightarrow \textit{Nothing}) \rangle \ \text{:\!+\!:} \ \langle C \ (\lambda \_ \rightarrow 5) \rangle \ )$

$=$ \qquad $\{ \textit{pure } f \ \langle E \ s \rangle \ = \ \langle E \ (\textit{fmap } f \circ s) \rangle \ \}$

$\lambda \_ \rightarrow \textit{vtail} \ (\ \langle E \ (\textit{fmap id} \circ (\lambda \_ \rightarrow \textit{Nothing})) \rangle \rangle \ \text{:\!+\!:} \ \langle C \ (\lambda \_ \rightarrow 5) \rangle \ )$

$=$ \qquad $\{ \textit{vtail} \ (\ \langle a \rangle \ \text{:\!+\!:} \ \textit{bs}) = \textit{bs} \}$

$\lambda \_ \rightarrow \ \langle C \ (\lambda \_ \rightarrow 5) \rangle$

$=$ \qquad $\{ \textit{constant } c = \lambda \_ \rightarrow \ \langle C \ (\lambda \_ \rightarrow c) \rangle \ \}$

$\textit{constant } 5$

7.6 CHANGE PROPAGATION

In general, as a signal function network grows larger, the size of the quiescent network regions (regions where signals remain unchanging during periods of time), grows in proportion to the overall network size. The present Yampa implementation, while in some cases being able to avoid redundant recomputation of unchanging signals, will nevertheless (redundantly) recompute a large fraction of these unchanging signals. The amount of wasted work thus grows in proportion to the size of the network, which is one reason Yampa does not scale well. In the following, we give a brief description of how the change classifications enable optimizations based on *change propagation* that eliminate *all* redundant computations of unchanging signals, thus addressing this particular scalability issue.

The intuition is that, at any given time sample, if a signal is known to be unchanging *before* we compute its value, then there is no need to perform that computation. Instead, we use either the value of the signal from the preceding time sample (for a continuous-time signal), or have no event occurrence (for an event signal).

$evalCSignal$ $:: CSignal\ a \rightarrow STime \rightarrow a$
$evalCSignal\ s\ t =$ **if** $unchanging\ \langle s \rangle\ t$ **then** $evalCSignal\ s\ (pred\ t)$ **else** $s\ t$

$evalESignal$ $:: ESignal\ a \rightarrow STime \rightarrow Maybe\ a$
$evalESignal\ s\ t =$ **if** $unchanging\ \langle s \rangle\ t$ **then** $Nothing$ **else** $s\ t$

This is of use in a signal function network where, at the implementation level, a signal is computed by executing a signal function. If, at any given time sample, we do not need to compute the value of a signal, then we may not need to execute the signal function that computes it. The set of signal functions where this is the case is SF_I, with the additional constraint that unchanging input must imply unchanging internal state. We will denote this set as $SF_{I'}$, but note that in many languages (including Yampa) SF_I and $SF_{I'}$ are equivalent.

$unchangingState :: SF\ as\ bs \rightarrow as \rightarrow STime \rightarrow Bool$

$SF_{I'}\ a\ b = \{\ sf :: SF\ as\ bs \mid \forall\ t :: STime, \forall\ ss :: as,$
$\qquad\qquad unchanging\ ss\ t \Rightarrow unchanging\ (sf\ ss)\ t \wedge unchangingState\ sf\ ss\ t\ \}$

Thus, provided we have a way of injecting change information into a signal function network, we can optimize the run-time execution of the network so as to avoid the execution of I' signal functions whenever their input is *unchanging*.

We will not go into further details about change propagation here.

7.7 RELATED WORK

Incremental evaluation and change propagation have been studied extensively as optimization techniques [27, 2]. The key difference between such work and ours is that the notion of time passing is inherent to our setting. Consequently, we have *varying* signal functions with output that can change even when their input does not, and *decoupled* signal functions which are conceptually connected to signals from previous time samples.

The synchronous data-flow languages [3, 15, 16] have long modelled reactive programs as synchronous data-flow networks with an inherent notion of time. These languages guarantee strong time and space bounds, and consequently have usually had static, first order structures. However, there has been recent work on allowing signal functions to be first class entities [8], though this does not yet have the same level of dynamism as FRP.

Many of the optimizations we achieve through applying the identities in Section 7.5 are used in the latest version of Yampa [10, 22]. However, because of the limitations of the arrows framework, some optimizations cannot be achieved. In particular, though Yampa tries to encourage the programmer to treat event signals differently to continuous-time signals, they are not inherently different.

Also because of the arrows framework, Yampa uses nested tuples rather than the flat vectors we advocate here. This hinders change propagation by creating incidental dependencies: if one component of a tuple changes, then the tuple as a whole is considered to have changed.

FrTime [9, 5] is another dynamic, hybrid functional reactive programming language that makes a clear distinction between continuous-time signals and event signals. It uses a variety of optimization techniques, including many of those described in this paper.

FrTime uses dynamic change propagation. When applying a lifted function to a continuous-time signal, the output is only recomputed when the input changes. When applying a signal function to an event signal, the output is only recomputed when an event occurs. This corresponds closely with the change propagation that we propose, though differs slightly in that FrTime performs run-time equality checks on recomputed signals to determine whether they have changed.

FrTime also uses a static optimization called *lowering*. Lowering reduces a signal function network by fusing together composite signal functions into single signal functions. This technique is only applied to signal functions that are lifted pure functions. For example, (in our setting) a typical lowering optimization would look like:

$$pure\, f \ggg pure\, g = pure\, (g \circ f)$$

FrTime's lowering optimizations are applied statically at compile time, which allows for substantial optimization of source code, but does not allow dynamic optimization of the network after structural changes.

Yampa also performs some lowering optimizations, but not to the extent of FrTime. However, Yampa can lower some stateful signal functions as well as stateless ones. Yampa performs its lowering optimizations dynamically, which suffers from additional run-time overhead, but does allow for continued optimization after structural changes.

We aim to incorporate lowering optimizations with our static optimizations, but have not done so in this paper (though there is some overlap). We advocate an initial optimization of the network, an initial optimization of each newly created network, and a (local) re-optimization after each structural change.

7.8   CONCLUSIONS AND FURTHER WORK

We have presented a means of classifying signal functions by their change properties, such that we can use these classifications for *static* network optimizations and *dynamic* change propagation. By treating *discrete-time* and *continuous-time* signals distinctly from each other, we can perform more precise optimizations than would otherwise be the case.

In this paper we have only considered *acyclic* networks. We are currently investigating how these optimizations interact with *cyclic* networks, and whether allowing only non-instantaneous feedback cycles would be beneficial. We currently believe that instantaneous cycles would greatly complicate an implementation based on change propagation, for little gain. The fixed-point computation required to compute the instantaneous values of a signal involved in such a cycle takes place completely *within* a time sample, and thus equally well could be carried out at the purely functional level.

We are in the process of developing a new Yampa prototype implementation. Our goal is to use the optimizations discussed in this paper to achieve an implementation that scales better than the current Yampa implementation.

ACKNOWLEDGEMENTS

We would like to thank Thorsten Altenkirch for his helpful suggestions, in particular in relation to the formulation of signal function properties.

We also thank the anonymous reviewers for their valuable feedback.

REFERENCES

[1] *Using Simulink, Version 7.2.* 3 Apple Hill Drive, Natick, MA, 2008. www.mathworks.com.

[2] U. A. Acar, G. E. Blelloch, and R. Harper. Adaptive functional programming. In *Principles of Programming Languages (POPL '02)*, pages 247–259. ACM, 2002.

[3] A. Benveniste, P. Caspi, S. Edwards, N. Halbwachs, P. Le Guernic, and R. de Simone. The synchronous languages twelve years later. *Proceedings of the IEEE, Special issue on embedded systems*, 91(1):64–83, 2003.

[4] G. Berry and G. Gonthier. The Esterel synchronous programming language: Design, semantics, implementation. *Science of Computer Programming*, 19(2):87–152, 1992.

[5] K. Burchett, G. H. Cooper, and S. Krishnamurthi. Lowering: A static optimization technique for transparent functional reactivity. In *Partial Evaluation and Program Manipulation (PEPM '07)*, pages 71–80. ACM, 2007.

[6] P. Caspi and M. Pouzet. Synchronous Kahn networks. In *International Conference on Functional Programming (ICFP '96)*, pages 226–238. ACM, 1996.

[7] M. H. Cheong. Functional programming and 3D games. BEng thesis, University of New South Wales, Sydney, Australia, 2005.

[8] J.-L. Colaço, A. Girault, G. Hamon, and M. Pouzet. Towards a higher-order synchronous data-flow language. In *Embedded Software (EMSOFT '04)*, pages 230–239. ACM, 2004.

[9] G. H. Cooper and S. Krishnamurthi. Embedding dynamic dataflow in a call-by-value language. In *European Symposium on Programming (ESOP '06)*, pages 294–308. Springer-Verlag, 2006.

[10] A. Courtney. *Modeling User Interfaces in a Functional Language*. PhD thesis, Yale University, 2004.

[11] A. Courtney and C. Elliott. Genuinely functional user interfaces. In *Haskell Workshop (Haskell '01)*, pages 41–69, 2001.

[12] A. Courtney, H. Nilsson, and J. Peterson. The Yampa arcade. In *Haskell Workshop (Haskell '03)*, pages 7–18. ACM, 2003.

[13] C. Elliott and P. Hudak. Functional reactive animation. In *International Conference on Functional Programming (ICFP '97)*, pages 263–273. ACM, 1997.

[14] G. Giorgidze and H. Nilsson. Switched-on Yampa: Declarative programming of modular synthesizers. In *Practical Aspects of Declarative Languages (PADL '08)*, pages 282–298. Springer-Verlag, 2008.

[15] N. Halbwachs. *Synchronous Programming of Reactive Systems*. The Springer International Series in Engineering and Computer Science. Springer-Verlag, 1993.

[16] N. Halbwachs. Synchronous programming of reactive systems, a tutorial and commented bibliography. In *Computer Aided Verification (CAV '98)*, pages 1–16. Springer-Verlag, 1998.

[17] N. Halbwachs, P. Caspi, P. Raymond, and D. Pilaud. The synchronous data-flow programming language Lustre. *Proceedings of the IEEE*, 79(9):1305–1320, 1991.

[18] T. A. Henzinger. The theory of hybrid automata. In *Logics in Computer Science (LICS '96)*, pages 278–292. IEEE Computer Society, 1996.

[19] J. Hughes. Generalising monads to arrows. *Science of Computer Programming*, 37(1–3):67–111, 2000.

[20] O. Kiselyov, R. Lämmel, and K. Schupke. Strongly typed heterogeneous collections. In *Haskell Workshop (Haskell '04)*, pages 96–107. ACM, 2004.

[21] E. A. Lee and D. G. Messerschmitt. Static scheduling of synchronous data flow programs for digital signal processing. *IEEE Transactions on Computers*, 36(1):24–35, 1987.

[22] H. Nilsson. Dynamic optimization for functional reactive programming using generalized algebraic data types. In *International Conference on Functional Programming (ICFP '05)*, pages 54–65. ACM, 2005.

[23] H. Nilsson, A. Courtney, and J. Peterson. Functional reactive programming, continued. In *Haskell Workshop (Haskell '02)*, pages 51–64. ACM, 2002.

[24] R. Paterson. A new notation for arrows. In *International Conference on Functional Programming (ICFP '01)*, pages 229–240. ACM, 2001.

[25] J. Peterson, P. Hudak, and C. Elliott. Lambda in motion: Controlling robots with Haskell. In *Practical Aspects of Declarative Languages (PADL '99)*, pages 91–105. Springer-Verlag, 1999.

[26] M. Pouzet. *Lucid Synchrone, version 3.0: Tutorial and reference manual*. Université Paris-Sud, LRI, 2006. www.lri.fr/~pouzet/lucid-synchrone.

[27] G. Ramalingam and T. Reps. A categorized bibliography on incremental computation. In *Principles of Programming Languages (POPL '93)*, pages 502–510. ACM, 1993.

Chapter 8

Short Cut Fusion of Recursive Programs with Computational Effects

Neil Ghani, Patricia Johann[1]
Category: Research

Abstract: Fusion is the process of improving the efficiency of modularly constructed programs by transforming them into monolithic equivalents. This paper defines a generalization of the standard `build` combinator which expresses uniform production of functorial contexts containing data of inductive types. It also proves correct a fusion rule which generalizes the `fold`/`build` and `fold`/`buildp` rules from the literature, and eliminates intermediate data structures of inductive types without disturbing the contexts in which they are situated. An important special case arises when this context is monadic. When it is, a second rule for fusing combinations of producers and consumers via monad operations, rather than via composition, is also available. We give examples illustrating both rules, and consider their coalgebraic duals as well.

8.1 GENERALIZING SHORT CUT FUSION

8.1.1 Introducing Short Cut Fusion

Fusion is the process of improving the efficiency of modularly constructed programs by transforming them into monolithic equivalents. Short cut fusion [6] is concerned with eliminating list traversals from compositions of components that are 'glued' together via intermediate lists. Short cut fusion uses a local transformation — known as the `foldr`/`build` rule — to fuse computations which can be written as compositions of applications of the uniform list-consuming function `foldr` and the uniform list-producing function `build` given by

---

[1]University of Strathclyde, Glasgow, Scotland
{Neil.Ghani,Patricia.Johann}@cis.strath.ac.uk.

```
newtype Mu f = In {unIn :: f (Mu f)}

fold :: Functor f => (f a -> a) -> Mu f -> a
fold h (In k) = h (fmap (fold h) k)

build :: Functor f =>
   (forall a. (f a -> a) -> c -> a) -> c -> Mu f
build g = g In

fold k . build g = g k
```

FIGURE 8.1. The `fold` and `build` **combinators and** `fold`/`build` **rule**

```
foldr :: (b -> a -> a) -> a -> [b] -> a
foldr c n [] = n
foldr c n (x:xs) = c x (foldr c n xs)

build :: (forall a. (b -> a -> a) -> a -> a) -> [b]
build g = g (:) []
```

The function `foldr` is standard in the Haskell prelude. Intuitively, `foldr c n xs` produces a value by replacing all occurrences of `(:)` in `xs` by `c` and the occurrence of `[]` in `xs` by `n`. Thus, `sum xs = foldr (+) 0 xs` sums the (numeric) elements of the list `xs`. Uniform production of lists, on the other hand, is accomplished using the combinator `build`, which takes as input a type-independent template for constructing 'abstract' lists and produces a corresponding 'concrete' list. Thus, `build (\c n -> c 4 (c 7 n))` produces the list `[4,7]`. Uniform list transformers can be written in terms of both `foldr` and `build`. For example, the function `map` can be implemented as

```
map :: (a -> b) -> [a] -> [b]
map f xs = build (\c n -> foldr (c . f) n xs)
```

The `foldr`/`build` rule capitalizes on the uniform production and consumption of lists to improve the performance of list-manipulating programs. It says

$$\text{foldr c n (build g)} = \text{g c n} \qquad (8.1)$$

If `sqr x = x * x`, then this rule can be used, for example, to transform the modular function `sum . map sqr :: [Int] -> Int` which produces an intermediate list into an optimized form which does not:

```
sum (map sqr xs) = foldr (+) 0
                        (build (\c n -> foldr (c . sqr) n xs))
                 = (\c n -> foldr (c . sqr) n xs) (+) 0
                 = foldr ((+) . sqr) 0 xs
```

8.1.2 Short Cut Fusion for Inductive Types

Inductive data types are fixed points of functors. Functors can be implemented in Haskell as type constructors supporting `fmap` functions as follows:

```
buildp :: Functor f =>
   (forall a. (f a -> a) -> c -> (a,z)) -> c -> (Mu f, z)
buildp g = g In

fmap (fold k) . buildp g = g k
```

FIGURE 8.2.   **The** `buildp` **combinator and** `fold`/`buildp` **fusion rule**

```
class Functor f where
  fmap :: (a -> b) -> f a -> f b
```

The function `fmap` is expected to satisfy the two semantic functor laws stating that `fmap` preserves identities and composition.It is well-known that analogues of `foldr` exist for every inductive data type. As shown in [4, 5], every inductive type also has an associated generalized `build` combinator; the extra type `c` in the type of `build` is motivated in those papers and to lesser extent in Section 8.3 below. These combinators can be implemented generically in Haskell as in Figure 8.1. There, `Mu f` represents the least fixed point of the functor `f`, and `In` represents the structure map for `f`, i.e. the 'bundled' constructors for the data type `Mu f`. The `fold`/`build` fusion rule for inductive types can be used to eliminate data structures of type `Mu f` from computations. The `foldr` and `build` combinators for lists can be recovered by taking `f` to be the functor whose fixed point is `[b]`. The `foldr`/`build` rule can be recovered by taking `c` to be the unit type as well. As usual, `fold` and `build` implement the isomorphisms between inductive types and their Church encodings.

8.1.3 Short Cut Fusion in Context

Short cut fusion handles compositions `g` . `f` in which the data structure produced by `f` is passed from `f` to `g`. But what if `f` produces not just a single data structure, but multiple such structures, embeds these data structures in a non-trivial context, and passes the result to `g` for consumption of these data structures 'in context'? Is it possible to eliminate these intermediate data structures from `g` . `f` while keeping the context information, which `g` may need to compute its result, intact? Standard fusion techniques cannot achieve this: the intermediate data structures produced by `f` cannot be decoupled from the context in which they are situated. In [2], Fernandes et al. introduce a technique for fusing compositions `g` . `f` in which `f` passes to `g` not only the intermediate data structure produced by `f`, but an additional datum as well. Although `g` requires this datum to compute its result, it is not used when processing the intermediate data structure, and so only the data structure itself needs to be eliminated from `g` . `f`. To do this, [2] uses a variant of the standard `fold`/`build` rule based on the combinator `buildp`, which captures the extra datum by returning a data structure embedded in a pair context. The data type-generic `buildp` combinator and its associated `fold`/`buildp` fusion rule are given in Figure 8.2. There, `fmap` is the map function

```
fmap :: (a -> b) -> (a,z) -> (b,z)
fmap f (a,z) = (f a, z)
```

which witnesses the fact that the type constructor `h` given by `h x = (x,z)` is a

```
superbuild :: (Functor f, Functor h) =>
    (forall a. (f a -> a) -> c -> h a) -> c -> h (Mu f)
superbuild g = g In

fmap (fold k) . (superbuild g) = g k
```

FIGURE 8.3. **The** `superbuild` **combinator and** `fold`/`superbuild` **fusion rule**

functor. The context information produced by `buildp` and used by the consumer in the left-hand side of the `fold`/`buildp` fusion rule is reflected in the pair return types of `buildp` and its template argument, as well as in the mapping of `fold` across the pair in the associated `fold`/`buildp` rule. This rule eliminates intermediate data structures within the context of pairing with an additional datum.

But now suppose we want to write a function

```
gsplitWhen :: (b -> Bool) -> [b] -> [[b]]
```

which splits a list into sublists at every element that satisfies a given p. Note that the function `gsplitWhen` splits lists into arbitrary numbers of sublists, depending on the data they contain, and that the type z in the type of `buildp` cannot be instantiated to allow the return of a number of lists which has the potential to change on each program run. This means that `gsplitWhen` cannot be written in terms of `buildp`. Moreover, compositions of `gsplitWhen` with functions that consume each of the individual 'inner' lists produced by `gsplitWhen` but require the information inherent in its 'context list' to compute their results cannot be fused using the `fold`/`buildp` rule. But why try to structure programs only with contexts of the form $(-, z)$? That is, why not consider a generalization of the `buildp` combinator, and a generalization of the `fold`/`buildp` fusion rule which can be used to eliminate intermediate data structures, like those returned by `gsplitWhen`, which appear in contexts other than just pairs? That is precisely what this paper does. We call these generalizations `superbuild` and the `fold`/`superbuild` rule, respectively. Like `buildp` and the `fold`/`buildp` rule, our `superbuild` combinator and `fold`/`superbuild` fusion rule are available at every inductive data type. Data type-generic versions are given in Figure 8.3; note that the type of superbuild is actually generic in both f and h. The generalization of the pair context in the type of `buildp` is captured by the replacement in the type of `superbuild` of the type (x, z) by the type h x for a more general 'context functor' h. This generalization is further reflected in the replacement of the `fmap` function for pairs in the `fold`/`buildp` rule by the `fmap` function for the more general context functor h in the `fold`/`superbuild` rule. The `fold` combinator in the `fold`/`superbuild` rule is the one for `Mu f`, as usual. These `fmap` and `fold` functions are guaranteed to be defined precisely because the type of `superbuild` requires both f and h to be functors. We argue in Section 8.3 that the `fold`/`superbuild` rule holds for a large class of functors h.

Taking h x = x gives the generalized `build` combinator and `fold`/`build` rule from Figure 8.1, while taking h x = (x, z) gives the `buildp` combinator and `fold`/ `buildp` rule from Figure 8.2. In general, the `fold`/`superbuild` rule can fuse compositions in which context information describable by non-pair functors is passed, along with intermediate data structures, from producer to consumer. Indeed, the fold/superbuild rule eliminates intermediate structures of type Mu f obtained by mapping a consumer expressed as a fold over the data of type Mu f stored in a context specified by a functor h. Thus, setting c = [b], h x = [x], and f to be the functor whose least fixed point is [b], we can write

```
gsplitWhen p = superbuild go where
go c n z = case z of
              []        -> []
              [w]       -> [c w n]
              (w : ws)  -> let xs = go c n ws
                           in if p w then (c w n) : xs
                                     else (c w (head xs)) : (tail xs)
```

If lgh = foldr (\x -> (1+)) 0 then using the fold/superbuild rule to fuse the composition evLghs = map lgh . gsplitWhen even gives

```
evLghs' z = case z of
              []        -> []
              [w]       -> [1]
              (w : ws)  -> let xs = evLghs' ws
                           in if even w then 1 : xs
                                        else (head xs + 1) : (tail xs)
```

Note that evLghs' trades production and consumption of the list of intermediate lists returned by gsplitWhen even in evLghs for production of the corresponding list of values obtained by applying lgh to each such list.

8.1.4 Short Cut Fusion in Effectful Contexts

The ability to fuse intermediate data structures in context turns out to be the key to extending short cut fusion to the effectful setting. Although fusion in the presence of computational effects has been studied by other researchers (see, e.g., [10, 12, 14, 16]), short cut fusion in particular has not previously been formally explored in this context. To perform short cut fusion in an effectful context, the functional argument to superbuild, and thus superbuild itself, must have a monadic return type. Monads can be implemented in Haskell as type constructors supporting >>= and return operations as follows; these operations are expected to satisfy the semantic monad laws.

```
class Monad m where
  return :: a -> m a
  (>>=)  :: m a -> (a -> m b) -> mb
```

If m is a monad, setting h to m in superbuild's type gives the msuperbuild combinator in Figure 8.4. The accompanying fold/msuper build rule is the natural 'monadification' of the fold/superbuild rule; we give an example of its use in Section 8.2. As we see in Section 8.3.3 the fold/msuper build rule follows from the fold/super build rule and standard properties of monad multiplication. This rule does not eliminate the monadic context described by m, but

```
msuperbuild :: (Functor f, Monad m) =>
   (forall a. (f a -> a) -> c -> m a) -> c -> m (Mu f)
msuperbuild g = g In

msuperbuild g c >>= fold k = g k c >>= id
```

FIGURE 8.4. The `msuperbuild` **combinator and** `fold`/`msuperbuild` **fusion rule**

does eliminate intermediate data structures of type `Mu f` within that monadic context. Moreover, although the rule does not change the type of the context containing the data structure, it can change the context itself, and so is more sophisticated than its non-monadic counterpart.

The remainder of this paper is structured as follows. In Section 8.2 we apply our new `fold`/`superbuild` and `fold`/`msuperbuild` rules to substantive examples. In Section 8.3 we show how the `superbuild` and `msuperbuild` combinators are derived from initial algebra semantics, and prove the correctness of their associated fusion rules. In Section 8.4 we give non-monadic and monadic `superdestroy`/`unfold` rules dual to our non-monadic and monadic `fold`/`super build` rules; our results for `superbuild` and `msuperbuild` are easily dualized to prove them correct. In Section 8.5 we discuss related work, and in Section 8.6 we conclude and offer directions for future research. A Haskell implementation of our results and an additional example highlighting the versatility of our rules are available at `http://www.cs.nott.ac.uk/~nxg`.

8.2 EXAMPLES

In this section we give some more sophisticated examples showcasing the power of the `fold`/`superbuild` and `fold`/`msuperbuild` fusion rules. Our first example shows that the `fold`/`superbuild` rule can be used to eliminate intermediate data structures other than lists. Our second example shows that the `fold`/`msuperbuild` rule can eliminate data structures within the state monad.

Example 8.1. Consider the simple arithmetic expression data type given by

```
data Opr = Add | Mul | Sub deriving (Eq, Show)
```

```
data Expr  = Lit Int | Op Opr Expr Expr deriving (Eq, Show)
```

The `fold` combinator for expressions, the instance of `superbuild` for expressions where `c` is `Expr` and `h x` is `[x]`, and the associated fusion rule are

```
foldExpr :: (Int -> a) -> (Opr -> a -> a -> a) -> Expr -> a
foldExpr l o e = case e of
                   Lit i -> l i
                   Op op e1 e2 -> o op (foldExpr l o e1)
                                       (foldExpr l o e2)
```

```
superbuildExpr :: (forall a. (Int -> a) ->
   (Opr -> a -> a -> a) -> Expr -> [a]) -> Expr -> [Expr]
```

```
superbuildExpr g = g Lit Op

map (foldExpr l o e) (superbuildExpr g) = g l o e
```

If we define `opToHas Add = (+)`, `opToHas Mul = (*)`, and `opToHas Sub = (-)`, then we can implement an interpreter which traces the evaluation steps taken in computing the integer values represented by expressions as

```
trace :: Expr -> [Expr]
trace = superbuildExpr g

g :: (Int -> a) -> (Opr -> a -> a -> a) -> Expr -> [a]
g l o e = case e of
            Lit i -> [l i]
            Op op e1 e2 -> let b1 = foldExpr l o e1
                               b2 = foldExpr l o e2
                               e' = o op b1 b2
                               Lit k = last (g Lit Op e1)
                               Lit j = last (g Lit Op e2)
                               b1s = g l o e1
                               b2s = g l o e2
                           in (e' : (map (\x -> o op x b2)
                                (tail b1s))
                              ++ (map (o op (last b1s))
                                (tail b2s))
                              ++ [l (opToHas op k j)])
```

For example, if

```
myexp = Op Mul (Op Add (Lit 5) (Lit 6))
               (Op Sub (Lit 7) (Lit 4))
```

then `trace myexp` generates the trace

```
[ Op Mul (Op Add (Lit 5) (Lit 6)) (Op Sub (Lit 7) (Lit 4)),
  Op Mul (Lit 11) (Op Sub (Lit 7) (Lit 4)),
  Op Mul (Lit 11) (Lit 3), Lit 33 ]
```

Once an interpreter trace is built, we can perform various analyses of it. For example, we can measure the computational effort required to compute the value represented by each expression arising in the evaluation of a given expression. For this we use `count`, which counts 0 units of effort to compute a literal, 2 to perform an addition, 3 to perform a subtraction, and 5 to perform a multiplication.

```
count Add x y = x + y + 2
count Sub x y = x + y + 3
count Mul x y = x + y + 5
```

We then have

```
costExprs :: Expr -> [Int]
costExprs expr = map (foldExpr (\x -> 0) count)
                     (superbuildExpr g expr)
```

Thus `costExprs myexp` generates the result `[10,8,5,0]`. Fusion using the `fold`/`superbuild` rule gives `costExprs' g (\x -> 0) count` — an equivalent function in which no intermediate list of expressions is constructed.

Example 8.2. Pardo [14] shows that graph traversal algorithms, such as depth-first and breadth-first traversal, can be written as calls to a monadic `unfold` combinator. We show that these algorithms can be written in terms of `msuper build`. The relationship between monadic and non-monadic `unfold` combinators, and between `superbuild` and `msuperbuild`, is discusssed in Section 8.5 below.

A graph traversal is represented as a function which takes as input a list of root vertices of a graph and returns a list containing the vertices met in order as the graph is traversed. We can represent the vertices of a graph by integers, and a graph by an adjacency list function for vertices as follows:

```
type V     = Int
type Graph = V -> [V]
```

In a graph traversal, each vertex is visited at most once. To avoid repeated visits to vertices we can use the state monad [13, 15] to maintain a list of vertices visited previously in the computation and thread this list through the traversal. We therefore define a data type of *visit-dependent data*, each element of which is a function taking a list of vertices already visited as input and returning a datum depending on that list together with an updated list of visited vertices. We have

```
data State s a = State {runstate :: s -> (s,a)}

instance Monad (State s) where
  return a = State (\s -> (s,a))
  t >>= f  = State (\s -> let (s',v) = runstate t s
                          in runstate (f v) s')

type Vis a = State [V] a
```

Visit-dependent data support the following useful auxiliary functions:

```
data Unit = Unit

emp :: Vis a -> a
emp xs = snd (runstate xs [])

sunion :: V -> Vis Unit
sunion v = State (\vs -> (v:vs, Unit))

mem :: V -> Vis Bool
mem v = State (\vs -> (vs, elem v vs))
```

With this machinery we can define depth-first traversal as in Figure 8.5. There, `dft` first allocates an empty list of visited vertices, then runs `depthFirst`, yielding a final list of visited vertices, and then de-allocates this visitation list and returns the list resulting from the traversal. At each iteration of the traversal, `df` explores the current list of roots in `vs` to find a vertex it has not reached before.

```
dft :: (V -> [V]) -> [V] -> [V]
dft g vs = emp (depthFirst g vs)


depthFirst :: (V -> [V]) -> [V] -> Vis [V]
depthFirst g = msuperbuild (df g)


df :: (V -> [V]) ->
        forall a. (V -> a -> a) -> a -> [V] -> Vis a
df g c n vs = case vs of
  []     -> return n
  (x:xs) -> mem x >>=
              (\b -> if b then df g c n xs
                     else sunion x >>=
                       (\z -> df g c n (g x ++ xs) >>=
                       (\ys -> return (c x ys))))
```

FIGURE 8.5.   Depth-first graph traversal functions

This is done by removing from the front of vs all vertices for which mem x is true
until either an unvisited vertex or the end of vs is encountered. When an unvisited vertex x is encountered, df adds x to the list of vertices visited, recursively
computes the depth-first traversals of the graphs rooted at x's children, as well as
those specified by the rest of the vertices in vs, and then returns the list of vertices
obtained by adding x to the list of vertices recording the order in which the rest of
the vertices are traversed. The code for breath-first search is identical, except that
the function bf corresponding to df uses xs ++ g x rather than g x ++ xs. To
traverse a particular graph we specify the desired traversal, the graph's adjacency
list function, and its root vertices. For example, if the graph *G* is modeled by g 0
= [2,1], g 1 = [], and g x = [x+1], then depthFirst g [0] computes
the depth-first search of *G* starting at root vertex 0.

For example, to consume the result of a traversal with filtergph odd where

```
filtergph :: (V -> Bool) -> [V] -> Vis [V]
filtergph p = foldr (\v i -> if p v then return (v : emp i)
                             else return (emp i))(return [])
```

we can write one of the following, depending on the desired traversal

```
dfFil g = emp (depthFirst g [0] >>= filtergph odd)

bfFil g = emp (breadthFirst g [0] >>= filtergph odd)
```

To perform the same computations without constructing the intermediate lists of
visit-dependent vertices, we can use the fold/msuperbuild rule to get

```
fn v i = if odd v then return (v : emp i)
                  else return (emp i)

dfFil' g = emp ((df g) fn (return []) [0] >>= id)

bfFil' g = emp ((bf g) fn (return []) [0] >>= id)
```

Note that the lists obtained by taking any non-empty initial segments of the results of `dfFil` `g` and `bfFil` `g` — and thus of `dfFil'` `g` and `bfFil'` `g` — reflect the distinction between the underlying depth-first and breadth-first traversals.

8.3 CORRECTNESS

8.3.1 Categorical Preliminaries

Let $\mathscr{C}$ be a category and F be an endofunctor on $\mathscr{C}$. An *F-algebra* is a morphism $h : FA \to A$ in $\mathscr{C}$. The object A is called the *carrier* of the F-algebra. The F-algebras for a functor F are the objects of a category called the *category of F-algebras* and denoted *F-$\mathscr{A}$lg*. In the category of F-algebras, a morphism from $h : FA \to A$ to $g : FB \to B$ is a morphism $f : A \to B$ such that the following diagram commutes:

$$
\begin{array}{ccc}
FA & \xrightarrow{\;Ff\;} & FB \\
{\scriptstyle h}\downarrow & & \downarrow{\scriptstyle g} \\
A & \xrightarrow{\;f\;} & B
\end{array}
$$

We call such a morphism an *F-algebra morphism*. If the category of F-algebras has an initial object then Lambek's Lemma ensures that this *initial F-algebra* is an isomorphism, and thus that its carrier is a fixed point of F. Initiality ensures that the carrier of the initial F-algebra is actually a *least* fixed point of F. If it exists, the least fixed point for F is unique up to isomorphism. Henceforth we write μF for the least fixed point for F and $in : F(\mu F) \to \mu F$ for the initial F-algebra.

Within the paradigm of initial algebra semantics, every data type is the carrier μF of the initial algebra of a suitable endofunctor F on a suitable category $\mathscr{C}$. The unique F-algebra morphism from *in* to any other F-algebra $h : FA \to A$ is given by the interpretation *fold* of the `fold` combinator for the interpretation μF of the data type `Mu F`. The *fold* operator for μF thus makes the following commute:

$$
\begin{array}{ccc}
F(\mu F) & \xrightarrow{\;F(fold\,h)\;} & FA \\
{\scriptstyle in}\downarrow & & \downarrow{\scriptstyle h} \\
\mu F & \xrightarrow{\;fold\,h\;} & A
\end{array}
$$

From this diagram, we see that *fold* has type $(FA \to A) \to \mu F \to A$ and that *fold h* satisfies *fold h* $(in\ t) = h\ (F\ (fold\ h)\ t)$. The uniqueness of the mediating map ensures that, for every F-algebra h, the map *fold h* is defined uniquely.

As shown in [5], the carrier of the initial algebra of an endofunctor F on $\mathscr{C}$ can be seen not only as the carrier of the initial F-algebra, but also as the limit of the forgetful functor $U_F : F\text{-}\mathscr{A}lg \to \mathscr{C}$ mapping each F-algebra $h : FA \to A$ to A. If $G : \mathscr{C} \to \mathscr{D}$ is a functor, then a *cone* $\tau : D \to G$ to the base G with vertex D is an object D of $\mathscr{D}$ and a family of morphisms $\tau_C : D \to GC$, one for every object

C of $\mathscr{C}$, such that for every arrow $\sigma : A \to B$ in $\mathscr{C}$, $\tau_B = G\sigma \circ \tau_A$ holds.

We usually refer to a cone simply by its family of morphisms, rather than the pair comprising the vertex together with the family of morphisms. A *limit* for $G : \mathscr{C} \to \mathscr{D}$ is an object $\lim G$ of $\mathscr{D}$ and a limiting cone $v : \lim G \to G$, i.e. a cone $v : \lim G \to G$ with the property that if $\tau : D \to G$ is any cone, then there is a unique morphism $\theta : D \to \lim G$ such that $\tau_C = v_C \circ \theta$ for all $C \in \mathscr{C}$.

The characterization of μF as $\lim U_F$ provides a principled derivation of the interpretation *build* of the `build` combinator for μF which complements the derivation of its *fold* operator from standard initial algebra semantics. It also guarantees the correctness of the standard `fold`/`build` rules. Indeed, the universal property that the carrier μF of the initial F-algebra enjoys as $\lim U_F$ ensures:

- The projection from the limit μF to the carrier of each F-algebra defines the *fold* operator with type $(FA \to A) \to \mu F \to A$.
- Given a cone $\theta : C \to U_F$, the mediating morphism from it to the limiting cone $v : \lim U_F \to U_F$ defines a map from C to $\lim U_F$. Since a cone to U_F with vertex C has type $\forall x.(Fx \to x) \to C \to x$, this mediating morphism defines the *build* operator with type $(\forall x.(Fx \to x) \to C \to x) \to C \to \mu F$.
- The correctness of the `fold`/`build` fusion rule then follows from the fact that *fold* after *build* is a projection after a mediating morphism, and thus is equal to the cone applied to the specific algebra. Diagrammatically, we have

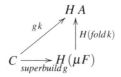

8.3.2 Correctness of the `fold/superbuild` Rule

To prove correctness of our `fold/superbuild` rule we are actually interested in the following variation of the preceding diagram:

$$
\begin{array}{c}
HA \\
\nearrow^{gk} \quad \uparrow^{H(fold\,k)} \\
C \xrightarrow[superbuild\,g]{} H(\mu F)
\end{array}
$$

Here, *superbuild* is the interpretation in $\mathscr{C}$ of superbuild. If the functor $H :$ $\mathscr{D} \to \mathscr{E}$ preserves limits — i.e. if, for every functor $G : \mathscr{C} \to \mathscr{D}$ and every limiting cone $v : \lim G \to G$, the cone $Hv : H(\lim G) \to H \circ G$ is also a limit, henceforth denoted $\lim (H \circ G)$ — then this is the diagram for the universal property of $\lim (H \circ U_F)$. We thus ask which functors H preserve limits. It is well-known that right adjoints preserve limits, but this is a more restrictive class of functors than we would like. On the other hand, H needn't preserve *all* limits, just $\lim U_F$.

A *connected category* is a non-empty category whose underlying graph is connected. A *connected limit* is a limit of a functor whose domain is a connected category. The limit $\lim U_F : F\text{-}\mathscr{A}lg \to \mathscr{C}$ is a connected limit since the category of F-algebras is connected (there is a morphism from the initial F-algebra $in : F (\mu F) \to \mu F$ to any other F-algebra), so knowing that the functor H interpreting the type constructor h in the type of superbuild preserves connected limits is sufficient to ensure correctness of the fold/superbuild rule. It is well-known that strictly positive functors preserve connected limits [3, 7]; in particular, all polynomial functors preserve them. More generally, all functors created by containers preserve connected limits [7]. The class of containers includes functors, such as those whose least fixed points are nested types, which are not strictly positive; the above proof thus covers many situations that are interesting in practice. To prove correctness of the fold/superbuild rule for functors H which do not preserve connected limits, it should be possible to give a formal argument based on logical relations [1]. However, a proof based upon logical relations would not cover examples such such as nested types which preserve connected limits but are not definable in the underlying type theory of the logical relation.

8.3.3 Correctness of the fold/msuperbuild **Rule**

To see that the fold/msuperbuild rule is correct, we consider the diagram

$$
\begin{array}{ccc}
M(MA) & \xrightarrow{\ id^*\ } & MA \\
\nearrow {\scriptstyle gk} & \uparrow {\scriptstyle M(fold\,k)} \ \ {\scriptstyle (fold\,k)^*} \nearrow & \\
C \xrightarrow[\,msuperbuild\,g\,]{} & M(\mu F) &
\end{array}
$$

where M is the interpretation of m in the type of msuperbuild, *bind* and *return* are the interpretations of the >>= and return operations for m, respectively, and $f^* x = bind\,x\,f$. Correctness of the fold/msuperbuild rule is exactly commutativity of the diagram's outer parallelogram. The diagram's left-hand triangle commutes because it is an instance of the previous diagram, and standard properties of monads ensure that its right-hand side commutes as well. Then

$$
\begin{aligned}
g\,k\,c \gg= id &= id^* (g\,k\,c) \\
&= (id^* \circ g\,k)\,c \\
&= ((fold\,k)^* \circ msuperbuild\,g)\,c \\
&= (fold\,k)^* (msuperbuild\,g\,c) \\
&= msuperbuild\,g\,c \gg= fold\,k
\end{aligned}
$$

It is worth noting here that many monads that arise in applications — including the exceptions monad, the state monad, and the list monad — preserve connected limits. The continuations monad, however, does not.

8.4 DUALITY

Our fold/superbuild and fold/msuperbuild rules dualize to the coinductive setting. Shortage of space prevents us from giving the corresponding constructs and results in detail here, so we simply present their implementation. We have

```
unfold :: Functor f => (a -> f a) -> a -> Mu f
unfold k x = In (fmap (unfold k) (k x))

superdestroy :: (Functor f, Functor h) =>
   (forall a. (a -> f a) -> h a -> c) -> h (Mu f) -> c
superdestroy g = g unIn

superdestroy g . fmap (unfold k) = g k
```

When c is Mu f, superdestroy returns an h-algebra which stores coalgebraic f-data. When h is a comonad, i.e. an instance of the Comonad class

```
class Comonad cm where
 coreturn :: cm a -> a
 (=<<)    :: cm b -> (cm b -> a) -> cm a
```

we have

```
cmsuperdestroy :: (Functor f, Comonad cm) =>
   (forall a. (a -> f a) -> cm a -> c) -> cm (Mu f) -> c
cmsuperdestroy g = g unIn

cmsuperdestroy g (x =<< unfold k) = g k (x =<< id)
```

8.5 RELATED WORK

The work most closely related to ours is that of Pardo and his coauthors. Like this paper, [14] also investigates conditions under which the composition of a function producing an expression of type $M(\mu F)$ for M a monad and F a functor, and a function *fold k* of type $\mu F \to A$ can be fused to produce an expression of type MA. But there are several crucial differences with our work. First, Pardo uses unfold rather than msuperbuild to construct the intermediate expression. This gives his fusion rule some additional logical generality over ours, since unfold can construct elements of its associated functor f's final coalgebra which are not in f's initial algebra, whereas msuperbuild can construct only elements of f's initial algebra. But when the initial and final algebras of each functor coincide, as in Haskell, this added logical generality yields no advantage in practice.

Secondly, Pardo's monadic hylofusion (and hylofusion in general) is only known to be correct in algebraically compact categories, i.e. categories in which the initial algebra and final coalgebra for each functor coincide. By contrast, our fold/superbuild rule is correct in any category supporting a parametric interpretation of `forall`, and this condition is independent of any compactness condition. The requirement that the interpreting category be algebraically compact is unfortunate since it generates strictness conditions that must be satisfied, and also requires the underlying monad to be strictness-preserving. This results in strictness condition propagation. By contrast, neither our `fold`/`superbuild` nor our `fold`/msuperbuild rules require the satisfaction of side conditions.

Thirdly, Pardo trades a composition of an `unfold` and a monadic `fold` for the computation of an equivalent fixed point. By contrast, our `fold`/msuperbuild rule trades a bind of a call to `msuperbuild` with a monadic `fold` for the bind of the application of the function argument to `msuperbuild` to the `fold`'s algebra with the identity function. Like all generalizations of the `fold`/`build` rule, our `fold`/msuperbuild rule requires 'payment up front' in that the producer in a composition to be fused must be expressed in terms of `msuperbuild`. (This is not very different from the price paid by expressing consumers in terms of `unfold`.) But our rule delivers a fused result which is simpler than that obtained using Pardo's technique. In particular, the functions obtained from our fusion rules involve only binds of applications involving data structure 'templates', rather than fixed point calculations. Their computation is thus guaranteed to terminate.

Finally, Pardo requires the existence of a distributivity law of the underlying monad over the underlying functor to construct the lifting of functors to the Kleisli category on which his monadic hylofusion rule depends. But distributivity laws for arbitrary functors, even those admitting fixed points, need not exist.

Recently, Manzino and Pardo [11] have proposed a fusion rule similar to the `fold`/msuperbuild rule given here. This rule seems to be interderivable with ours in the presence of distributivity. Meijer and Jeuring [12] have also developed fusion laws in the monadic setting, including a short cut fusion law for eliminating intermediate structures of type $F A$ in a monadic context M. Many fusion methods, including those of [12] and [14], eliminate data structures in the carriers of initial algebras for only restricted classes of functors. By contrast, our method can eliminate data structures of *any* inductive type, and can handle non-monadic contexts as well. In addition, Jürgensen [10] and Voigtländer [16] have each defined fusion combinators based on the uniqueness of the map from a free monad to any other monad. These techniques give very different forms of fusion from ours.

8.6 CONCLUSION AND DIRECTIONS FOR FUTURE WORK

In this paper we defined a `superbuild` combinator which generalizes the standard `build` combinator and expresses uniform production of functorial contexts containing data of inductive types. We also proved correct a `fold`/`super build` fusion rule which generalizes the `fold`/`build` and `fold`/`buildp` rules from the literature, and eliminates intermediate data structures of inductive types without disturbing the contexts in which they are situated. An important special case arises when this context is monadic. When it is, our `fold`/msuperbuild rule fuses combinations of producers and consumers via monad operations, rather than via composition. We have given examples illustrating both the `fold`/`superbuild` and `fold`/msuperbuild rules, and considered their coalgebraic duals as well.

The standard `fold` combinator can consume data structures in any context describable by a functor, but the algebra it uses cannot depend on the context in a non-trivial way. By contrast, context information can be used by algebras to partially determine how the `pfold` combinator given in [2] will consume the data structures, but unfortunately the contexts are limited to pairs. Interestingly, the `pfold`/`buildp` rule given there for context-dependent `folds` derives from the `fold`/`buildp` rule from Figure 8.2 for standard `folds`. As already noted, it is the `fold`/`buildp` rule that our `fold`/`superbuild` and `fold`/`msuperbuild` rules generalize. One direction for future work is to generalize these rules even further to accommodate *both* context-dependent algebras and non-pair contexts.

Another direction for future work is suggested by considering an even more monadic fusion rule based on `fold`- and `build`-like combinators which manipulate algebra-like functions of type `f a -> m a`. Such a rule would produce intermediate data structures using 'templates' based on so-called monadic algebras and, in the presence of a distributivity rule `delta` for m over f, would consume data structures using them via a monadic `mafold` combinator. We'd have

```
mafold :: (Functor f, Monad m) =>
                             (f a -> m a) -> Mu f -> m a
mafold k = fold (\x -> fmap k (delta x) >>= id)

masuperbuild :: (Functor f, Monad m) =>
   (forall a. (f a -> m a) -> c -> m a) -> c -> m (Mu f)
masuperbuild g = g (return . In)
```

```
masuperbuild  g c >>= mafold k = g k c
```

Although a data type-generic `masuperbuild` combinator is not defined in [12], several instances of the above fusion rule are given. Yet no correctness proofs for any of these specific instances — let alone any formulation of, or correctness proof for, a data type-generic fusion rule — are given. We believe an independent proof of the `mafold`/`masuperbuild` rule similar to those in Section 8.3 is possible. Although it is not entirely clear how such a proof would go, a proof for monads which preserve connected limits will likely require independent verification that $\lim(M U_{F,M}) = M(\mu F)$ for the forgetful functor $U_{F,M}$ mapping each monadic algebra $h : F a \to M a$ to a, and a proof for monads which do not preserve connected limits will likely be based on logical relations.

The facts that `mafold` is defined in terms of `fold` and that `masuperbuild g` can be expressed as `msuperbuild (\k -> g (return . k))` together suggest that the `mafold`/`masuperbuild` rule might be derivable from (distributivity and) the `fold`/`msuperbuild` rule. However, we believe the two rules to offer distinct fusion options in the presence of distributivity; it would be interesting to see which is more useful for programs that arise in practice.

REFERENCES

[1] T. Altenkirch, P. Levy, and M. Hasagawa, 2008. Personal communication, and message 1192 from the TYPES mailing list archive.

[2] J. P. Fernandes, A. Pardo, and J. Saraiva. A shortcut fusion rule for circular program calculation. In *Proceedings, Haskell Workshop*, pages 95–106, 2007.

[3] N. Ghani, M. Abbott, and T. Altenkirch. Containers - constructing strictly positive types. *Theoretical Computer Science*, 341(1):3–27, 2005.

[4] N. Ghani, P. Johann, T. Uustalu, and V. Vene. Monadic augment and generalised short cut fusion. In *Proceedings, International Conference on Functional Programming*, pages 294–305, 2005.

[5] N. Ghani, T. Uustalu, and V. Vene. Build, augment and destroy. Universally. In *Proceedings, Asian Symposium on Programming Languages*, pages 327–347, LNCS 3302, Springer, 2003.

[6] A. Gill, J. Launchbury, and S. L. Peyton Jones. A short cut to deforestation. In *Proceedings, Functional Programming Languages and Computer Architecture*, pages 223–232, 1993.

[7] R. Hasegawa. Two applications of analytic functors. *Theoretical Computer Science*, 272(1-2):113–175, 2002.

[8] P. Johann and N. Ghani. Initial algebra semantics is enough! In *Proceedings, Typed Lambda Calculus and Applications*, pages 207–222, LNCS 4583, Springer, 2007.

[9] P. Johann and N. Ghani. Foundations for structured programming with GADTs. In *Proceedings, Principles of Programming Languages*, pages 297–308, 2008.

[10] C. Jürgensen. Using monads to fuse recursive programs (extended abstract), 2002.

[11] C. Manzino and Pardo. Shortcut fusion of monadic programs. In *Presented at Simposio Brasiliero de Linguagens de Programacao*, 2008.

[12] E. Meijer and J. Jeuring. Merging monads and folds for functional programming. In *Proceedings, Advanced Functional Programming*, pages 228–266, Springer, 1995.

[13] E. Moggi. Notions of computation and monads. *Information and Computation*, 93(1):55–92, 1991.

[14] A. Pardo. Fusion of recursive programs with computational effects. *Theoretical Computer Science*, 260(1-2):165–207, 2001.

[15] S. L. Peyton Jones, editor. *Haskell 98 Language and Libraries: The Revised Report*. Cambridge University Press, 2003.

[16] J. Voigtländer. Asymptotic improvement of computations over free monads. In *Proceedings, Mathematics of Program Construction*, pages 388–403, 2008.

Chapter 9

Towards a Verified Implementation of Software Transactional Memory

Liyang HU,[1] Graham Hutton[1]
Category: Research

Abstract: In recent years there has been much interest in the idea of concurrent programming using *transactional memory*, for example as provided in STM Haskell. While programmers are provided with a simple high-level model of transactions in terms of a stop-the-world semantics, the low-level implementation is rather more complex, using subtle optimization techniques to execute multiple concurrent transactions efficiently, which is essential to the viability of the programming model.

In this article, we take the first steps towards a formally verified implementation of transactional memory. In particular, we present a stripped-down, idealized concurrent language inspired by STM Haskell, and show how a low-level implementation of this language can be justified with respect to a high-level semantics, by means of a compiler and its correctness theorem, mechanically tested using QuickCheck and the HPC (Haskell Program Coverage) toolkit. The use of these tools proved to be invaluable in the development of our formalization.

9.1   INTRODUCTION

In recent years, traditional uniprocessors have reached a plateau in terms of raw operating speed, and we now have entered the era of multi core processors [18]. However, traditional techniques for concurrent programming, in particular the use of explicit locks, are notoriously error prone and hinder code reuse.

---

[1] School of CS, University of Nottingham, UK; {lyh, gmh}@cs.nott.ac.uk.

One approach to addressing this problem is to adopt a lock-free model of concurrency and specify the desired behaviour of programs in a declarative manner, without requiring the programmer to be concerned about how this is achieved in practice. In the context of Haskell, this idea has been explored in the form of *software transactional memory* [7], in which sequences of read and write operations on memory can be specified to run atomically, in the sense that their intermediate states are not observable to other concurrent computations.

While atomicity provides programmers with a simple yet powerful mechanism to write concurrent programs, the actual implementation of this mechanism is rather more complex, using the notion of *transactions* [4] to better exploit the available multi core hardware. In this article, we take the first steps towards a formally verified implementation of software transactional memory, inspired by STM Haskell. In particular, we make the following contributions:

- Identification of a simplified subset of STM Haskell and a semantics for this language, suitable for exploring design issues.
- A low-level virtual machine for this language in which transactions are made explicit, along with a semantics for this machine.
- A compiler from the language to the virtual machine, along with a correctness theorem, tested using QuickCheck [3] and HPC [5].

To the best of our knowledge, this is the first time that the correctness of a compiler for a language with transactions has been considered in a formal setting. This article is aimed at the functional programmers who are interested in the implementation and formalization of software transactional memory. We require only a basic familiarity with Haskell, to the level of Bird's textbook [2]. An implementation of the model described in this paper may be found on the authors' websites.

9.2   STM IN HASKELL

Harris et al. [7] first introduced transactional memory to Haskell as an extension to the Glasgow Haskell Compiler. Notable is the fact that no modification to the Haskell language specification was necessary: its higher-order constructs are sufficient to implement the required control structures, whereas previous attempts [6] made changes to the language syntax.

The standard Haskell approach to sequencing read and write operations on memory is to use the IO monad to handle sequencing, and IORefs to represent mutable variables. STM Haskell provides analogous operations on TVars (transactional variables) within the STM monad:

$$(\gg\!\!=) \quad :: \mathsf{STM}\ \alpha \to (\alpha \to \mathsf{STM}\ \beta) \to \mathsf{STM}\ \beta$$
$$return \quad :: \alpha \to \mathsf{STM}\ \alpha$$
$$newTVar \quad :: \alpha \to \mathsf{STM}\ (\mathsf{TVar}\ \alpha)$$
$$readTVar :: \mathsf{TVar}\ \alpha \to \mathsf{STM}\ \alpha$$
$$writeTVar :: \mathsf{TVar}\ \alpha \to \alpha \to \mathsf{STM}\ ()$$

In this manner, the STM monad provides just the relevant operations within transactions (a term we use synonymously with 'STM action'), and precludes arbitrary and potentially irreversible side-effects. Executing transactions involves first converting them to IO actions using the *atomically* operation, and these actions can then be run concurrently using *forkIO* [16]:

$$atomically :: \mathsf{STM}\ \alpha \rightarrow \mathsf{IO}\ \alpha$$
$$forkIO \qquad :: \mathsf{IO}\ \alpha \rightarrow \mathsf{IO\ ThreadId}$$

Finally, STM Haskell supports a novel form of transaction composition, using a choice operator *orElse* that behaves as the first transaction if it succeeds and as the second transaction if the first fails, together with a *retry* primitive that forces failure:

$$orElse :: \mathsf{STM}\ \alpha \rightarrow \mathsf{STM}\ \alpha \rightarrow \mathsf{STM}\ \alpha$$
$$retry \quad :: \mathsf{STM}\ \alpha$$

Example

Suppose we represent the current balance of a bank account by a transactional variable *account* :: TVar Integer. Using the above operations, it is straightforward to implement a function that deposits a given amount:

$$deposit :: \mathsf{Integer} \rightarrow \mathsf{STM}\ ()$$
$$deposit\ amount = \mathbf{do}$$
$$\quad balance \leftarrow readTVar\ account$$
$$\quad writeTVar\ account\ (balance + amount)$$

Now if the following program is executed, the two deposits are guaranteed to take place, in either order. In particular, a deposit cannot be lost due to unexpected interleavings of *readTVar* and *writeTVar* in the definition of *deposit*.

$$\mathbf{do}\ forkIO\ (atomically\ (deposit\ 10))$$
$$\quad forkIO\ (atomically\ (deposit\ 20))$$

9.3 A SIMPLE TRANSACTIONAL LANGUAGE

Our goal in this article is to formalize the low-level implementation details of software transactional memory. In order to focus on the essence of the problem, we abstract from the details of a real language such as STM Haskell, and consider a minimal language in which to explain and verify the basic implementation techniques. This section presents the syntax and semantics of our minimal language.

9.3.1   Language Syntax

The syntax of the language we consider can be defined by the following Haskell data types, where Tran represents transactions in the STM monad, Proc represents the desired aspects of concurrent processes in the IO monad, and Var represents a finite but unspecified collection of transactional variables:

> **data** Tran = Val$_T$ Integer | Tran +$_T$ Tran | Read Var | Write Var Tran
> **data** Proc = Val$_P$ Integer | Proc +$_P$ Proc | Atomic Tran | Fork Proc

This language of expressions provides the essential computational features of STM Haskell, in a simplified form. On both levels, we replace sequencing ($\ggeq$) and *return* with left-to-right addition ($+.$) and integers. This has the advantage of avoiding the issues of name binding, yet still retains the fundamental monadic idea of sequencing computations and combining their results [11]. More formally, the use of integers and addition is justified by the fact that they form a monoid, a degenerate form of monads.

Read and Write are intended to mimic *readTVar* and *writeTVar*. We omit *newTVar* to once again avoid the issue of binding, and assume all variables are initialized to zero. Atomic runs a transaction to completion, delivering a value, while Fork spawns off its argument as a concurrent process, in the style of *forkIO*.

For simplicity, we do not consider *orElse* or *retry*, as they are not strictly necessary to illustrate the basic implementation of a log-based transactional memory system.

Example

Assuming a transactional variable *account* :: Var, our *deposit* function from the previous section can now be defined using our language as follows:

> *deposit* :: Integer $\rightarrow$ Tran
> *deposit n* = Write *account* (Read *account* +$_T$ Val$_T$ *n*)

In turn, our example program of two concurrent deposits becomes:

> Fork (Atomic (*deposit* 10)) +$_P$ Fork (Atomic (*deposit* 20))

9.3.2   Transactional Semantics

We specify the meaning of transactions in this language using a mostly small-step operational semantics, following the approach of [7, 15]. Formally, we give a reduction relation $\mapsto_T$ on pairs $\langle h, e \rangle$ consisting of a heap h (a total map of type Var $\rightarrow$ Integer from variable names to their values) and a transaction expression e :: Tran. In this section we explain each of the inference rules defining $\mapsto_T$.

First of all, reading a variable v looks up its value in the heap:

$$\langle h,\ \text{Read } v \rangle \mapsto_T \langle h,\ \text{Val}_T\ h(v) \rangle \tag{READ}$$

Writing to a variable is taken care of by two rules: (WRITE$\mathbb{Z}$) updates the heap with the new integer value for a variable in the same manner as the published semantics of STM Haskell [7], while (WRITET) allows its argument expression to be repeatedly reduced until it becomes a value:

$$\langle h,\ \mathsf{Write}\ v\ (\mathsf{Val_T}\ n)\rangle \mapsto_\mathsf{T} \langle h[v \mapsto n],\ \mathsf{Val_T}\ n\rangle \qquad \text{(WRITE}\mathbb{Z}\text{)}$$

$$\frac{\langle h,\ e\rangle \mapsto_\mathsf{T} \langle h',\ e'\rangle}{\langle h,\ \mathsf{Write}\ v\ e\rangle \mapsto_\mathsf{T} \langle h',\ \mathsf{Write}\ v\ e'\rangle} \qquad \text{(WRITET)}$$

Because we replace $\ggg$ with addition in our language, it is important to force a sequential evaluation order. The following three rules define reduction for $+_\mathsf{T}$, and ensure left-to-right evaluation:

$$\langle h,\ \mathsf{Val_T}\ m +_\mathsf{T} \mathsf{Val_T}\ n\rangle \mapsto_\mathsf{T} \langle h,\ \mathsf{Val_T}\ (m+n)\rangle \qquad \text{(ADD}\mathbb{Z}_\mathsf{T}\text{)}$$

$$\frac{\langle h,\ b\rangle \mapsto_\mathsf{T} \langle h',\ b'\rangle}{\langle h,\ \mathsf{Val_T}\ m +_\mathsf{T} b\rangle \mapsto_\mathsf{T} \langle h',\ \mathsf{Val_T}\ m +_\mathsf{T} b'\rangle} \qquad \text{(ADDR}_\mathsf{T}\text{)}$$

$$\frac{\langle h,\ a\rangle \mapsto_\mathsf{T} \langle h',\ a'\rangle}{\langle h,\ a +_\mathsf{T} b\rangle \mapsto_\mathsf{T} \langle h',\ a' +_\mathsf{T} b\rangle} \qquad \text{(ADDL}_\mathsf{T}\text{)}$$

9.3.3 Process Semantics

The reduction relation $\mapsto_\mathsf{P}$ for processes acts on pairs $\langle h,\ s\rangle$ consisting of a heap h as before, and a 'soup' s of running processes [15]. The soup itself is a multiset, which we represent as a list of type $[\mathsf{Proc}]$ for implementation reasons. The process rules are in general defined by matching on the first process in the soup. However, we begin by giving the (PREEMPT) rule, which allows the rest of the soup to make progress, giving rise to non-determinism in the language:

$$\frac{\langle h,\ s\rangle \mapsto_\mathsf{P} \langle h',\ s'\rangle}{\langle h,\ p:s\rangle \mapsto_\mathsf{P} \langle h',\ p:s'\rangle} \qquad \text{(PREEMPT)}$$

Executing Fork p adds p to the process soup, and evaluates to $\mathsf{Val_P}$ 0 (which corresponds to *return* () in Haskell) as the result of this action:

$$\langle h,\ \mathsf{Fork}\ p:s\rangle \mapsto_\mathsf{P} \langle h,\ \mathsf{Val_P}\ 0:p:s\rangle \qquad \text{(FORK)}$$

Next, the (ATOMIC) rule has a premise which evaluates the given expression until it reaches a value (where $\mapsto_\mathsf{T}^*$ denotes the reflexive / transitive closure of $\mapsto_\mathsf{T}$), and a conclusion which encapsulates this as a single transition on the process level:

$$\frac{\langle h,\ e\rangle \mapsto_\mathsf{T}^* \langle h',\ \mathsf{Val_T}\ n\rangle}{\langle h,\ \mathsf{Atomic}\ e:s\rangle \mapsto_\mathsf{P} \langle h',\ \mathsf{Val_P}\ n:s\rangle} \qquad \text{(ATOMIC)}$$

In this manner we obtain a *stop-the-world* semantics for atomic transactions, preventing interference from other concurrently executing processes. Note that while the use of $\mapsto_T^*$ may seem odd in an otherwise small-step semantics, it expresses the intended semantics in a clear and concise manner [7].

Finally, it is straightforward to handle $+_P$ on the process level using three rules, in an analogous manner to $+_T$ on the transaction level:

$$\langle h,\ \mathsf{Val_P}\ m +_P \mathsf{Val_P}\ n : s \rangle \mapsto_P \langle h,\ \mathsf{Val_P}\ (m+n) : s \rangle \qquad (\text{ADD}\mathbb{Z}_P)$$

$$\frac{\langle h,\ b : s \rangle \mapsto_P \langle h',\ b' : s' \rangle}{\langle h,\ \mathsf{Val_P}\ m +_P b : s \rangle \mapsto_P \langle h',\ \mathsf{Val_P}\ m +_P b' : s' \rangle} \qquad (\text{ADDR}_P)$$

$$\frac{\langle h,\ a : s \rangle \mapsto_P \langle h',\ a' : s' \rangle}{\langle h,\ a +_P b : s \rangle \mapsto_P \langle h',\ a' +_P b : s' \rangle} \qquad (\text{ADDL}_P)$$

In summary, the above semantics for transactions and processes mirror those for STM Haskell, but for a simplified language. Moreover, while the original semantics uses evaluation contexts to identify the point at which transition rules such as $(\text{ADD}\mathbb{Z}_P)$ can be applied, our language is sufficiently simple to allow the use of explicit structural rules such as (ADDL_P) and (ADDR_P), which for our purposes have the advantage of being directly implementable.

9.4   A SIMPLE TRANSACTIONAL MACHINE

The (ATOMIC) rule of the previous section simply states that the evaluation sequence for a transaction may be seen as a single indivisible transition with respect to other concurrent processes. However, to better exploit the available multi core hardware, an actual implementation of this rule would have to allow multiple transactions to run concurrently, while still maintaining the illusion of atomicity. In this section we consider how this notion of concurrent transactions can be implemented, and present a compiler and virtual machine for our language.

9.4.1   Instruction Set

Let us consider compiling expressions into code for execution on a stack machine, in which Code comprises a sequence of Instructions:

```
type Code       = [Instruction]
data Instruction = PUSH Integer | ADD | READ Var | WRITE Var
                 | BEGIN | COMMIT | FORK Code
```

The PUSH instruction leaves its argument on top of the stack, while ADD replaces the top two numbers with their sum. The behaviour of the remaining instructions is more complex in order to maintain atomicity, but conceptually, READ pushes the value of the named variable onto the stack, while WRITE updates the variable with the topmost value. In turn, BEGIN and COMMIT mark the start and finish of a transaction, and FORK executes the given code concurrently.

9.4.2 Compiler

We define the *compile*$_T$ and *compile*$_P$ functions to provide translations from Tran and Proc to Code, both functions taking an additional Code argument to be appended to the instructions produced by the compilation process; using such a *code continuation* both simplifies reasoning and results in more efficient compilers [10, §13.7]. In both cases, integers and addition are compiled into PUSH and ADD instructions, while the remaining language constructs map directly to their analogous machine instructions. The intention is that executing a compiled transaction or process always leaves a single result value on top of the stack.

$$compile_T :: \text{Tran} \rightarrow \text{Code} \rightarrow \text{Code}$$
$$compile_T \; e \; cc = \textbf{case } e \textbf{ of}$$

Val$_T$ i	$\rightarrow$ PUSH $i:cc$
$x +_T y$	$\rightarrow compile_T \; x \; (compile_T \; y \; (\text{ADD}:cc))$
Read v	$\rightarrow$ READ $v:cc$
Write $v \; e'$	$\rightarrow compile_T \; e' \; (\text{WRITE } v:cc)$

$$compile_P :: \text{Proc} \rightarrow \text{Code} \rightarrow \text{Code}$$
$$compile_P \; e \; cc = \textbf{case } e \textbf{ of}$$

Val$_P$ i	$\rightarrow$ PUSH $i:cc$
$x +_P y$	$\rightarrow compile_P \; x \; (compile_P \; y \; (\text{ADD}:cc))$
Atomic e'	$\rightarrow$ BEGIN $:compile_T \; e' \; (\text{COMMIT}:cc)$
Fork x	$\rightarrow$ FORK $(compile_P \; x \; [\,]):cc$

For example, applying *compile*$_P$ to our earlier program

$$compile_P \; (\text{Fork } (\text{Atomic } (deposit \; 10)) +_P \text{Fork } (\text{Atomic } (deposit \; 20))) \; [\,]$$

gives the following result:

    [FORK [BEGIN, READ account, PUSH 10, ADD, WRITE account, COMMIT]
    , FORK [BEGIN, READ account, PUSH 20, ADD, WRITE account, COMMIT]
    , ADD]

9.4.3 Implementing Transactions

The simplest method of implementing transactions would be to suspend execution of all other concurrent processes on encountering a BEGIN, and carry on with the current process until we reach the following COMMIT. In essence, this is the approach used in the high-level semantics presented in the previous section. Unfortunately, this does not allow transactions to execute concurrently, one of the key aspects of transactional memory. This section introduces the log-based approach to implementing transactions, and discusses a number of design issues.

Transaction Logs

In order to allow transactions to execute concurrently, we utilize the notion of a *transaction log*. Informally such a log behaves as a cache for read and write operations on transactional variables. Only the first read from any given variable accesses the heap, and only the last value written can potentially modify the heap; all intermediate reads and writes operate solely on the log. Upon reaching the end of the transaction, and provided that that no other concurrent process has 'interfered' with the current transaction, the modified variables in the log can then be committed to the heap. Otherwise, the log is discarded and the transaction is restarted afresh.

Note that restarting a transaction relies on the fact that it executes in complete isolation, in the sense that all its side-effects are encapsulated within the log, and hence can be revoked by simply discarding the log. For example, it would not be appropriate to 'launch missiles' [7] during a transaction.

Interference

But what constitutes *interference*? When a transaction succeeds and commits its log to the heap, all of its side-effects are then made visible in a single atomic step, as if it had been executed in its entirety at that point with a stop-the-world semantics. Thus when a variable is read for the first time and its value logged, the transaction is essentially making the following bet: at the end of the transaction, the value of the variable in the heap will still be the same as that in the log.

In this manner, interference arises when any such bet fails, as the result of other concurrent processes changing the heap in a way that invalidates the assumptions about the values of variables made in the log. In this case, the transaction fails and is restarted. Conversely, the transaction succeeds if the logged values of all the variables read are 'equal' to their values in the heap at the end of the transaction.

Equality

But what constitutes *equality*? To see why this is an important question, and what the design choices are, let us return to our earlier example of a transaction that deposits a given amount into an account. Consider the following timeline:

Suppose that *account* starts with a balance of zero, which is read by the first transaction and logged. Prior to its final COMMIT, a second concurrent trans-action successfully makes a deposit, which is subsequently withdrawn by a third transaction. When the first finally attempts to commit, the balance is back to zero as originally logged, even though it has changed in the interim. Is this acceptable?

i.e. are the two zeros 'equal'? We can consider a hierarchy of notions of equality, in increasing order of permissiveness:

- The most conservative choice is to increment a global counter every time the heap is updated. Under this scheme, a transaction fails if the heap is modified at any point during its execution, reflected by a change in the counter, even if this does not actually interfere with the transaction itself.

- A more refined approach is provided by the notion of *version equality*, where a separate counter is associated with each variable, and is incremented each time the variable is updated. In this case, our example transaction would still fail to commit, since the two zeros would have different version numbers, and hence be considered different.

- For a pure language such as Haskell, in which values are represented as pointers to immutable structures, *pointer equality* can be used as an efficient but weaker form of version equality. In this case, whether the two zeros are considered equal or not depends on whether the implementation created a new instance of zero, or reused the old zero by sharing.

- We can also consider *value equality*, in which two values are considered the same if they have the same representation. In this case, the two zeros are equal and the transaction succeeds.

- The most permissive choice would be a *user-defined equality*, beyond that built-in to the programming language itself, in order to handle abstract data structures in which a single value may have several representations, e.g. sets encoded as lists. Haskell provides this capability via the Eq typeclass.

Which of the above is the appropriate notion of equality when committing transactions? Recall that under a stop-the-world semantics, a transaction can be considered to be executed in its entirely at the point when it successfully commits, and any prior reads are bets on the state of the heap at this point. Any intermediate writes that may have been committed by other transactions do not matter, as long as the final heap is consistent with the bets made in the log. Hence, there is no need at commit time to distinguish between the two zeroes in our example, as they are equal in the high-level expression language.

From a semantics point of view, therefore, value or user-defined equality are the best choices. Practical implementations may wish to adopt a more efficient notion of equality (e.g. STM Haskell utilizes pointer equality), but for the purposes of this article, we will use value equality.

9.4.4 Virtual Machine

The state of the virtual machine is given by a pair $\langle h, s \rangle$, comprising a heap h mapping variables to integers, and a soup s of concurrent *threads*. Each Thread consists of a tuple of the form (c, σ, f, r, w), where c is the code to be executed, σ is the local stack, f gives the code to be rerun if a transaction fails to commit, and finally, r and w are two logs (partial maps from variables to integers) acting as read and write caches between a transaction and the heap.

type Thread $=$ (Code, Stack, Code, Log, Log)
type Stack $=$ [Integer]
type Log $=$ Var $\hookrightarrow$ Integer

We specify the behaviour of the machine using a transition relation $\mapsto_{\mathsf{M}}$ between machine states, defined via a collection of transition rules that proceed by case analysis on the first thread in the soup. As with the previous semantics, we begin by defining a (PREEMPT) rule to allow the rest of the soup to make progress, giving rise to non-determinism in the machine:

$$\frac{\langle h,\, s \rangle \mapsto_{\mathsf{M}} \langle h',\, s' \rangle}{\langle h,\, t : s \rangle \mapsto_{\mathsf{M}} \langle h',\, t : s' \rangle} \qquad \text{(PREEMPT)}$$

This rule corresponds to an idealized scheduler that permits context switching at every instruction, as our focus is on the implementation of transactions rather than scheduling policies. We return to this issue when we consider the correctness of our compiler in §9.5.1.

Executing FORK adds a new thread t to the soup, comprising the given code c' with an initially empty stack, restart code and read and write logs:

$$\langle h,\, (\text{FORK } c' : c,\, \sigma,\, f,\, r,\, w) : s \rangle \mapsto_{\mathsf{M}} \langle h,\, (c,\, 0 : \sigma,\, f,\, r,\, w) : t : s \rangle \quad \text{(FORK)}$$

where $t = (c',\, [\,],\, [\,],\, \emptyset,\, \emptyset)$

The PUSH instruction places the integer n on top of the stack, while ADD takes the top two integers from the stack and replaces them with their sum:

$$\langle h, (\text{PUSH } n : c, \qquad\;\; \sigma,f,r,w) : s \rangle \mapsto_{\mathsf{M}} \langle h, (c, \qquad n : \sigma,f,r,w) : s \rangle \quad \text{(PUSH)}$$
$$\langle h, (\text{ADD} \quad : c, n : m : \sigma,f,r,w) : s \rangle \mapsto_{\mathsf{M}} \langle h, (c, m+n : \sigma,f,r,w) : s \rangle \quad \text{(ADD)}$$

Executing BEGIN starts a transaction, which involves clearing the read and write logs, while making a note of the code to be executed if the transaction fails:

$$\langle h,\, (\text{BEGIN} : c,\, \sigma,\, f,\, r,\, w) : s \rangle \mapsto_{\mathsf{M}} \langle h,\, (c,\, \sigma,\, \text{BEGIN} : c,\, \emptyset,\, \emptyset) : s \rangle \quad \text{(BEGIN)}$$

Next, READ places the appropriate value for the variable v on top of the stack. The instruction first consults the write log. If the variable has not been written to, the read log is then consulted. Otherwise, if the variable has also not been read, its value is looked up from the heap and the read log updated accordingly:

$$\langle h,\, (\text{READ } v : c,\, \sigma,\, f,\, r,\, w) : s \rangle \mapsto_{\mathsf{M}} \langle h,\, (c,\, n : \sigma,\, f,\, r',\, w) : s \rangle \quad \text{(READ)}$$

$$\text{where } \langle n,\, r' \rangle = \begin{cases} \langle w(v),\, r \rangle & \text{if } v \in \text{dom}(w) \\ \langle r(v),\, r \rangle & \text{if } v \in \text{dom}(r) \\ \langle h(v),\, r[v \mapsto h(v)] \rangle & \text{otherwise} \end{cases}$$

In turn, WRITE simply updates the write log for the variable v with the value on the top of the stack, without changing the heap or the stack:

$$\langle h,\, (\text{WRITE } v : c,\, n : \sigma,\, f,\, r,\, w) : s \rangle \mapsto_{\mathsf{M}} \langle h,\, (c,\, n : \sigma,\, f,\, r,\, w') : s \rangle \quad \text{(WRITE)}$$
where $w' = w[v \mapsto n]$

Finally, COMMIT first checks the read log r for consistency with the current heap h, namely that the logged value for each variable read is equal to its value in the heap. Note that the write log may contain variables not in the read log, for which no check is necessary. Using our representation of logs and heaps, this condition can be concisely stated as $r \subseteq h$. If they are consistent, then the transaction has succeeded, so it may commit its write log to the heap. This update is expressed in terms of the overriding operator on maps as $h \oplus w$. Otherwise the transaction has failed, in which case the heap is not changed, the result on the top of the stack is discarded, and the transaction is restarted at f:

$$\langle h, (\text{COMMIT}:c, n:\sigma, f, r, w):s \rangle \mapsto_{\mathsf{M}} \langle h', (c', \sigma', f, r, w):s \rangle$$

$$\text{where } \langle h', c', \sigma' \rangle = \begin{cases} \langle h \oplus w, c, n:\sigma \rangle & \text{if } r \subseteq h \\ \langle h, f, \sigma \rangle & \text{otherwise} \end{cases} \qquad \text{(COMMIT)}$$

There is no need to explicitly clear the logs in the above rule, since this is taken care of by the first instruction of f always being a BEGIN.

9.5 CORRECTNESS OF IMPLEMENTATION

As we have seen, the high-level semantics of atomicity is both clear and concise, comprising a single inference rule (ATOMIC) that wraps up a complete evaluation sequence as a single transition. On the other hand, the low-level implementation of atomicity using transactions is rather more complex and subtle, involving the management of read and write logs, and careful consideration of the conditions that are necessary in order for a transaction to commit. How can we be sure that these two different views of atomicity are consistent? Our approach to establishing the correctness of the low-level implementation is to formally relate it to the high-level semantics via a compiler correctness theorem.

9.5.1 Statement of Correctness

In order to formulate our correctness result, we utilize a number of auxiliary definitions. First of all, since our semantics is non-deterministic, we define a relation *eval* that encapsulates the idea of completely evaluating a process using our high-level semantics:

$$p \; \underline{eval} \; \langle h, s \rangle \quad \Leftrightarrow \quad \langle \emptyset, [p] \rangle \mapsto_{\mathsf{P}}^{*} \langle h, s \rangle \not\mapsto_{\mathsf{P}}$$

That is, a process $p :: \mathsf{Proc}$ can evaluate to any heap h and process soup s that results from starting with the empty heap and completely reducing p using our high-level semantics, where $\not\mapsto$ expresses that no further transitions are possible. Similarly, we define a relation *exec* that encapsulates complete execution of a thread $t :: \mathsf{Thread}$ using our virtual machine, resulting in a heap h and a thread soup s:

$$t \; \underline{exec} \; \langle h, s \rangle \quad \Leftrightarrow \quad \langle \emptyset, [t] \rangle \mapsto_{\mathsf{M}}^{*} \langle h, s \rangle \not\mapsto_{\mathsf{M}}$$

Next, we define a function $load :: \mathsf{Proc} \rightarrow \mathsf{Thread}$ that converts a process into a corresponding thread for execution, which comprises the compiled code for the process, together with an empty stack, restart code and read and write logs:

$$load\ p = (compile_\mathsf{P}\ p\ [\,]\,,[\,]\,,[\,]\,,\emptyset,\emptyset)$$

Dually, we define a partial function $unload :: \mathsf{Thread} \hookrightarrow \mathsf{Proc}$ that extracts the resulting integer from a completely executed thread into our process language:

$$unload\ ([\,],[n],f,r,w) = \mathsf{Val}_\mathsf{P}\ n$$

Using these definitions, the correctness of our compiler can now be expressed by the following relational equation, in which $;$ denotes composition of relations, and the functions $load$ and $unload$ are viewed as relations by taking their graph:

Theorem 9.1 (Compiler Correctness).

$$eval\ =\ load\ ;\ exec\ ;\ (id \times map\ unload)$$

That is, evaluating a process using our high-level semantics is equivalent to compiling and loading the process, executing the resulting thread using the virtual machine, and unloading each of the final values.

The above theorem can also be split into two inclusions, where $\supseteq$ corresponds to soundness, and states that the compiled code will always produce a result that is permitted by the semantics. Dually, $\subseteq$ corresponds to completeness, and states that the compiled code can produce every result permitted by the semantics.

In practice, some language implementations are not complete with respect to the semantics for the language by design, because implementing every behaviour that is permitted by the semantics may not be practical. For example, a real implementation may utilize a scheduler that only permits a context switch between threads at particular intervals, rather than after every transition as in our semantics, because doing so would be prohibitively expensive.

9.5.2   Validation of Correctness

Proving the correctness of programs in the presence of concurrency is notoriously difficult. Ultimately we would like to have a formal proof of Theorem 9.1, but to date we have adopted a mechanical approach to validating this result, using randomized testing.

QuickCheck [3] is a system for testing properties of Haskell programs. It is straightforward to implement our semantics, virtual machine, and compiler in Haskell, and to define a property $prop\_Correctness :: \mathsf{Proc} \rightarrow \mathsf{Bool}$ that corresponds to Theorem 9.1. Non-deterministic transitions in our system are implemented as set-valued functions, which are used to build up a tree that captures all possible evaluation sequences, thus ensuring all possible interleavings are accounted for. QuickCheck can then be used to generate a large number of random test processes, and check that the theorem holds in each one of these cases:

```
*Main> quickCheck prop_Correctness
OK, passed 100 tests.
```

Having performed many thousands of tests in this manner, we gain a high degree of confidence in the validity of our compiler correctness theorem. However, as with any testing process, it is important to ensure that all the relevant parts of the program have been exercised during testing.

The Haskell Program Coverage (HPC) toolkit [5] supports just this kind of analysis, enabling us to quickly visualize and identify unexecuted code. Using HPC confirms that testing our compiler correctness result using QuickCheck does indeed give 100% code coverage, in the sense that every part of our implementation is actually executed during the testing process:

module	Top Level Definitions		Alternatives		Expressions	
	%	covered / total	%	covered / total	%	covered / total
module Main	100%	20/20	100%	58/58	100%	531/531
Program Coverage Total	100%	20/20	100%	58/58	100%	531/531

In combination, the use of QuickCheck for automated testing and HPC to confirm complete code coverage, as pioneered by the XMonad project [17], provides high assurance of the correctness of our implementation of transactions.

9.6 CONCLUSION AND FURTHER WORK

In this article we have shown how to implement software transactional memory correctly, for a simplified language based on STM Haskell. Using QuickCheck and HPC, we tested a low-level, log-based implementation of transactions with respect to a high-level, stop-the-world semantics, by means of a compiler and its correctness theorem. This appears to be the first time that the correctness of a compiler for a language with transactions has been mechanically tested.

The lightweight approach provided by QuickCheck and HPC was indispensable in allowing us to experiment with the design of the language and its implementation, and to quickly check any changes. Our basic definitions were refined many times during the development of this work, both as a result of correcting errors, and streamlining the presentation. Ensuring that our changes were sound was simply a matter of rerunning QuickCheck and HPC.

On the other hand, it is important to be aware of the limitations of this approach. First of all, randomized testing does not constitute a formal proof, and the reliability of QuickCheck depends heavily on the quality of the test-case generators. Secondly, achieving 100% code coverage with HPC does not guarantee that all possible interactions between parts of the program have been tested. Nonetheless, we have found the use of these tools to be invaluable in our work.

In terms of expanding on the work presented in this article, we have identified a number of possible directions for further work:

Proof. The most important step now is to consider how our correctness result can be formally proved. The standard approach [20] to compiler correctness for concurrent languages involves translating both the source and target languages into a common process language such as the π-calculus, where compiler correctness then amounts to establishing a bisimulation. We are in the process of developing a new, simpler approach that avoids the introduction of an intermediate language, by establishing a bisimulation directly between the source and target languages.

Generalization. Our simplified language focuses on the essence of implementing transactions. However, it is important to take into account other features in the core language of STM Haskell, namely binding, input / output, exceptions and *retry / orElse*. Previous work by Huch and Kupke [9] describes a full implementation of the STM Haskell semantics given in [7], using existing Concurrent Haskell primitives, but they do not address the correctness of their implementation.

We could go further, and consider the implications of allowing limited effects within transactions, such as the creation of nested transactions or concurrent processes, with a view to investigate a more liberal variant of STM in Haskell.

Mechanization. Just as QuickCheck and HPC were of great benefit for testing our compiler correctness theorem, we may similarly expect to benefit from the use of mechanical support when proving this result. Indeed, in the presence of concurrency it would not be surprising if the complexity of the resulting bisimulation proof necessitated some form of tool support. We are particularly interested in the use of automated proof-checkers such as Epigram [12] or Agda [14], in which the provision of dependent types allows proof to be conducted directly on the program terms, which helps to shift some of the work from the user to the type-checker [13]. Work on proving our correctness theorem in Agda is currently under way.

Other approaches. We have mechanically tested the basic log-based implementation of transactions, but it would also be interesting to consider more sophisticated techniques, such as suspending a transaction that has retried until a relevant part of the heap has changed. Finally, it is also important to explore the relationship to other semantic approaches to transactions, such as the use of functions [19] and processes [1], as well as relevant semantic properties, such as linearizability [8].

Acknowledgements

We would like to thank Nils Anders Danielsson, Peter Hancock, Tim Harris, James McKinna, Henrik Nilsson, Wouter Swierstra, the FP Lab at Nottingham, and the anonymous TFP referees for their useful comments and suggestions.

REFERENCES

[1] L. Acciai, M. Boreale, and S. D. Zilio. A Concurrent Calculus with Atomic Transactions. In *ETAPS Proceedings*. Springer-Verlag, April 2007.

[2] R. Bird. *Introduction to Functional Programming*. Prentice Hall, 2nd edition, 1998.

[3] K. Claessen and J. Hughes. QuickCheck: A Lightweight Tool for Random Testing of Haskell Programs. In *ICFP Proceedings*, 2000.

[4] C. J. Date. *An Introduction to Database Systems.* Addison-Wesley, 6th edition, 1995.

[5] A. Gill and C. Runciman. Haskell Program Coverage. In *Haskell Workshop Proceedings*, September 2007.

[6] T. Harris and K. Fraser. Language Support for Lightweight Transactions. In *OOPSLA Proceedings*, October 2003, ACM.

[7] T. Harris, S. Marlow, S. Peyton Jones, and M. P. Herlihy. Composable Memory Transactions. In *PPoPP Proceedings*, June 2005.

[8] M. P. Herlihy and J. M. Wing. Linearizability: A Correctness Condition for Concurrent Objects. *ACM Transactions on Programming Languages and Systems*, 12(3):463–492, July 1990.

[9] F. Huch and F. Kupke. A High-Level Implementation of Composable Memory Transactions in Concurrent Haskell. In *Implementation and Application of Functional Languages, Lecture Notes in Computer Science*, volume 4015, pages 124–141, 2005.

[10] G. Hutton. *Programming in Haskell.* Cambridge University Press, January 2007.

[11] G. Hutton and J. Wright. What is the Meaning of These Constant Interruptions? *Journal of Functional Programming*, 17(6):777–792, November 2007.

[12] C. McBride and J. McKinna. The View from the Left. *Journal of Functional Programming*, 14(1):69–111, 2004.

[13] J. McKinna and J. Wright. A Type-Correct, Stack-Safe, Provably Correct Expression Compiler in EPIGRAM. To appear in the Journal of Functional Programming, 2009.

[14] U. Norell. *Towards a Practical Programming Language Based on Dependent Type Theory.* PhD thesis, Chalmers University of Technology, September 2007.

[15] S. Peyton Jones. Tackling the Awkward Squad. In *Engineering Theories of Software Construction*, pages 47–96. IOS Press, 2001.

[16] S. Peyton Jones, A. Gordon, and S. Finne. Concurrent Haskell. In *POPL Proceedings*, pages 295–308, 1996.

[17] D. Stewart and S. Janssen. XMonad: A Tiling Window Manager. In *Haskell Workshop*, September 2007.

[18] H. Sutter. The Free Lunch is Over: A Fundamental Turn Toward Concurrency in Software. *Dr Dobb's Journal*, 30(3), March 2005.

[19] W. Swierstra. IOSpec: A Pure Specification of the IO Monad. Available from http://cs.nott.ac.uk/~wss/repos/IOSpec/, 2008.

[20] M. Wand. Compiler Correctness for Parallel Languages. In *Functional Programming Languages and Computer Architecture*, pages 120–134, June 1995.

Chapter 10

Complexity Certification of C++ Template Metaprogramming

Emanuele Covino,[1] Giovanni Pani[1]
Category: Research

Abstract: Any partial recursive function can be computed at compile time, using C++ templates to define primitive recursion, composition, and minimalization. In this paper, we define a restricted language based on C++ templates, and we prove that it characterizes the set of polynomial-time computable functions, that is the set of functions computed by a Turing machine with time bounded by a polynomial.

10.1 INTRODUCTION

Templates were introduced to C++ to support generic programming and code reuse through parameterization. This is done by defining generic functions and objects whose behaviour is customized by means of parameters that must be known at compile time. For example, a generic vector class can be declared in C++ as follows:

```
template <class T, int N> class vector { ... private: T data[N] ... }
```

The class has two parameters: T, the type of the vector's elements, and N, the length of the vector. The command line vector<int,5> instantiates the template by replacing all occurrences of T and N in the definition of vector with int and 5, respectively. Unintentionally, templates can write code generators or perform static computation. This ability is largely described by Czarnecki and Eisenecker

---
[1]Dipartimento di Informatica, Università di Bari, via Orabona 4, Bari, Italy; (covino|pani)@di.uniba.it.

[7], and Veldhuizen [28]: C++ may be regarded as a two-level language, in which types are first-class values, and template instantiation mimics off-line partial evaluation (see Jones [12]). The first example of this behaviour was reported by Unruh [25] [26], where a program that forces the compiler to calculate (at compile time) a list of prime numbers is written. Another example is the following recursive definition of the template which multiplies the values of parameters Y and X:

template <int Y, int X> struct times
        {enum {result=X+times<Y-1,X>::result };};

template <int X> struct times<0,X> {enum {result=0};};

The command line int z=times<3,5>::result produces the value 15. This happens because the operator A::B refers to the symbol B in the scope of A; when reading the command times<3,5>::result (a full instantiation), the compiler recursively instantiates the template with the intermediate values <2,5>, <1,5>, until it eventually hits <0,5>. This final case is handled by the partially specialized template times<0,X>, which returns 0. The whole computation happens at compile time, because C++ compilers include a pattern-matching system to select among templates, and since enumeration values are not l-values (that is, they don't have an address); thus, no static memory is used during the recursive call of a template (see Stroustrup [24], and Vandevoorde and Josuttis [27], Chapter 17).

Following Veldhuizen [29], we say that

> a restricted metalanguage *captures* a property when every restricted program has the property and, conversely, for every unrestricted program with the property, there exists a functionally equivalent restricted program.

In this paper we define a restricted metalanguage by means of C++ templates, and we show that it captures the set of polynomial-time computable functions, that is, functions computable by a Turing machine in which the number of moves — the time complexity — is bounded by a polynomial. This result makes three kinds of contributions. First, since C++ templates can be considered a functional language evaluated at compile time, our result could represent an approach to the certification of upper bounds for time consumption of functional languages. The compilation process certifies the complexity of the program, returning an error when the complexity is not polynomial. Second, this is among the very few characterizations of a complexity class made by means of metaprogramming. Finally (see Section 10.6), our approach copes with a theoretical problem raised by Colson and Fredholm [4] [5] [8] that cannot be solved by means of standard characterizations of complexity classes.

The paper is organized as follows: in Section 10.2 we discuss some related works and we recall some known results that we will use later; in Section 10.3 we define the *Poly-Temp* language; in Section 10.4 we prove that *Poly-Temp* is equivalent to the class of polynomial-time computable functions; in Section 10.5 we show how our language fixes the so-called *minimum problem*; conclusions and further work are in Section 10.6.

10.2   RELATED WORKS

Despite its baroque and perhaps clumsy nature, C++ template metaprogramming has been used in many different ways; we recall here some work related with our result.

10.2.1   C++ Metaprogramming and Functional Programming

The prevailing style of programming in C++ is imperative. However, template metaprogramming may be seen as a functional programming language, where all metaprograms are evaluated at compile time. This is clearly stated by Sheard and Peyton Jones [22]: they extended the purely functional language Haskell with compile-time metaprogramming (i.e. with a template system *à la* C++), with the purpose to support the algorithmic construction of programs at compile-time, program reification, and conditional compilation. Recently, Segura and Torrano [21] used Template Haskell to implement abstract interpretation analysis.

Modern Scheme systems support language extensions based on macros. Hilsdale and Friedman [10] defined a syntactic extension of Scheme, by means of syntax transformers written in a continuation-passing style, and they claimed that they can get Turing-complete computations out of their system. Our restricted metalanguage does a bit more, with respect to the previous approaches. It characterizes a complexity property of a fragment of Turing-computable functions, and this is achieved with a real, industrial template language, one that was constructed for doing real programming and that has had great success. Moreover, we do not define any extension of the language; we simply use the existing C++ type system to perform the computation.

It is not the first time that C++ templates are used in a functional programming way: Läufer [14] recalls how function closure can be modelled in C++ by enclosing a function inside an object such that the local environment is captured by data members of the object; this idiom can be generalized to a type-safe framework of C++ class templates for higher-order functions that supports composition and partial application, showing that object-oriented and functional idioms can coexist productively.

McNamara and Smaragdakis [17] [18] describe a rich library supporting functional programming in C++, in which templates and C++ type inference are used to represent polymorphic functions. Another similar approach is that of Striegnitz [23], that provides a functional language inside C++ by means of templates and operator overloading. Both approaches provide functional-like libraries in run-time, while computations made by means of our metalanguage are performed at compile-time, totally.

10.2.2   Capturing Computational Classes by Metaprogramming

The first attempt to use C++ metaprogramming to capture a significant class of functions has been made by Böhme and Manthey [2]; they presented a way to specify primitive recursion, composition, and μ-recursion by means of C++ templates, proving that *any partial recursive function can be computed at compile-time*, returning an error message that contains the result of the function, written in unary. *Number types* are constructed recursively:

class zero { }

represents zero, and

template<class T> class suc {typedef T pre;}

represents the unary successor of any number type T. For instance, number 2 is represented by suc<suc<zero>>, and T::pre is the predecessor of any number type T which is not zero. A function is represented by a C++ class template, in which the template's arguments are the arguments of the function. In particular, given a two-variable function f defined by primitive recursion from g and h,

$$\begin{cases} f(0,x) = & g(x) \\ f(y+1,x) = & h(y,x,f(y,x)) \end{cases}$$

function type F of f is expressed by templates in Figure 10.1 (where G and H are the class templates which compute g and h).

```
template <class Y, class X> class F
  {typedef typename H<typename Y::pre, X,
                 typename F<typename Y::pre, X>::val >::val val;};

template<class X> class F<zero,X> {typedef typename G<X>::val val; };
```

FIGURE 10.1.   Templates for primitive recursion

Similar templates can be written to represent composition and μ-recursion, and they can be extended to the the general case on n variables; thus, the whole class of partial recursive functions can be expressed by template metaprogramming. For instance, the template times introduced in Section 10.1 can be redefined accordingly, as in Figure 10.2 (enumeration values and typedef typename mechanism are equivalent), where add returns the sum of its two arguments and is defined in the same way.

10.2.3   Capturing Complexity Classes by Metaprogramming

Syntactical characterizations of relevant classes of functions have been introduced by the *Implicit Computational Complexity* approach (see [1], [11], [13], [15], [16], among the others), that studies how restricted functional languages can capture complexity classes; in general, several restricted recursion schemes have been introduced, all sharing the same feature: no explicit bounds (as in Cobham [3])

```
template <class Y, class X> class times
  {typedef typename
  add<X, typename times<typename Y::pre, X>::result>::result result;};

template <class X> class times<zero,X> {typedef zero result};
```

FIGURE 10.2.   Templates for the product between two numbers

are imposed in the definition of functions by recursion. Bellantoni and Cook [1] characterized the class of polytime computable functions (functions computable by a Turing machine in which the number of moves is bounded by a polynomial) as the smallest class of functions B containing some initial functions (constant, projection, binary successors, predecessor, conditional), and closed under *safe* recursion on notation and *safe* composition. The result is obtained by imposing a syntactic restriction on variables used in recursion and composition; they are distinguished in normal or safe variables, and the latter cannot be used as the principal variable of a function defined by recursion. Normal inputs are written to the left, and they are separated from safe inputs by means of a semicolon. A function in B can be written as $f(x_1 \ldots x_n; y_1 \ldots y_n)$; in this case, variables x_i are normal, whereas variables y_j are safe. Formally, The class B is defined as follows:

1. *constant*: 0 (it is 0-ary function).

2. *projection*: $\pi_j^{n,m}(x_1, \ldots, x_n; x_{n+1}, \ldots, x_{n+m}) = x_j$, for $1 \leq j \leq m+n$.

3. *successor*: $s_i(;a) = 2a + i = ai$, for $i \in \{0,1\}$.

4. *predecessor*: $p(;0) = 0$, $p(;ai) = a$.

5. *conditional*: $C(;a,b,c) = b$ if $a \bmod 2 = 0$; $C(;a,b,c) = c$ otherwise.

6. the function f is defined by *safe recursion on notation* from functions g and h_i if
$$\begin{cases} f(0,x;a) = & g(x;a) \\ f(yi,x;a) = & h_i(y,x;a,f(y,x;a)). \end{cases}$$
   for $i \in \{0,1\}$, g and h_i in B; y is called the *principal variable* of the recursion.

7. the function f is defined by *safe composition* from functions h, r and t if
$$f(x;a) = h(r(x;);t(x;a))$$
   for h, r and t in B.

When defining a function $f(yi,x;a)$ by safe recursion from g and h_i, the value $f(y,x;a)$ is in a safe position of h_i; and a function having safe variables cannot be substituted into a normal position of any other function, according to the definition of safe composition; thus, the recursive call $f(y,x;a)$ cannot control the depth of any other inner recursion. Moreover, normal variables can be moved into a safe position, but not viceversa. By constraining recursion and composition variables in such a way, class B is equivalent to the class of polynomial-time computable functions. The same class is captured by the authors in [6], where basic functions, recursion and composition are represented by C++ templates; the normal/safe behaviour is mimicked by besiding a two-value flag to each variable occurring in a template. The values of flags are defined according to the following three rules:

1. flags associated to variables assigned with recursive calls are set to safe;

2. a compiler error must be generated whenever a variable labelled with a safe flag is moved into the principal variable of a recursion; this is done by adding a *negative specialization* (see below);

3. all other flags are set to normal.

The safe version of the previous times template is in Figure 10.3, where add is a template defined according to the same rules. By rule 1, the flag associated with the recursive call of times which occurs into add is set to safe. The instruction times<2, normal, 3, normal>::result instantiates the template add for values 3, normal, times<1, normal, 3, normal>::result, and safe, respectively; thus, the product is recursively evaluated. The last template specialization in Figure 10.3

```
template<int Y, int flagy, int X, int flagx> class times
   {typedef typename add<
       X, flagx,
       typename times<typename Y::pre, flagy, X, flagx>::result, safe
       >::result result};

template<int flagy, int X, int flagx> class times<zero, flagy, X, flagx>
   {typedef zero result };

template<int Y, int X, int flagx> class times<Y, safe, X, flagx>
   {typedef typename times<Y, safe, X, flagx>::result result};
```

FIGURE 10.3.   Safe templates for the product

is called a *negative specialization*, and it is introduced because the programmer is not allowed to assign a recursive call or function to the principal variable of the recursion Y (rule 2); if this happens, the compiler stops by producing the error 'result' is not a member of type 'times<spec-arg's>'. For instance, if the templates representing the exponential function are defined as in Figure 10.4, the instruction exp<2,normal,3,normal>::result instantiates the template times for the values exp<1,normal, 3,normal>::result, safe, 3, and normal, respectively; this matches the third template of times's definition, and a compiler

```
template<int Y, int flagy, int X, int flagx> class exp
  {typedef typename times<
     typename exp<typename Y::pre, flagy, X, flagx>::result, safe,
     X, flagx>::result result};

template<int flagy, int X, int flagx> class exp<0, flagy, X, flagx>
  {public: enum {result=1 };};
```

FIGURE 10.4. **Safe templates for the exponent**

error 'result' is not a member of type 'times<1,safe,3,normal$>$' is produced[2]. An intrinsic limit of these languages is that a number of natural algorithms cannot be defined with the appropriate time complexity (see Section 10.5).

10.3 THE LANGUAGE *POLY-TEMP*

Let normal and safe be notations for constants 0 and 1, respectively (this means, in C++ code, ♯define normal 0 and ♯define safe 1). *Binary number types* represent binary numbers, and are constructed recursively. We use the typedef typename mechanism (following Böhme and Manthey [2]) instead of enumerated values; this allows us to write natural definitions of binary successors and predecessor and, in what follows, of composition and recursion on notation.

Number types representing the constant function 0 and binary successors of any number type T are in Figure 10.5; those representing the predecessor of any number type T are in Figure 10.6. According to these definitions, and using the composition template defined in Figure 10.8, the number 1101 can be represented by suc_1 <suc_0 <suc_1 < suc_1 <zero,safe>,safe>,safe>,safe>. The predecessor of any type number T is represented by pre<T, safe>::result. Moreover, note that each specialization implements a safe/normal behaviour on templates arguments (that is, on functions' variables). For example, it is mandatory in our system that the binary successors and the predecessor operate on safe arguments: thus, we add negative specializations to templates suc_0, suc_1 and pre, forcing them to produce a significant compiler error when the flag associated with the argument T is normal.

---

[2]The general form of negative specialization is

```
template<arg's> class error <spec-arg's>
       {typedef typename error<spec-arg's>::result result}.
```

```
template<> class zero { typedef zero result;}

template<class T> class suc₀ <T, safe> {typedef suc₀ <T, safe> result;};

template<class T> class suc₁ <T, safe> {typedef suc₁ <T, safe> result;};

template<class T> class suc₀ <T, normal>
     {typedef typename suc₀ <T, normal>::result result;}

template<class T> class suc₁ <T, normal>
     {typedef typename suc₁ <X, normal>::result result;}
```

FIGURE 10.5.   Templates for zero and binary successors

```
template<> class pre<zero,safe> {typedef zero result;};

template<class T> class pre<suc₀ <T, safe>, safe> {typedef T result;}

template<class T> class pre<suc₁ <T, safe>, safe> {typedef T result;}

template<class T> class pre<suc₀ <T, safe>, normal>
     {typedef typename pre<suc₀ <T, safe>, normal>::result result;}

template<class T> class pre<suc₁ <T, safe>, normal>
     {typedef typename pre<suc₁ <T, safe>, normal>::result result;}
```

FIGURE 10.6.   Templates for predecessor

Templates for projection and conditional are defined in Figure 10.7. The first three specializations in if definition are introduced to handle the cases in which the first argument C ends with 1 or 0, and the three arguments are safe, simultaneously. The fourth specialization returns an error when at least one of the arguments is normal. The class template F that represents the *safe composition* of templates H, R and T is defined in Figure 10.8. Flags associated with R and T into H have values normal and safe, respectively; this implies that the value of T cannot be used by H as a principal variable of a recursion. The last specialization produces a compiler error if the variable X in R is safe, and R is used into H, simultaneously (X can be assigned with a safe value into R, harmlessly; but this cannot be done when R is substituted into a normal variable of H). This definition matches the definition of safe composition given in section 10.2.3, and can be extended to the general case, when X and A are tuples of values, and R and T are tuples of templates.

template< class X_1, int F_1, ..., class X_n, int F_n > class Π_j
  {typedef X_j result }

template<class C, class X, class Y> class if
  <suc_1 <typename pre<C,safe>::result,safe>, safe, X, safe, Y, safe>
  {typedef Y result;};

template<class C, class X, class Y> class if
  <suc_0 <typename pre<C,safe>::result, safe>, safe, X, safe, Y, safe>
  {typedef X result;};

template<class C, class X, class Y> class if
  <zero, safe, X, safe, Y, safe> {typedef X result;};

template<class C, int F_C, class X, int F_X, class Y, int F_Y > class if
  {typedef typename myif<C, F_C, X, F_X, Y, F_Y >:: result result;};

FIGURE 10.7. **Templates for projections and conditional**

template<template<class X, int F_X > class R,
          class X, int F_X, class A, int F_A > class F
          {typedef typename H< typename R<X, F_X >::result, normal,
                              typename T<X, F_X, A, F_A >::result, safe
                              >::result result };

template<template <class X> class R, class X, int F_X, class A, int F_A >
  class F <R<class X, safe>, X, F_X, A, F_A >
  {typedef typename F<R<class X, safe>, X, F_X, A, F_A >::result result};

FIGURE 10.8. **Templates for safe composition**

In order to define our version of recursive template, we recall that a function
f is defined by *double recursion on notation* from functions g, h and α if

$$\begin{cases} f(x,y) = & g(x,y) & \text{if } x = 0 \text{ or } y = 0 \\ f(xi,yi) = & h(x,y,f(x,\alpha(x,y,f(xi,y))),f(xi,y)) & \text{otherwise} \end{cases}$$

The class template F that represents the *n-ple safe recursion on notations* from
templates H, G_1, ..., G_n and M_1, ..., M_n is defined in Figure 10.9, where each
M_i ($i = 1 \ldots n$) is a sequence of predecessors applied to a binary number type
which is not zero, and where we write template$<X_1, F_1, \ldots, X_n, F_n >$ instead
of template$<$class X_1, int F_1, ..., class X_n, int $F_n >$, for sake of simplicity.
This definition can be extended to the general case, when X is a tuple of variables.

---

template $<Y_1, F_1, \ldots, Y_n, F_n, X, F_X, A, F_A >$ class F
  {typedef typename H$<$typename $M_1 <Y_1 >$::result, F_1,

           ...

        typename $M_n <Y_n >$::result, F_n,
        X, F_X, A, F_A,
        typename F$<$typename $M_1 <Y_1 >$::result, F_1,

              ...

             typename $M_n <Y_n >$::result, F_n,
             X, F_X, A, $F_A >$::result,
     safe$>$::result result};

template $<Y_1, F_1, \ldots, Y_{i-1}, F_{i-1}, F_i, Y_{i+1}, F_{i+1}, \ldots Y_n, F_n, X, F_X, A, F_A >$
class F$<Y_1, F_1, \ldots, Y_{i-1}, F_{i-1}$, zero, $F_i, Y_{i+1}, F_{i+1}, \ldots Y_n, F_n, X, F_X, A, F_A >$
  {typedef typename $G_i <X, F_X, A, F_A >$::result result};

template $<Y_1, F_1, \ldots, Y_{i-1}, F_{i-1}, Y_i, Y_{i+1}, F_{i+1}, \ldots Y_n, F_n, X, F_X, A, F_A >$
class F$<Y_1, F_1, \ldots, Y_{i-1}, F_{i-1}, Y_i$, safe, $Y_{i+1}, F_{i+1}, \ldots Y_n, F_n, X, F_X, A, F_A >$
  {typedef typename
  F$<Y_1,F_1,\ldots,Y_{i-1},F_{i-1},Y_i$,safe, $Y_{i+1},F_{i+1},\ldots Y_n,F_n,X,F_X,A,F_A >$::result result};

FIGURE 10.9.   Templates for *n*-ple safe recursion

We set to safe the value of the flag associated with the recursive call of F
into H (rule 1, Section 10.2.3); we specialize F to compute the base cases of the
recursion; and we introduce the last n templates because the programmer is not
allowed to assign a recursive call to one of the principal variables Y_1, ..., Y_n (rule
2).

We define the language *Poly-Temp* as the smallest class of templates containing zero, suc_0, suc_1, pre, if, Π_j and closed under safe composition and n-ple
safe recursion on notations. The polynomial-time functions will be represented
exactly by those templates in *Poly-Temp* with all normal flags.

10.4 *POLY-TEMP* CAPTURES POLYTIME

In this section, we show that every function computable within polynomial time by a Turing machine can be expressed in *Poly-Temp*; in order to do this, we recall that Polytime is captured by Bellantoni & Cook's class B, and we prove that B is represented by templates in *Poly-Temp* (Theorem 10.1). Conversely, we show that any template in *Poly-Temp* is polynomial-time bounded (Theorem 10.2)

Theorem 10.1. *For each function f in B, there exists a C++ template program* F *such that* F *computes f (at compile time).*

Proof. (By induction on the construction of f.) We denote binary number types with the capital letters X, Y, A, C, and the related flags with F_X, F_Y, F_A, F_C; we write template$<X_1, F_1, \ldots, X_n, F_n>$ instead of the sequence of template arguments (and flags) template$<$class X_1, int $F_1, \ldots,$ class X_n, int $F_n>$.

Base. Templates defined in Section 10.3 (constant, binary successors, predecessor, conditional and projections) trivially compute the basic functions of B.

Step. Case 1. Let f be defined by safe recursion on notations from functions $g(x;a)$, $h_0(y,x;a,s)$ and $h_1(y,x;a,s)$, that are computed, by the inductive hypotheses, by templates G, H_0 and H_1, respectively. f is represented in *Poly-Temp* by the following template F:

```
template <Y, F_Y, X, F_X, A, F_A > class F
{typedef typename if<Y, safe
    typename H_0 <typename pre<Y, safe>::result, F_Y,
            X, F_X, A, F_A,
            typename F<typename pre<Y, safe>::result, F_Y,
                    X, F_X, A, F_A >::result,
            safe>::result, safe
    typename H_1 <typename pre<Y, safe>::result, F_Y,
            X, F_X, A, F_A,
            typename F<typename pre<Y, safe>::result, F_Y,
                    X, F_X, A, F_A >::result,
            safe>::result, safe
                    >::result result };
```

```
template <F_Y, X, F_X, A, F_A > class F<zero, F_Y, X, F_X, A, F_A >
    {typedef typename G<X, F_X, A, F_A >::result result};
```

```
template <Y, X, F_X, A, F_A > class F<Y, safe, X, F_X, A, F_A >
    {typedef typename F<Y, safe, X, F_X, A, F_A >::result result};
```

F is obtained by *n*-ple safe recursion (Figure 10.9), where (1) $n = 1$, (2) M_1 is pre$<$Y,safe$>$::result, and (3) the template H is obtained by safe composition from if, H_0 and H_1.

Case 2. Let f be defined by safe composition from functions $h(p;q)$, $r(x;)$ and $t(x;a)$, that are computed, by the inductive hypotheses, by templates H, R and T, respectively. The template F computing f is defined in Figure 10.8.

To prove that any template in our language is polynomial-time bounded, we find a polynomial-space bound for the length of any template belonging to *Poly-Temp*. For sake of brevity, we omit the flags and we write safe inputs to the right of a semicolon, and normal ones to the left, following the notation used by Bellantoni and Cook. We also use '$(\ldots)$' instead of '$<\ldots>$'. This implies that if a template F is defined by n-ple safe recursion from templates H, G_1, ..., G_n and M_1, ..., M_n, we write

$$
\begin{aligned}
\mathsf{F}(\overline{Y},\overline{X};\overline{A}) &= \mathsf{G}_i(\overline{X};\overline{A}) && \text{if one of } Y_i \text{ is } \mathsf{zero} \\
&= \mathsf{H}(\overline{\mathsf{M}(Y)},\overline{X};\overline{A},\mathsf{F}(\overline{\mathsf{M}(Y)},\overline{X};\overline{A})) && \text{otherwise}
\end{aligned}
$$

where $\overline{\mathsf{M}(Y)}$ stands for $\mathsf{M}_1(Y_1),\ldots,\mathsf{M}_n(Y_n)$, and each M_i is a sequence of predecessors.

Theorem 10.2. *For each template* F *in Poly-Temp, there exists a polynomial* q_F *such that*

$$
|\mathsf{F}(\overline{X};\overline{A})| \le q_\mathsf{F}(|\overline{X}|) + \max_i |A_i|
$$

where $\overline{X}$ *and* $\overline{A}$ *are the variables labelled with* normal *and* safe, *respectively, and* $q_\mathsf{F}(|\overline{X}|)$ *stands for* $q_\mathsf{F}(|X_1|,\ldots,|X_n|)$.

Proof. (By induction on the construction of F.)

Base. If F is a constant, binary successors, predecessor, conditional or projection template, then we have $|\mathsf{F}(\overline{X};\overline{A})| \le 1 + \sum_i |X_i| + \max_i |A_i|$.

Step. Case 1. If F is defined by n-ple safe recursion we have, by induction hypotheses, the polynomials $q_{\mathsf{G}_1},\ldots,q_{\mathsf{G}_n}$ and q_H bounding $\mathsf{G}_1,\ldots,\mathsf{G}_n$ and H, respectively; that is,

$$
\begin{aligned}
&|\mathsf{F}(\ldots,\mathsf{zero},\ldots,\overline{X};\overline{A})| \le q_{G_j}(|\overline{X}|) + \max_i |A_i|, \text{ and} \\
&|\mathsf{F}(\overline{Y},\overline{X};\overline{A})| \le q_H(|\overline{\mathsf{M}(Y)}|,|\overline{X}|) + \max(\max_i |A_i|, |\mathsf{F}(\overline{\mathsf{M}(Y)},\overline{X};\overline{A})|).
\end{aligned}
$$

Define q_F such that

$$
q_\mathsf{F}(|\overline{Y}|,|\overline{X}|) = |\overline{Y}| \cdot q_\mathsf{H}(|\overline{Y}|,|\overline{X}|) + \sum_j q_{\mathsf{G}_j}(|\overline{X}|).
$$

We have that $|\mathsf{F}(\ldots,\mathsf{zero},\ldots,\overline{X};\overline{A})| \le q_\mathsf{F}(|\overline{\mathsf{zero}}|,|\overline{X}|) + \max_i(A_i)$. We also have

$$
\begin{aligned}
|\mathsf{F}(\overline{Y},\overline{X};\overline{A})| &= |\mathsf{H}(\overline{\mathsf{M}(Y)},\overline{X};\overline{A},\mathsf{F}(\overline{\mathsf{M}(Y)},\overline{X};\overline{A}))| \\
&\le q_\mathsf{H}(|\overline{\mathsf{M}(Y)}|,|\overline{X}|) + \max(\max_i |A_i|, |\mathsf{F}(\overline{\mathsf{M}(Y)},\overline{X};\overline{A})|) \\
&\le q_\mathsf{H}(|\overline{\mathsf{M}(Y)}|,|\overline{X}|) + \max(\max_i |A_i|, q_\mathsf{F}(|\overline{\mathsf{M}(Y)}|,|\overline{X}|) + \max_i |A_i|) \\
&\le q_\mathsf{H}(|\overline{\mathsf{M}(Y)}|,|\overline{X}|) + q_\mathsf{F}(|\overline{\mathsf{M}(Y)}|,|\overline{X}|) + \max_i |A_i| \\
&\le q_\mathsf{H}(|\overline{\mathsf{M}(Y)}|,|\overline{X}|) + |\overline{\mathsf{M}(Y)}| \cdot q_\mathsf{H}(|\overline{\mathsf{M}(Y)}|,|\overline{X}|) + \sum_j q_{\mathsf{G}_j}(|\overline{X}|) + \\
&\quad + \max_i |A_i| \\
&\le (|\overline{\mathsf{M}(Y)}| + 1) \cdot q_\mathsf{H}(|\overline{\mathsf{M}(Y)}|,|\overline{X}|) + \sum_j q_{\mathsf{G}_j}(|\overline{X}|) + \max_i |A_i| \\
&\le |\overline{Y}| \cdot q_\mathsf{H}(|\overline{\mathsf{M}(Y)}|,|\overline{X}|) + \sum_j q_{\mathsf{G}_j}(|\overline{X}|) + \max_i |A_i| \\
&\le |\overline{Y}| \cdot q_\mathsf{H}(|\overline{Y}|,|\overline{X}|) + \sum_j q_{\mathsf{G}_j}(|\overline{X}|) + \max_i |A_i| \\
&\le q_\mathsf{F}(|\overline{Y}|,|\overline{X}|) + \max_i |A_i|
\end{aligned}
$$

Case 2. If f is defined by safe composition we have, by induction hypotheses, q_H, q_R and q_T bounding H, R and T, respectively; we have

$$
\begin{aligned}
|\mathsf{F}(\overline{\mathsf{X}};\overline{\mathsf{Y}})| &= |\mathsf{H}(\mathsf{R}(\overline{\mathsf{X}};);\mathsf{T}(\overline{\mathsf{X}};\overline{\mathsf{Y}}))| \\
&\leq q_\mathsf{H}(|\mathsf{R}(\overline{\mathsf{X}};)|) + |\mathsf{T}(\overline{\mathsf{X}};\overline{\mathsf{Y}})| \\
&\leq q_\mathsf{H}(q_\mathsf{R}(\overline{|\mathsf{X}|})) + |\mathsf{T}(\overline{\mathsf{X}};\overline{\mathsf{Y}})| \\
&\leq q_\mathsf{H}(q_\mathsf{R}(\overline{|\mathsf{X}|})) + q_\mathsf{T}(\overline{|\mathsf{X}|}) + \max_j |\mathsf{Y}_j|
\end{aligned}
$$

Let $q_\mathsf{F}(\overline{|\mathsf{X}|},\overline{|\mathsf{Y}|})$ be $q_\mathsf{H}(q_\mathsf{R}(\overline{|\mathsf{X}|})) + q_\mathsf{T}(\overline{|\mathsf{X}|})$. We have the result.

Note that templates in *Poly-Temp* are polynomially time-bounded, when evaluated. Indeed, base templates zero, Π_j, suc$_0$, suc$_1$, if are bounded by the length of their arguments; for composition templates, observe that the composition of two polynomial-time templates is still a polynomial-time template; for recursion templates, it is well known that recursion on notation can be executed in polynomial time if the result of the recursion is polynomially length bounded and the step and base functions are polytime, as in our case.

10.5 A LIMIT TO PRIMITIVE RECURSION

The *intension* of an algorithm, its computational behavior, has to be distinguished from its *extension*, the function computed by the algorithm. Two algorithms can be extensionally equal (that is, they compute the same function) but intentionally distinct (they have different behaviours on the same input). In recent years, the problem of studying functional systems from the intensional point of view has been raised.

In Colson [4] and in Fredholm [9], the problem of representing the natural algorithm for computing the minimum of two numbers has been analyzed. The algorithm is written with the following Herbrand-Gödel equations:

$$min(0,y) = 0; \quad min(s(x),0) = 0; \quad min(s(x),s(y)) = s(min(x,y)).$$

The natural computation time of this algorithm for $min(n,p)$ is $O(min(n,p))$, but it is established [4] that no primitive recursive algorithm (evaluated in call-by-name) can simulate the previous algorithm and, in particular, that there is no primitive recursive program computing the *min* function in time $O(min(n,p))$. The same result was established for call-by-value computation [8].

The following program min'' of type $N \to (N \to N)$ is written in Gödel system T (primitive recursion extended with functional parameters):

$$
\begin{cases}
min''0 = & Z \\
min''(S(x)) = & H(min'').
\end{cases}
$$

where Z (of type $N \to N$) is the constant zero function defined by $Z(z) = 0$ and H (of type $(N \to N) \to (N \to N)$) is defined by:

$$
\begin{cases}
Hu0 = & 0 \\
Hu(S(y)) = & S(uy).
\end{cases}
$$

Such a program evaluated in call-by-name computes the minimum in time proportional to the minimum, since $min''S(x)S(y)$ rewrites to $H(min''x)S(y)$ which is reduced to $S(min''xy)$. But if the same program is evaluated call-by-value, we note that to compute $min''S(x)$, we have to compute $H(min''x)$ in call-by-value, and hence to compute $min''x$ ect.; the computation time is in $\Omega(x)$ i.e. at least proportional to the first input (so the computation time is $O(max(x,y))$). It is shown by Colson and Fredholm [5] that this example is general, that is that in the call-by-value case there is no program in system T (thus, in [1] or [6]) computing the minimum of two natural numbers in time the minimum.

In this paper, we have redefined the recursive template language presented in Covino et al. [6], using an extended form of recursion instead of primitive recursion. We are now able to write the following templates, according to the definitions introduced in section 10.3:

template $<$class X, int F_X, class Y, int $F_Y >$ class min
   {typedef typename
   suc_1 $<$typename min$<$typename pre$<$X,safe$>$::result, F_X,
                        typename pre$<$Y,safe$>$::result, F_Y
                    $>$::result, safe$>$::result result};

template $<$int F_X, class Y, int $F_Y >$ class min$<$zero, F_X, Y, $F_Y >$
   {typedef zero result};

template $<$class X, int F_X, int $F_Y >$ class min$<$X, F_X, zero, $F_Y >$
   {typedef zero result};

template $<$class X, int F_X, class Y, int $F_Y >$ class min$<$X, safe, Y, $F_Y >$
   {typedef typename min$<$X, safe, Y, $F_Y >$::result result};

template $<$class X, int F_X, class Y, int $F_Y >$ class min$<$X, F_X, Y, safe$>$
   {typedef typename min$<$X, F_X, Y, safe$>$::result result};

Template min$<$X,Y$>$, computes the function *min* within time $O(min(x,y))$; thus, our system is able to express more intensions (that is, more algorithms) than previous approaches.

10.6   CONCLUSIONS AND FURTHER WORK

In summary, we have defined a restricted metalanguage by means of C++ templates, and we have shown that it captures at compile time the set of polynomial-time computable functions. As we mentioned in the Introduction, a contribution of this result is that it could provide tools for the formal certification of upper bounds for time consumption of functional languages. Nevertheless, even if our template language is admissible C++, there is no doubt that programming in it should be hard, due to the extra annotations encoded as templates parameters; one may think to hide them into *traits* [20] containing representation of numbers and of related flags; in this way we'd be able to obtain a neater functional language. However, obscure error messages from C++ compilers could inhibit this as a workable approach. The programmer is not able to understand why and where in the program he used a recursive variable in the wrong way; *static interfaces* techniques [19] could help us to provide a clearer meaning to error messages.

Even if this is a clumsy characterization of a complexity class, it is worth noting that the three rules introduced above can produce polynomial time bounded templates when applied to *any* recursive definition, not only to primitive recursion or *n*-ple recursion; it seems that our approach improves the understanding of polynomial-time computation's nature, allowing us to use more expressive recursive schemes.

Finally, our approach copes with the *minimum problem*, a problem that cannot be solved within the standard framework of complexity classes characterization.

Acknowledgements. We wish to express our gratitude to the anonymous reviewers for their helpful comments and suggestions on the draft version of this paper.

REFERENCES

[1] S. Bellantoni and S. Cook. A new recursion-theoretic characterization of the polytime functions. *Computational Complexity*, 2:97–110, 1992.

[2] M. Böhme and B. Manthey. The computational power of compiling C++. *Bull. of the EATCS*, 81:264–270, 2003.

[3] A. Cobham. The intrinsic computational difficulty of functions. *Y. Bar-Hillel (ed), Proceedings of the International Conference on Logic, Methodology, and Philosophy of Science, North-Holland, Amsterdam*, pages 24–30, 1962.

[4] L. Colson. About primitive recursive algorithms. *Theoretical Computer Science*, 83:57–69, 1991.

[5] L. Colson and D. Fredholm. System T, call by value and the minimum problem. *Theoretical Computer Science*, 206:301–315, 1998.

[6] E. Covino, G. Pani, and D. Scrimieri. Compile-time computation of polytime functions. *Journal of Universal Computer Science*, 13.4:468–478, 2007.

[7] K. Czarnecki and U. Eisenecker. *Generative Programming: Methods, Tools, and Applications*. Addison-Wesley, 1999.

[8] D. Fredholm. Intensional aspects of functions definitions, PhD Thesis. *Theoretical Computer Science*, 152:1–66, 1995.

[9] D. Fredholm. Computing minimun with primitive recursion over lists. *Theoretical Computer Science*, 163:269–276, 1996.

[10] E. Hilsdale and D. P. Friedman. Writing macros in continuation-passing style. *Proceedings of the Workshop on Scheme and Functional Programming*, pages 53–59, 2000.

[11] M. Hofmann. Linear type and non-size-increasing polynomial time computation. *Proceedings of the 14th IEEE Symposium on Logic in Computer Science*, pages 464–473, 1999.

[12] N. D. Jones. An introduction to partial evaluation. *ACM Computing Surveys*, 28,3:480–503, 1996.

[13] N. D. Jones. LOGSPACE and PTIME characterized by programming languages. *Theoretical Computer Science*, 228:151–174, 1999.

[14] K. Läufer. A framework for higher-order functions in C++. *Proceedings of the Conf. on Object-Oriented Technologies (COOTS), Monterey, CA*, June 1995.

[15] D. Leivant. Ramified recurrence and computational complexity I: word recurrence and polytime. *P. Clote and J. Remmel (eds), Feasible Mathematics II, Birkauser*, pages 320–343, 1994.

[16] D. Leivant and J.-Y. Marion. Ramified recurrence and computational complexity II: substitution and polyspace. *J. Tiuryn and L. Pocholsky (eds), Computer Science Logic, LNCS*, 933:486–500, 1995.

[17] B. McNamara and Y. Smaragdakis. Functional programming in C++. *Proceedings of the 5th ACM SIGPLAN International Conference on Functional Programming, ICFP '00, New York, NY*, pages 118–129, 2000.

[18] B. McNamara and Y. Smaragdakis. Functional programming with the FC++ library. *J. Funct. Program.*, 14(4):429–472, 2004.

[19] B. McNamara and Y. Smaragdakis. Static interfaces in C++. *First Workshop on C++ Template Programming, Erfurt, Germany*, October 2000.

[20] N. Myers. A new and useful template technique: 'Traits'. *C++ Report*, 7,5:32–35, 1995.

[21] C. Segura and C. Torrano. Using template Haskell for abstract interpretation. *Proceedings of the 15th Workshop on Functional and (Constraint) Logic Programming (WFLP 2006), Electronic Notes in Theoretical Computer Science*, 177:201–217, June 2007.

[22] T. Sheard and S. Peyton Jones. Template meta-programming for Haskell. *Proceedings of the 2002 Haskell Workshop (Haskell '02), Pittsburgh, PA*, pages 1–16, October 2002.

[23] J. Striegnitz. FACT! The functional side of C++. http://www.fz-juelich.de/zam/FACT.

[24] B. Stroustrup. *The C++ programming language*. Addison-Wesley, 1997.

[25] E. Unruh. Prime number computation, ANSI X3J16-94-0075/ISO WG21-462.

[26] E. Unruh. Template Metaprogrammierung, http://www.erwin-unruh.de/meta.html, 2002.

[27] D. Vandevoorde and N. M. Josuttis. *C++ templates: the complete guide*. Addison-Wesley, 2003.

[28] T. Veldhuizen. C++ templates as partial evaluation. *Proceedings of the 1999 ACM SIGPLAN Symposium on Partial Evaluation and Semantic-Based Program Manipulation*, ACM Press:13–18, 1999.

[29] T. Veldhuizen. Tradeoffs in metaprogramming. *Proceedings of the 2006 ACM SIGPLAN Symposium on Partial Evaluation and Semantic-Based Program Manipulation*, ACM Press:150–159, 2006.

Chapter 11

Lightweight Invariants with Full Dependent Types

Edwin Brady,[1] Christoph Herrmann,[1] Kevin Hammond[1]
Category: Position Paper

Abstract: Dependent types allow a programmer to express invariant properties of functions, such as the relationship between the input and output lengths of a list. Several 'lightweight' approaches to dependent types have been proposed for existing systems, such as Haskell's Generalized Algebraic Data Types or Type Families. Such approaches are lightweight in the sense that they require minimal modifications to existing systems. However, while these extensions are apparently simple, we find that we often run into limitations fairly quickly. In this paper we will explore these limitations, and show that a full dependent type system allows more straightforward implementation of simple invariants without restricting expressivity.

11.1 INTRODUCTION

Dependent types, which allow types to be predicated on *values*, allow us to specify in advance both precisely what a program is intended to do and the invariants that it is expected to maintain. Dependent types have become a very active area of research, and various 'lightweight' approaches have been proposed that either extend existing functional programming languages, e.g. GADTs in Haskell [17, 10] or Ωmega [19], interact with a theorem prover like Concoqtion [9], or that exploit existing language features in creative ways, e.g. [12, 13].

While these approaches are indeed lightweight in the sense that they require little or no change to existing production programming languages, as the complexity of functions increases, so it becomes more difficult to explain the required program invariants using these lightweight systems. Even an apparently simple

---

[1] School of Computer Science, University of St Andrews, St Andrews, Scotland;
Phone: +44 1334-461629; Email: {eb,ch,kh}@cs.st-andrews.ac.uk.

example, partitioning a list for sorting, in a way akin to the quicksort divide-and-conquer schema, can be difficult to encode since it requires reasoning about the behaviour of addition and defining a strong link between the representation of the list and the partitions. While these lightweight approaches are certainly powerful, they require a deep understanding of the underlying type system on the part of the programmer in order to explain the necessary reasoning for such programs.

We believe that the addition of such advanced features to functional languages is a big step forward. However, in this paper we will argue that *lightweight* should mean that the programmer has to do *as little work as possible* to demonstrate that a program satisfies the required invariants. The full dependently typed approach gives flexibility to allow the *programmer* to decide on the level of safety that is required, rather than be limited by what is expressible within the type system.

11.2 THE IDRIS LANGUAGE

We introduce IDRIS, an experimental functional language with full dependent types.[2] IDRIS is similar to EPIGRAM [14] or AGDA [16], in that it supports dependent pattern matching. It is built on top of the IVOR [2] theorem proving library, and is a pure functional language with a syntax similar to Haskell with GADTs. The purpose of the language is to provide a platform for practical programming with dependent types. We have used our own implementation, rather than an existing tool, as this gives complete freedom to experiment with abstractions and language features beyond the type system, such as I/O and concurrency. Additionally, although unrelated to the work we present in this paper, the core language of IDRIS is intended as an important step towards a fully dependently typed implementation of Hume [11].

11.3 THE BASIC QUICKSORT ALGORITHM

We will take a functional variant of the standard *quicksort* sorting algorithm as a running example to illustrate our argument. For this example, several different invariants may be desirable, depending on context:

1. sorting must return a list of the same element type as the input;[3]

2. sorting must be size preserving;

3. sorting must return a permutation of the original list; and

4. sorting must return an ordered permutation of the original list.

In this paper, we will explore which of these invariants may be specified and guaranteed both in Haskell, with various extensions, and in IDRIS. We will use the same functional variant of *quicksort*, named `qsort` throughout the paper. It

---

[2]http://www.cs.st-and.ac.uk/%7Eb/Idris/

[3]This is, of course, easily enforced using conventional type checking.

first partitions the argument list around the pivot into two sets, values that are less than the pivot, and values that are greater than or equal to the pivot, then sorts each set, and finally appends the two sorted partitions to form the result of the sort. The IDRIS implementation is written in a similar style to the expected Haskell version, although the current implementation lacks type classes or syntactic sugar for lists. Lists can be declared using Haskell-style notation:

```
data List a = Nil | Cons a (List a);
```

`qsort` and `partition` can then be defined as follows:

```
qsort :: (a->a->Bool) -> List a -> List a;
qsort lt Nil = Nil;
qsort lt (Cons x xs)
 = let part = partition lt x xs
    in append (qsort lt (fst part))
              (Cons x (qsort lt (snd part)));

partition :: (a->a->Bool) -> a -> List a -> (List a, List a);
partition lt pivot Nil = (Nil, Nil);
partition lt pivot (Cons x xs)
 = let prec = partition lt pivot xs
    in if (lt x pivot) then (Cons x (fst prec), snd prec)
                       else (fst prec, Cons x (snd prec));
```

In principle, any valid Haskell 98 program can be implemented in IDRIS, except that IDRIS requires top-level type declarations on all but nullary functions. This is because type inference for dependent types is, in general, undecidable.

11.4 SIZE PRESERVATION

An important abstract program property concerns the sizes of data structures. Apart from the obvious contribution to program verification this property could also be exploited, for example, by a compiler to improve program performance by using static instead of dynamic memory allocation. Sorting functions deliver a data structure which has the same size as the input — in this section, we will attempt to implement a size-preserving list partition function, as would be used to implement a functional variant of quicksort, named `qsort`, using GADTs and type families in Haskell and a full dependently typed approach in IDRIS.

The GADT Approach

GADTs [17, 10, 19] are a generalization of Haskell algebraic data types which allow more flexible parameterization of data constructor types. The following example defines two type constructors `Z` (zero) and `S` (successor) to represent natural numbers in the type language; plus a GADT to define a corresponding type of natural numbers `Nat` which reflects the value of data objects in the type and uses the data constructors `Zero` and `Succ`:

```
data Z
data S n

data Nat :: * -> * where
   Zero :: Nat Z
   Succ :: Nat n -> Nat (S n)
```

Now it is possible to enforce compile-time restrictions on natural numbers when they are used as function arguments and to automatically perform compile-time calculations on such numbers, for example.

In order to define type-level addition by induction on the type, we use a type class so that there is a single name (`plus`) which works for all natural numbers. Note that 0 (`Zero`) and 1 (`Succ Zero`) now have different types.

```
class Plus m n s | m n -> s where
   plus :: Nat m -> Nat n -> Nat s
```

The extended type-class definition generalizes the type of the function with the parameters m, n and s and contains a functional dependency m n -> s telling the compiler that s depends on (i.e, is calculated from) m and n.

We express the definition of `Plus` inductively with two type-class instances, depending on whether the first argument is Z or S m. In the second instance definition the context `Plus a b c => Plus (S a) b (S c)` tells the compiler about the logic of recursion within the type itself, i.e. it exposes that induction is performed on the first argument. Note that type-class instances have to be stated as predicates, so the third type argument of `Plus` here corresponds to the result of the function `plus`.

```
instance Plus Z b b where
   plus Zero y = y

instance Plus a b c => Plus (S a) b (S c) where
   plus (Succ x) y = Succ (plus x y)
```

Instead of lists we now use vectors which carry their length as a type parameter. We simply state that the length increases by one with every new element.

```
data Vect :: * -> * -> * where
   Nil  :: Vect a Z
   Cons :: a -> Vect a k -> Vect a (S k)
```

In the `qsort` example we have to maintain an invariant stating that the sum of the length of both partitions and the pivot element equals the length of the original vector. Since the decision about which part an element will be assigned to, and thus the absolute size of each part, is not known at compile time, in order to preserve the information about the sum of the sizes, we have to calculate both partitions in a single function. We do this by defining a new GADT for partitions which carries this information as a type context (`Plus l r x`).

```
data Partition :: * -> * -> * where
   MkPart :: Plus l r x =>
              Vect a l -> Vect a r -> Partition a x
```

During partitioning, we have to insert an element either into the left part of the partition or into the right part. Insertion into the left part of the partition is simple:

```
mkPartL :: Plus l r x =>
             a -> Vect a l -> Vect a r -> Partition a (S x)
mkPartL x left right = MkPart (Cons x left) right
```

This typechecks because the instance of the `Plus` type class is defined by analysis of its first argument, and we insert the item into the first argument of the partition. However, insertion into the right part causes a problem, because the `Cons` on the right list puts the `S` symbol in the wrong place:

```
mkPartR :: Plus l r x =>
             a -> Vect a l -> Vect a r -> Partition a (S x)
mkPartR x left right = MkPart left (Cons x right)
```

The obvious way to resolve this is to add another instance of the type class:

```
instance Plus a b c => Plus a (S b) (S c) where
   plus x (Succ y) = Succ (plus x y)
```

While this is clearly a reasonable statement, it yields overlapping instances of the type class. Although compiler flags exist which circumvent the problem, this dirty hack would eventually lead to a run-time error — the type classes must be resolved at some point, and the run-time system does not have enough information to do this. This is not static safety!

What we need is a way to teach the type checker a weak form of commutativity for `plus`. However, even if we only want to *pretend* that we are always increasing the first argument of `plus` (even though in the definition of `mkPartR`, we actually increase the second argument), we are unable do this here. It turns out that syntactic equality on type parameters is not enough to allow us to write such functions — although we might expect to be able to write this function with GADTs, it turns out we need to extend the Haskell type system further to allow it.

Type Families

Type families are an experimental feature in Haskell which allow the definition of functions over types [18]. This goes beyond the application of type constructors, as with GADTs. In particular, these type functions can be used by the Haskell type checker to normalize type expressions to a semantically equivalent syntactic structure. Using type families, we can define a new version of the quicksort algorithm. The difference with the previous GADT-based example is that addition can now be defined in the type language itself, and we can define our own addition symbol, `:+`, for use within type expressions. The `type family` syntax allows us to define the : + symbol and its arity, and the `type instance` syntax allows us to specify the corresponding normalization rules, i.e. how the type checker should proceed with eliminating the : + symbol.

```
type family n :+ m
type instance Z       :+ m = m
type instance (S n) :+ m = S (n :+ m)
```

We can now use the type operator : + to specify the length of the partition:

```
data Partition :: * -> * -> * where
   MkPart :: Vect a l -> Vect a r -> Partition a (l :+ r)
```

As in our previous attempt, appending two vectors and extending the left part is straightforward, since the `mkPartL` function recurses on its first argument.

```
app :: Vect a m -> Vect a n -> Vect a (m :+ n)
app Nil ys = ys
app (Cons x xs) ys = Cons x (app xs ys)

mkPartL :: a -> Vect a l -> Vect a r ->
           Partition a (S (l :+ r))
mkPartL x left right = MkPart (Cons x left) right
```

Before defining `mkPartR` and the partitioning function, we need to define a set of lemmas that express semantic equalities for types. The `rewrite` function converts the type of its first argument using the appropriate equality proof term for the equality as its second argument. We omit the definitions for space reasons, but give the types below:

```
data EQ2 :: * -> * -> * -> * -> * where
   EQ2 :: EQ2 x y a a

plus_Z   :: EQ2 n m (n :+ Z)   (n)
plus_nSm :: EQ2 n m (n :+ S m) (S n :+ m)
rewrite  :: c a -> EQ2 x y a a' -> c a'
```

Insertion into the right part of the partition requires a rewrite on the type expression so that we can normalize the first argument of : +.

```
mkPartR :: forall a l r. a -> Vect a l -> Vect a r ->
           Partition a (S (l :+ r))
mkPartR x left right =
  MkPart left (Cons x right)
  `rewrite` (plus_nSm :: EQ2 l r (l :+ S r) (S l :+ r))
```

Function `partInsert` inserts one element, `insertN` a vector of elements and `partition` initializes the `Partition` data type.

```
partInsert :: Ord a => a -> a -> Partition a n ->
              Partition a (S n)
partInsert pivot val (MkPart left right)
  | val < pivot = mkPartL val left right
  | otherwise   = mkPartR val left right

insertN :: Ord a => Vect a m -> a -> Partition a n ->
           Partition a (m :+ n)
insertN Nil _ part = part
insertN (Cons x xs) pivot part
       = let part' = insertN xs pivot part
         in partInsert pivot x part'

partition :: Ord a => Vect a m -> a -> Partition a m
partition vec pivot
      = (insertN vec pivot (MkPart Nil Nil))
        `rewrite` (plus_Z :: EQ2 m n (m :+ Z) m)
```

Putting it all together, the qsort function is defined as follows:

```
qsort :: Ord a => Vect a m -> Vect a m
qsort Nil = Nil
qsort (Cons x xs) =
 case partition xs x of
  MkPart (l::Vect a ll) (r::Vect a rl)
      -> (app (qsort l) (Cons x (qsort r)))
             `rewrite` (plus_nSm
                :: EQ2 ll rl (ll :+ S rl) (S ll :+ rl))
```

Full Dependent Types Approach

We have already seen some simple types in IDRIS declared using the Haskell-style syntax, e.g. unary natural numbers:

```
data Nat = Z | S Nat;
```

Dependent types are declared using GADT-style syntax, using # as the type of types.[4] The indices are not restricted to being types, however — unlike with GADTs, we can use *data* constructors such Z and S. e.g. Vectors:

```
data Vect : # -> Nat -> # where
   nil  : Vect a Z
 | cons : a -> (Vect a k) -> (Vect a (S k));
```

For the type of Partition, we can use an ordinary function plus to give the length of the pair of vectors. It is convenient to be able to lift plus directly into the type, so giving a strong and machine checkable link between partitions, vectors and their sizes:

---

[4]The reason for choosing # instead of the more conventional $\star$ is to avoid syntactic conflict with the multiplication operator!

```
data Partition : # -> Nat -> # where
   mkPartition : (left:Vect a l) ->
                 (right:Vect a r) ->
                 (Partition a (plus l r));
```

In adding a value to a partition, we need to decide whether the value goes in the
left or right of the partition, depending on a pivot value. We encounter the same
difficulties as with the GADT and type family approaches in that the type of the
resulting partition will also vary according to whether we insert into the left or
right part of the partition:

- Insertion on the left,
  ```
  mkPartition (cons x xs) ys : Partition (plus (S l) r)
  ```

- Insertion on the right,
  ```
  mkPartition xs (cons x ys) : Partition (plus l (S r))
  ```

To make it easy to write a well-typed partition function, it is therefore necessary
to be able to explain to the typechecker that these are really the same length. We
achieve this by using a type rewriting function and a lemma to show that adding a
successor to the second argument is equivalent to adding a successor to the first.
These are provided by the standard library:

```
plus_nSm : ((plus n (S m)) = (plus (S n) m)));
rewrite  : {A:B->#} -> (A m) -> (m = n) -> (A n);
```

The {} syntax indicates that the first argument to `rewrite` can be omitted, since
it can be inferred by the typechecker. We can then write a function which inserts a
value into the right of a partition, but which rewrites the type so that it is the same
as if it were inserted into the left:

```
mkPartitionR : a -> (Vect a l) -> (Vect a r) ->
            (Partition a (plus (S l) r));
mkPartitionR x left right
    = rewrite (mkPartition left (cons x right))
              plus_nSm;
```

Now that insertion into the left and right have the same type, it is simple to write
an insertion function based on a pivot and a comparison function:

```
partInsert: (lt:a->a->Bool) -> (pivot:a) -> (val:a) ->
            (p:Partition a n) -> (Partition a (S n));
partInsert lt pivot val (mkPartition left right)
    = if lt val pivot
         then mkPartition (Cons val left) right
         else (mkPartitionR val left right);
```

Length-preserving partitioning then simply iterates over a vector, inserting each
element into the partition.

```
partition : (lt:a->a->Bool)->(pivot:a)->
            (xs:Vect a n)->(Partition a n);
partition lt pivot Nil = mkPartition Nil Nil;
partition lt pivot (Cons x xs)
    = partInsert lt pivot x (partition lt pivot xs);
```

To complete a `qsort` program, we will need to glue two partitions back together, along with their pivot.

```
qsort : (lt:a->a->Bool)->(Vect a n)->(Vect a n);
qsort lt Nil = Nil;
qsort lt (Cons x xs) = glue lt x (partition lt x xs);
```

The `glue` function takes a partition and the pivot, and reassembles them into a list. Again, because we insert the pivot at the start of the right list, we will need to rewrite the type, since `plus` is defined by recursion on its first argument:

```
glue : (lt:a->a->Bool)->
       a -> (Partition a n) -> (Vect a (S n));
glue lt val (mkPartition left right)
  = let lsort = qsort lt left,
        rsort = qsort lt right in
    rewrite (append lsort (Cons val rsort)) plus_nSm;
```

The complete IDRIS program we have outlined here, including test cases, is available online.[5] The approach we have taken here is similar to that for a conventional functional `qsort`. We need to define an intermediate type, `Partition`, to ensure the total length of the partition is the same as the length of the vector being partitioned, but otherwise we can program in the usual functional style.

Discussion

We initially attempted to use GADTs, a small extension to Haskell, to represent the relatively simple invariant that sorting a list preserves size. However, this approach ran into difficulties since there is no obvious way to do verifiable equational reasoning with GADTs. A further extension to Haskell, type families, is sufficient to verify this invariant. The full dependent type version in IDRIS is defined in a similar way to the type family version, indexing lists by their length and rewriting the type to insert into the right of a partition. The key conceptual difference is that with full dependent types, data may appear in a type or a value, whereas the Haskell version with type families maintains a strict separation between types and values.

Size, represented by natural numbers, is a common invariant on many data structures and it is therefore important to be able to represent and manipulate sizes effectively. Using sizes we can, for example, represent the depth of a tree structure or guarantee that a tree is balanced. However, we would sometimes

---

[5]http://www-fp.cs.st-and.ac.uk/%7Eeb/TFP08/partition.idr.

like to represent more sophisticated invariants. In the case of `qsort`, a fully guaranteed version would not only maintain the length invariant, but also that the output is ordered and is a permutation of the input.

11.5 PERMUTATIONS

To show the flexibility of our fully dependently typed approach, let us consider how we can represent list permutations. Informally, an empty list is a permutation of an empty list. A non-empty list is a permutation of another list, if its tail is a permutation of that other list with its head removed. We revert to standard polymorphic lists, without the size index, since lists which are permutations of each other are naturally the same size:

```
data List a = Nil | Cons a (List a);
```

We need a predicate to represent list membership:

```
data Elem : A -> (List A) -> # where
   now    : {x:A} -> {xs:List A} -> (Elem x (Cons x xs))
 | later : {x:A} -> {ys:List A} -> {y:A} ->
           (Elem x ys) -> (Elem x (Cons y ys));
```

We can use this predicate to remove an element from a list safely. The predicate is effectively an index into the list, with `now` indicating the element is at index zero, and `later` x indicating the element is at index $x+1$. Removing an element is then by induction over the index. We also match on the (implicit) argument `xs`:

```
remove : {x:A} -> {xs:List A} -> (Elem x xs) -> (List A);
remove {xs=(Cons x ys)} now = ys;
remove {xs=(Cons x (Cons y ys))} (later p)
       = Cons x (remove p);
```

We can then represent permutations as a predicate on two lists, so making our informal description above precise:

```
data Perm : (List A) -> (List A) -> # where
   PNil  : Perm {A} Nil Nil
 | PCons : {x:A} -> {xs:List A} -> {xs':List A} ->
           (e:Elem x xs') -> (Perm xs (remove e)) ->
           (Perm (Cons x xs) xs');
```

Full dependent types allow us to write such predicates in terms of the actual data structures, and index them in terms of arbitrary functions such as `remove`.

In our previous definition, partitions were indexed over their total length. We now need to ensure that in building the partition we maintain knowledge about how the permutations are built. In order to achieve this, we carry the left and right lists in the partition *in the type*, and require a proof that inserting an element into the partition maintains the permutation.

```
data Partition : (l:List A) -> (r:List A) ->
                 (xs:List A) -> # where
   nilPart : Partition Nil Nil Nil
 | lCons   : {x:A} -> {xs,ys,zs:List A} ->
             (Partition xs ys zs) ->
             (Perm (Cons x (app xs ys)) (Cons x zs)) ->
             (Partition (Cons x xs) ys (Cons x zs))
 | rCons   : {x:A} -> {xs,ys,zs:List A} ->
             (Partition xs ys zs) ->
             (Perm (app xs (Cons x ys)) (Cons x zs)) ->
             (Partition xs (Cons x ys) (Cons x zs));
```

This is indexed over both sublists and the result, which allows us to maintain all the information we need throughout the structure. However, we cannot know in advance what the sublists will be given the original list, so we wrap this in a less informative type indexed only over the original list:

```
data Part : (xs:List A) -> # where
   mkPart : {ls,rs,xs:List A} -> (Partition ls rs xs) ->
            (Part xs);
```

Then our partition function has the following type, expressing that the partition arises from the input list. The types of Part and Permutation ensure that we will be able to extract a proof that the resulting list is a permutation of the original.

```
partition : (lt:a->a->Bool) -> (pivot:a) ->
            (xs:List a) -> (Part xs);
```

We can always extract a permutation proof from a partition:

```
getPartPerm : {xs,ys,zs:List A} ->
    (Partition xs ys zs) -> (Perm (app xs ys) zs);
getPartPerm nilPart = PNil;
getPartPerm (lCons part perm) = perm;
getPartPerm (rCons part perm) = perm;
```

Building a partition requires an explanation of what to do when inserting into the left and right parts of the partition, as before. We write a helper function rConsP so that insertion into the left and right parts of a partition have the same type:

```
rConsP : {xs,ys,zs:List A} ->
         (Perm (app xs ys) zs) ->
         (Perm (app xs (Cons x ys)) (Cons x zs));
rConsP {xs=Nil} p = PCons now p;
rConsP {xs=Cons w ws} {ys} {zs=Cons z' zs} (PCons e p)
     = PCons (later e) (consRPerm p);
```

We use rConsP to show that adding an element to the right list and then appending maintains a permutation with adding an element to the left of the whole list. This allows us to write partInsert:

```
partInsert : {xs:List a} ->
             (lt:a->a->Bool) -> (pivot:a) -> (x:a) ->
             (p:Part xs) -> (Part (Cons x xs));
partInsert lt pivot val (mkPart p)
   = if lt val pivot
       then (mkPart (lCons p (PCons now (getPartPerm p))))
     else (mkPart (rCons p (rConsP (getPartPerm p))));
```

The partitioning function itself has a very similar definition to the size preserving version (only the `Nil` case and the type differ):

```
partition : (lt:a->a->Bool)->(pivot:a)->
            (xs:List a)->(Part xs);
partition lt pivot Nil = mkPart nilPart;
partition lt pivot (Cons x xs)
   = partInsert lt pivot x (partition lt pivot xs);
```

This definition (and the corresponding definition of `glue` which we omit here) requires a certain amount of reasoning about the construction of permutations. This is to be expected — the more static information we want to express, the more we have to explain to the typechecker.

Comparison with GADTs and Type Families

The above definition gives even more static guarantees — not only is it size preserving, but it also guarantees that the output is a permutation of the input. We could go further and guarantee that the output is ordered, if required and we were prepared to do the required reasoning. Although it is conceivable that such proofs could also be done using a combination of GADTs, type families and type classes, some technical problems would need to be overcome first:

- Lists are polymorphic, and we are using lists both as data *and* as an index to partitions. When we restricted the invariant to list length, the length was treated independently of the data. Permutations, however, are directly linked to the real, polymorphic data in a fundamental way. It is not clear how to represent this conveniently if a strict separation between types and values is to be maintained.

- Although we have used it in the index to a type, the `remove` function operates on data. It may be possible to write this function with type families, but not generically for use on types and data.

While we do not make the claim that a permutation preserving quicksort is *impossible* in (extended) Haskell, we do believe that once invariants become sufficiently complex, they also become too difficult to express easily. The difficulty is in expressing properties of types which are themselves parametrized (e.g. the permutation property of lists) and, it is not at all clear how to express types which themselves depend on dependent types. There are fairly simple examples of such types, e.g. in the implementation of an interpreter, an environment of well-typed, well-scoped values could depend on a sized list of types as described in [3].

11.6 RELATED WORK

In this paper we have used a new experimental dependently typed language, IDRIS, which is closely related to EPIGRAM [14, 7] and AGDA [16]. In IDRIS, we have the full flexibility of dependent types, but also allow conventional polymorphic functional programming.

An advantage of dependent types is that, in linking a data type's representation directly with its meaning, we can provide strong static guarantees about the underlying data. In some of our own previous work [4, 6] we have used this to show properties of complex functions in a theorem proving environment [2]. We do not always want or need total correctness, however, and checking of 'lightweight' invariants in a partial language may be sufficient in many cases. A number of recent approaches to lightweight static invariant checking have been based on small extensions to existing languages [17, 10] or use of existing features [13, 12]. As we have seen, such approaches are, however, usually limited in their expressivity. Recent work by Schrijvers et al. [18] describes an extension of Haskell with restricted type-level functions which improves the level of expressivity, but still requires separate implementations at the type and value levels. While we can express the partition example with this extension, we anticipate difficulties encoding properties of parametrized types such as Lists.

The language Ωmega [20] combines reduction of type-level expressions and unification in a narrowing process [19] in which bindings of variables enable type terms to reduce to a normal form. It leaves termination issues as the responsibility of the programmer. On the other hand, type terms in Haskell are not simplified in the presence of free type variables, leading to a type error when $x:+Z$ is found where x is expected.

In Concoqtion [9], checking dependent types relies on an application of the proof checker Coq [8] to type level constraints which are integrated in the MetaO-Caml language [22].

Both Ωmega and Concoqtion have independent languages of program expressions and type terms which forces the programmer to repeat parts from the expression level at the type level. As types become more complex, and especially when types depend themselves on parametrized or dependent types (such as our list permutation example), this becomes increasingly difficult.

11.7 DISCUSSION

The direction being taken in the development of GHC is encouraging, especially the recent experimental addition of type families. The introduction and development of GADTs, and more recently type families, allows increasing expressivity in the type system, which, in turn, allows several invariants to be verified by the typechecker. In the short term, this is an effective way of introducing some of the benefits of dependent types to functional programmers, by incorporating them into a familiar system with familiar (and extensive) libraries.

However, as demonstrated by the example of list partitioning, this general methodology has clear limits. Using only GADTs, we run into difficulties manipulating even simple equations. Type families improve the situation, but as the invariants become more complex (e.g. with list permutations) even these present some difficulties which do not arise in a full dependently typed system. However lightweight or small the invariant we wish to keep may seem at first, there is always a possibility that we may run into some limitation which requires a more expressive type system, or a *property* which can be represented more easily in a more expressive type system. For this reason, we believe that in the longer term, new languages with full dependent types offer a more promising approach to writing programs which satisfy machine checkable invariants. Nevertheless, several challenges remain if dependently typed programming is to continue to develop as a trend in functional programming. In particular, we must address software engineering considerations such as modularity and code reuse:

Modularity: As we have presented it, the proofs that invariants are maintained are developed alongside the program. As far as possible, we would prefer proof obligations to be solved separately. Additionally, a programmer using a library implemented with dependent types may prefer to use a simply typed interface. The first problem is more serious; while it is always possible to expose a simpler interface which hides the details of the invariants, we would like any proof obligations which arise to be solved separately, and ideally automatically. Sozeau's Russell system [21] is a promising line of research in this direction.

Reuse: We have seen by implementing quicksort with several different invariants that decorating a data type with different properties can require significant rewriting of code even in situations where the program remains the same, and the reasons for correctness remain the same. This is related to some extent to modularity, in that we would like to write one program and have the language generate (and solve, if possible) appropriate proof obligations for different invariants.

Our research to date has focussed on solving *programming* problems [3, 4, 6], and the benefits of full dependent types have been argued elsewhere, e.g. [1]. We believe that *full* dependent types give the most flexibility in that we can still write simply typed programs or use a GADT based approach. Also, although we have not considered it in this paper, we can write post-hoc proofs of desired properties, in a similar way to an external theorem prover, e.g. Sparkle [15]. However it is clear that further research is necessary to demonstrate that full dependent types can be applied to larger scale *software engineering* problems.

There are several theoretical details we have not yet explored or only briefly touched on in our comparison of the full dependent type approach with the various Haskell extensions. For example, we have not mentioned decidability of type checking, termination analysis or the presence of side effects in types. Such theoretical considerations will, ultimately, be important in an industrial-strength dependently typed programming language. Our goal with IDRIS, however, is to explore the practical possibilities of programming with full dependent types. We are already beginning to explore domain-specific language implementation for concurrency [5], and we are integrating the type system of IDRIS into Hume [11] in order to investigate functional correctness of embedded systems.

11.8 CONCLUSION

We have taken a relatively simple and well-known program, *quicksort*, and considered how to represent some invariants; firstly length preservation, and secondly that the output is a permutation of the input. We consider these to be *lightweight* invariants in the sense that they do not guarantee *total* correctness of the implementation, but they do *verify* some important aspects. With full dependent types, we can protect against several potential programming errors in this way, with small programmer overhead — there are two places in the size-preserving example where a `rewrite` must be made. If the programmer has sufficient understanding of the function, such rewrites are easy to define.

In contrast, implementing the algorithm with GADTs has proved difficult, and to finish the implementation in Haskell required an additional extension, type families. The implementation required not only understanding of the algorithm, but also details of an increasingly complex type system. We believe that if dependent types are to be taken seriously in practical programming, and if programmers are to be encouraged to increase confidence in program correctness via types, there *must* be more support for reasoning about invariants. While there are obvious short-term advantages of adding less powerful type dependency to existing systems (namely, the existing code base and extensive library support Haskell offers), we believe that in the long term full dependent types will allow the programmer the greatest flexibility, e.g. to write the program with minimal invariant checking (the output merely has the same element type as the input), lightweight checking (the output shares some property with the input such as length or permutation) or, potentially, a full specification (the output must also be ordered).

ACKNOWLEDGEMENTS

We thank James Caldwell and James McKinna, and the anonymous reviewers for their valuable comments. This work is generously supported by EPSRC grant EP/C001346/1 and by EU Framework VI Grant IST-2004-510255.

REFERENCES

[1] Thorsten Altenkirch, Conor McBride, and James McKinna. Why dependent types matter. http://www.cs.nott.ac.uk/~txa/publ/ydtm.pdf, Manuscript, April 2005.

[2] Edwin Brady. Ivor, a proof engine. In *Proc. Implementation of Functional Languages (IFL 2006)*, volume 4449 of *LNCS*. Springer, 2007.

[3] Edwin Brady and Kevin Hammond. A Verified Staged Interpreter is a Verified Compiler. In *Proc. Conf. Generative Programming and Component Engineering (GPCE '06), Portland, Oregon*, ACM, 2006.

[4] Edwin Brady and Kevin Hammond. A dependently typed framework for static analysis of program execution costs. In *Proc. Implementation of Functional Languages (IFL 2005)*, volume 4015. Springer, 2006.

[5] Edwin Brady and Kevin Hammond. Correct by construction concurrency, 2008. In Preparation.

[6] Edwin Brady, James McKinna, and Kevin Hammond. Constructing Correct Circuits: Verification of Functional Aspects of Hardware Specifications with Dependent Types. In *Trends in Functional Programming*. Intellect, 2007.

[7] James Chapman, Thorsten Altenkirch, and Conor McBride. Epigram reloaded: a standalone typechecker for ETT. In *Trends in Functional Programming*. Intellect, 2005.

[8] Coq Development Team. The Coq proof assistant — reference manual. http://coq.inria.fr/, 2001.

[9] Seth Fogarty, Emir Pasalic, Jeremy Siek, and Walid Taha. Concoqtion: Indexed types now! In *ACM SIGPLAN 2007 Workshop on Partial Evaluation and Program Manipulation*, 2007.

[10] Jeremy Gibbons, Meng Wang, and Bruno C. d. S. Oliveira. Generic and index programming. In *Draft proceedings of TFP 2007*, Seton Hall University, 2007.

[11] Kevin Hammond and Greg Michaelson. Hume: a Domain-Specific Language for Real-Time Embedded Systems. In *Proc. Conf. Generative Programming and Component Engineering (GPCE '03)*, LNCS. Springer-Verlag, 2003.

[12] Oleg Kiselyov and Chung-Chieh Shan. Lightweight static capabilities. ENTCS, Volume 174 , Issue 7 (June 2007).

[13] Conor McBride. Faking it – simulating dependent types in Haskell. *Journal of Functional Programming*, 12(4+5):375–392, 2002.

[14] Conor McBride and James McKinna. The view from the left. *Journal of Functional Programming*, 14(1):69–111, 2004.

[15] Maarten De Mol, Marko Van Eekelen, and Rinus Plasmeijer. Theorem proving for functional programmers - Sparkle: A functional theorem prover. In *The 13th International Workshop on Implementation of Functional Languages, IFL 2001, Selected Papers, volume 2312 of LNCS*, pages 55–72. Springer, 2001.

[16] Ulf Norell. *Towards a practical programming language based on dependent type theory*. PhD thesis, Chalmers University of Technology, 2007.

[17] Simon Peyton Jones, Dimitrios Vytiniotis, Stephanie Weirich, and Geoffrey Washburn. Simple Unification-Based Type Inference for GADTs. In *Proc. International Conf. on Functional Programming (ICFP 2006)*, 2006.

[18] Tom Schrijvers, Simon Peyton Jones, Manuel Chakravarty, and Martin Sulzmann. Type checking with open type functions. In *Proc. International Conf. on Functional Programming (ICFP 1008)*, 2008.

[19] Tim Sheard. Type-level computation using narrowing in Ωmega. ENTCS, Volume 174 , Issue 7 (June 2007).

[20] Tim Sheard. Languages of the Future. In *Object Orientated Programming Systems, Languages and Applications (OOPSLA 2004)*. ACM, 2004.

[21] Matthieu Sozeau. Programming finger trees in Coq. In *International Conference on Functional Programming 2007*.

[22] Walid Taha. *Multi-stage Programming: Its Theory and Applications*. PhD thesis, Oregon Graduate Institute of Science and Technology, 1999.